IMAGES
of America

LAKE HAVASU CITY

IMAGES
of America

LAKE HAVASU CITY

Frederic B. Wildfang

ARCADIA
PUBLISHING

ISBN 978-0-7385-3012-3

Published by Arcadia Publishing
Charleston, South Carolina

Printed in the United States of America

Library of Congress Catalog Card Number: 2005928798

For all general information contact Arcadia Publishing at:
Telephone 843-853-2070
Fax 843-853-0044
E-mail sales@arcadiapublishing.com
For customer service and orders:
Toll-Free 1-888-313-2665

Visit us on the Internet at www.arcadiapublishing.com

To Betty Haskel, doyenne of Durango, Colorado, and Sedona, Arizona, who kindly donated funds for this project, and to A. E. "Bud" Graham (1911–2004), prominent resident of Lake Havasu City, who first inspired this history.

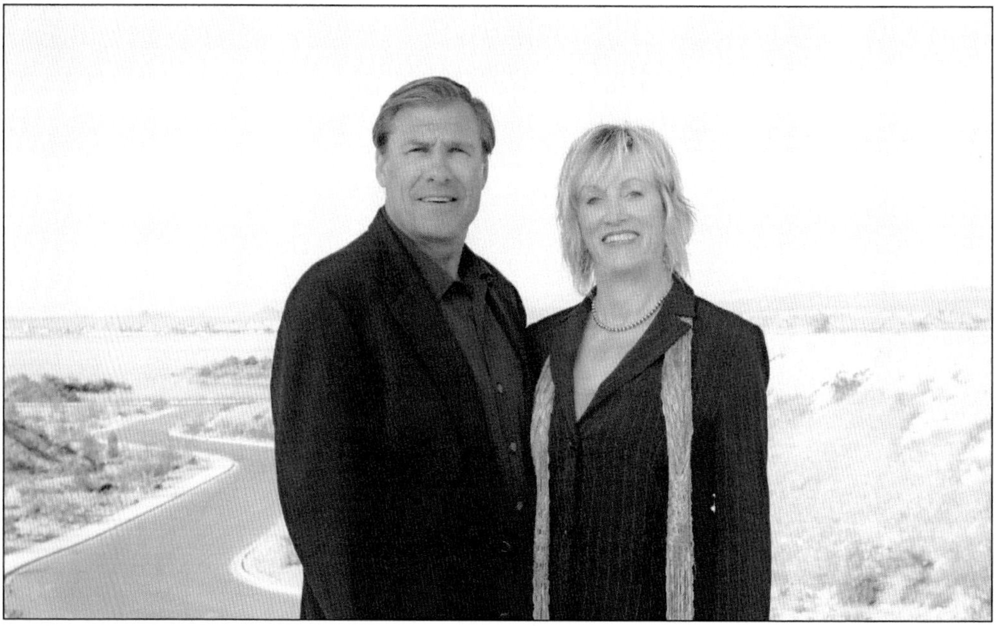

Author Fred Wildfang and his wife, Diane Wildfang, pose at Sailing Hawks, the latest addition to Lake Havasu City. (Courtesy On the Lake Photography.)

CONTENTS

Acknowledgments

When my wife, Diane, first brought me to Lake Havasu City, Arizona, to help her out with her latest development project (The Villages at Sailing Hawks, a beautiful master-planned residential community overlooking the lake), I didn't have any idea there was a history here. After all, the town was founded in 1963. Since becoming involved with the Lake Havasu City Historical Society, however, I have found out differently. As I wrote in the following excerpt from a brochure I put together for the historical society, "Mohave County has been literally at the crossroads of history for hundreds of years: Indian trails, wagon roads, the Atchison, Topeka & Santa Fe and Route 66 crisscross it. The Colorado River runs down the length of it. Mohaves and Chemehuevis, Spanish explorers, trappers, miners, ranchers and rivermen have worked its surfaces and plumbed its depths. Men like the missionary Francisco Garces (passing through the territory in 1776), the explorer Joseph Ives (mapping the river in 1858), and the adventurer Johnny Moss (discovering gold in 1862) have made Mohave County famous."

Add the anachronism of the London Bridge, built in England in 1831 and moved to Lake Havasu City in 1971, and this area becomes a true historical anomaly. Thanks to my wife, Diane, for giving me the opportunity to become a part of it.

And thanks to Judy Whelan, Ruth Brydon, and especially Phyllis Wagner at the Lake Havasu Museum of History for all their support and hard work. And special thanks to Matt Goin, the computer nerd. Gratitude is also due to a number of other organizations, publications, and individuals for information and photographs provided in this book, including Roseanne Rosenberg and Paul Carson, Mohave Museum of History and Art; Richard Simms and Scott Anderson, Sharlot Hall Museum; Clare Olson, Arizona Historical Society, Southern Arizona Division; Robert Spindler and Elizabeth Bentley, Arizona State University; Nancy Sawyer and Laurie Devine, Arizona State Library; Karen Underhill, Northern Arizona University; Simon Elliott and Genie Guerard, University of California, Los Angeles; Mike Dunning's "Havasu's Gold: The Chemehuevi Mining District"; Donald Judson Foust's "The Man Who Bought The London Bridge"; Gary W. McCarthy's *A. E. "Bud" Graham: A Life Well Lived*; Roger A. Johnson's *New City, Old Bridge*; Richard E. Lingenfelter's *Steamboats on the Colorado River*; Roman Malach's *Land of Chemehuevis* and *London Bridge Miracle*; Dan W. Messersmith's *The History of Mohave County to 1912*; William C. Sturtevant's *Handbook to the North American Indians*; Lee Arnon; John Bergman; Sherry and Don Butler; David Chavez; Irene Esquerra; Patty Fritz; Ruth Graham; Kathy and Don Hodel; June Levis; Rodney Lewis; Jim Massey; Wayne and Pat Patch; Dotty Quiggle, Hal and Julie Roach; Shirley and Abner Schultz; Lee Shoblom; Ernie Smith; Cynthia Skinner; Nancy and Jim Smith; Joe Stankus; Lori and Larry Wade; and Jim Wilson.

INTRODUCTION

Little did I know how my life would change back in 1967 when I spotted a copy of *Time* magazine someone had left on my news desk at Channel 9 in Denver. A headline caught my eye: "Instant City Rises in the Desert on the Colorado River." Intrigued, after finishing my newscast, I picked up the magazine and started reading. At 27 years old, with 10 years of broadcasting experience, I was dreaming of having my own radio station one day, but I had no clue as to where it might be.

Reading further, I learned of some other dreams—big dreams—including dreams of building a brand-new city.

Robert McCulloch Sr., after acquiring the Scott-Atwater outboard motor company in Minneapolis and moving it to Los Angeles, was looking for a site to test his outboard engines. That was one of his dreams. Robert McCulloch Sr., Robert McCulloch Jr., and C. V. Wood Jr. of the McCulloch Corporation, probably best-known worldwide for the McCulloch chain saw, decided to relocate all operations on the California-Arizona border, on the lake known as Lake Havasu. That was another dream. Finally, yet another dream evolved: "If you build it, they will come." A brand-new city was built on the edge of the lake known as Lake Havasu.

Well, the developers did everything they said they would do and a lot more, and we came. We came from all directions of the compass. We came from cities and towns, large and small, all over the country. We drove in. We flew in on the fleet of new airplanes owned by Holly Development, a subsidiary of the McCulloch Corporation, appropriately renamed McCulloch Airlines. We looked at property, we cruised the lake, we stayed lakeside at the wonderful Nautical Inn and inland at the exotic Havasu Hotel, which featured a waterfall over and across the front entrance. Then the life-changing wild ride, the Havasu adventure, began.

In my case, project manager Fred Schumaker showed me five acres of commercial property reserved for a 225-foot tower that would broadcast from Lake Havasu City's first radio station, KFWJ. It took a few years for the FCC to grant our license, but eventually it arrived in March 1970, and we moved quickly and began broadcasting on September 23, 1970—the only radio signal on the entire AM and FM bands. As I said when I coined our slogan, "It's easy to be number one when you are the *only* one!"

As one of the "BB" ("before bridge") residents, the adventure compounded with a population growth I never would have believed possible. When I arrived, there were fewer than 2,000 people here, in contrast to the almost 60,000 people here now. When I arrived, everything was fresh and new, everyone worked together, and everyone spread the word about Havasu. We were ready to extol the virtues of Havasu everywhere we went. Then the purchase and relocation of the world-famous London Bridge put us on the international map.

Lake Havasu City is unique for so many reasons, but one reason stands out: the city was founded in 1963. That means that although Havasu's developers have left us, most of the rest of us "town founders" are still around. Would you like to know what life was like "way back then"? Just ask us. We'd be happy to tell you. We were there!

We are thrilled that Fred Wildfang chose to write this book and do all of the research necessary to bring our history to life. You are now about to experience a fine writer's true labor of love. Fred captures the times and the passions of the people of Lake Havasu City and their accomplishments. As Fred has said, the pioneering dreams of Robert McCulloch Sr. and C. V. Wood Jr. have come true. And as their dreams became reality, so did ours.

Enjoy and be sure to tell others about this marvelous new book. For more information, visit the Lake Havasu Museum of History or go to their Website at www.havasumuseum.com.

—Lee Shoblom

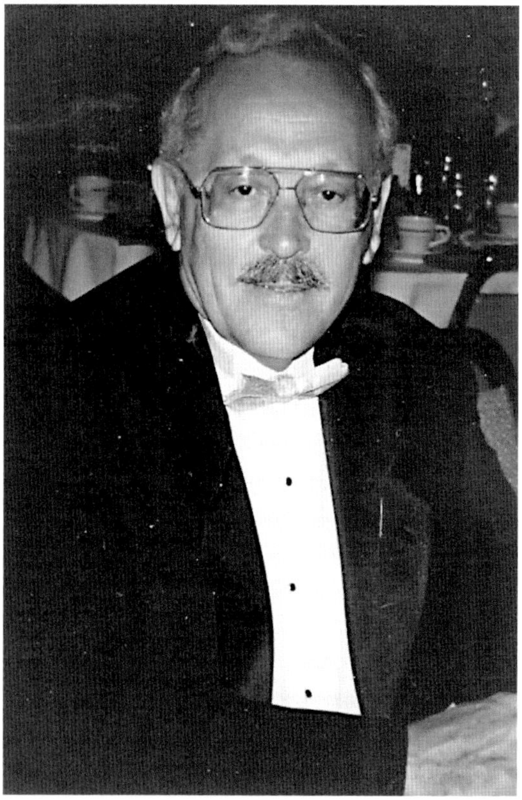

Lee Shoblom, founding director of the Lake Havasu Museum of History, was the owner/manager of the first radio station in Lake Havasu City, KFWJ AM, in 1970. Later he would add two more stations, KBBC FM in 1972 and TV45 in 1982. Lee was elected president of the Arizona Broadcast Association in 1982 and inducted into the Broadcast Hall of Fame in 1999. Lee and his wife, Lynne, currently reside in Prescott, Arizona, where Lee is chairman of Access 13 TV. (Courtesy Lee Shoblom.)

One

The Mohaves and the Chemehuevis

The Mohaves were here first, living up and down the Colorado River, as far north as the Black Canyon and as far south as the Picacho Mountains. They lived in seasonal homes constructed of the materials at hand. They made pottery and baskets and had a fondness for seashells obtained in trade with the coastal Native Americans. Though semi-nomadic, they were successful flood-land farmers—raising corn, beans, wheat, squash, and melons—and had domesticated turkeys and dogs.

Then, down from the north, came the Chemehuevis. These people were hunters and gatherers, surviving off the land, living in small groups. The Chemehuevis were known for their work with buckskin and fine willow baskets—twined, coiled, and decorated with devil's claw.

During his contact with the Mohaves in 1776, Franciscan missionary Francisco Garces described the Mohave women as "the most comely on the river" and the men as "very healthy and robust" (*On the Trail of a Spanish Pioneer* by Elliott Coues, editor). During his travels in 1826, Jedediah Strong Smith agreed that the Mohave women were "fleshy with tolerable features" and the men were "tall and well-formed . . . complexion not dark" (*The Southwest Expedition of Jedediah S. Smith* by George R. Brooks, editor). Lt. Joseph Christmas Ives, on his expedition up the river in 1858, described the Chemehuevis as having "small figures" and "delicate, nicely-cut features" and remarked that "they have been perfectly friendly," "behaved very well," and have "given little trouble" (*Report Upon the Colorado River*). Generally speaking, early European explorers in the area characterized both the Mohaves and Chemehuevis as friendly and peaceable. Both tribes tolerated the Anglos until the James Ohio Pattie and Ewing Young party of 1826–1827 retaliated for a stolen horse, killed a band of Mohaves in a series of attacks and counterattacks, and strung the victims' bodies up in trees as a warning. Then all hell broke loose.

In 1859, the U.S. Army marched in and established a military post on the river, later named Fort Mohave, which ultimately became a Mohave reservation homeland. In 1865, the Colorado River Indian Tribes Reservation, 40 miles south of Lake Havasu City near present-day Parker, Arizona, was created to provide for the Mohaves as well as for the Chemehuevis, and is now shared with the Hopis and Navajos. Today the Chemehuevis also occupy a reservation of 36,000 acres on the western shores of Lake Havasu.

Though pretty much relegated to reservations, the influence of the Mohaves and Chemehuevis is still evidenced by place names in the area—Mohave County, the Mohave and Chemehuevi Mountains, the Chemehuevi Valley, and most notably Chemehuevi Landing, the Indian village buried under the waters of Lake Havasu but now relocated directly across the lake from Lake Havasu City.

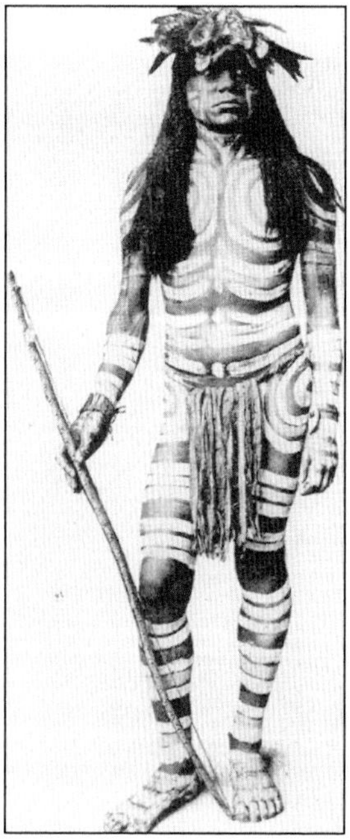

The Mohaves, or Mojaves ("Aha-makave"), believed to be descendants of the ancient Patayan, are Yuman speakers and share a common linguistic heritage with the Quechan, Cocopah, Yavapai, Maricopa, and Havasupai tribes. The Patayans (a Hualapai word for "The Old Ones") and their subgroups were located as far east as the Cerbat Mountains and the Coconino plateau. (Courtesy Mohave Museum of History and Art, No. 452.)

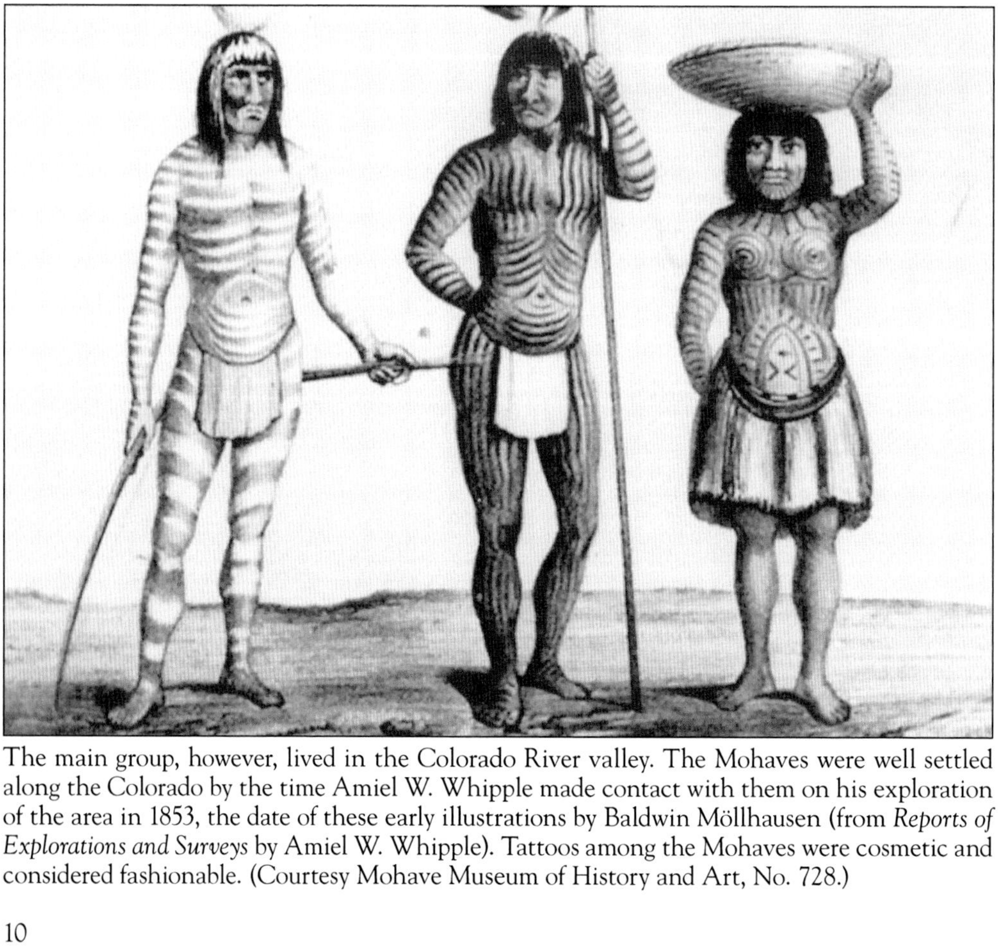

The main group, however, lived in the Colorado River valley. The Mohaves were well settled along the Colorado by the time Amiel W. Whipple made contact with them on his exploration of the area in 1853, the date of these early illustrations by Baldwin Möllhausen (from *Reports of Explorations and Surveys* by Amiel W. Whipple). Tattoos among the Mohaves were cosmetic and considered fashionable. (Courtesy Mohave Museum of History and Art, No. 728.)

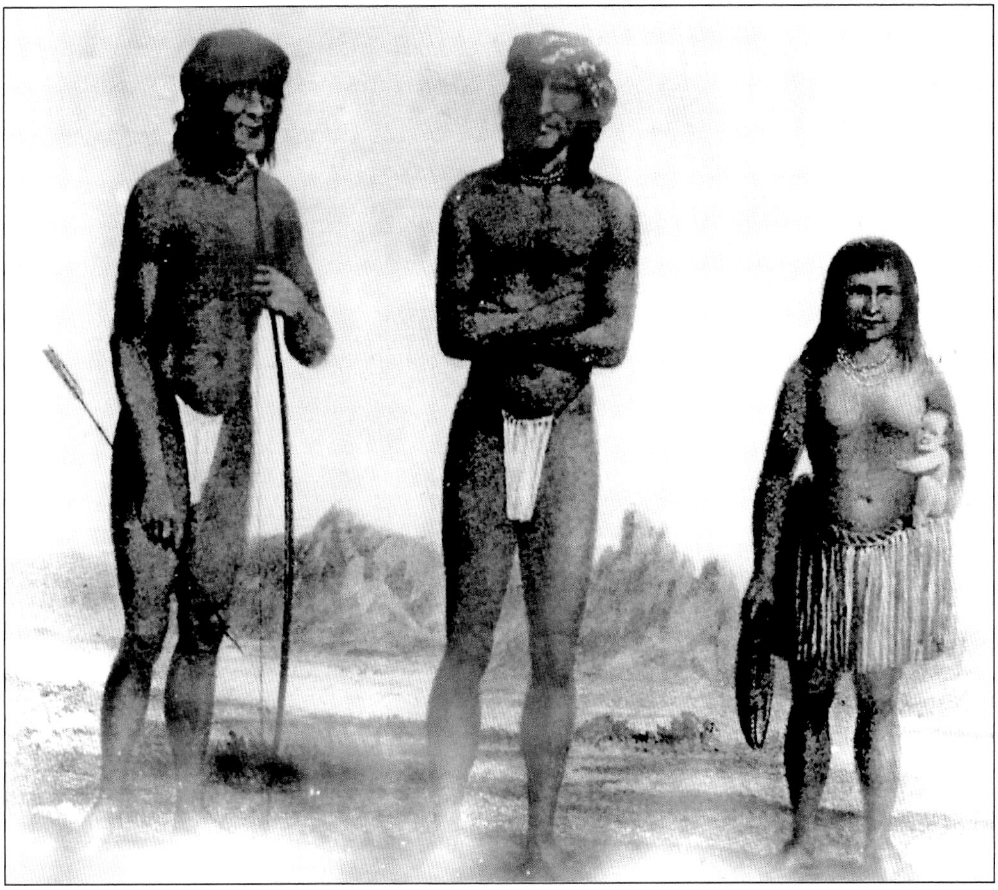

In his journals (unedited here), Jedediah Smith provided a description of Mohave dress. "The men when dressed at all," he wrote, "have a Spanish Blanket thrown over the left shoulder and passing under the right arm it is pined on the brest with a wooden pin. They wear no head dress mocasins or leggings." "The dress of the women," continued Smith, "is a peticoat made of a material like flax just Broken which is Banded with a plat on the upper edge like corn husks. It is fastened around the waist extending down to the knee and constitutes with whole of their clothing." He also noted, "The bows are 5 feet long and thee arrows verry long and made of cane grass with a wooden splice 6 inches long for a head." In this Möllhausen lithograph, Chief Cairook of the Mohaves (center) stands next to Iretaba (left), his successor. Ives befriended Cairook on the 1858 expedition, but the very next year Cairook was taken hostage by Lt. Col. William Hoffman and sent to Fort Yuma. (Courtesy Richard E. Lingenfelter Collection, Charles E. Young Research Library, Department of Special Collections, UCLA.)

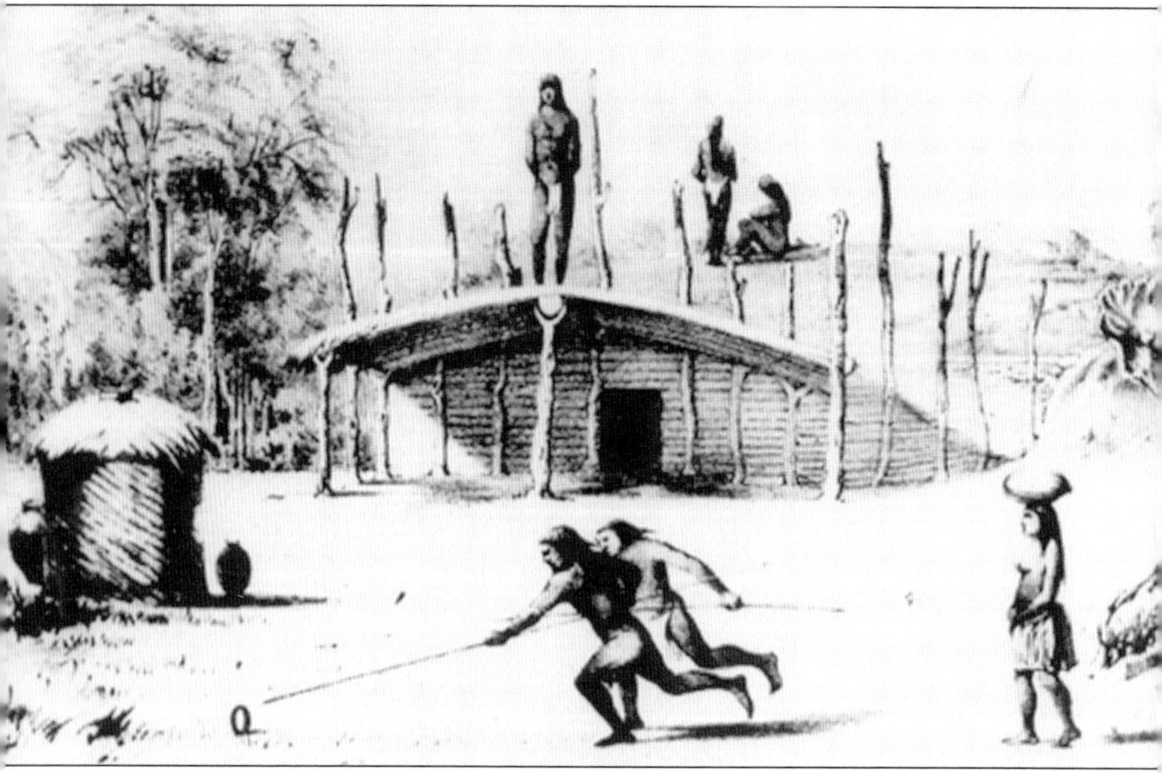

Smith described a popular hoop game played by the Mohaves: "A piece of ground 30 or 40 feet long and 8 feet wide is made level and smooth. Each man has a pole ten feet long and one of them a hoop 4 inches in diameter. The hoop is set rolling from one end of the floor and at the instant both start and sliding their poles endeavor to intersect the hoop. The one that pierces the hoop or when hoop and poles stop is the nearest to the spot is the winner [*sic*]." This illustration by Möllhausen shows a game in progress. (Courtesy Richard E. Lingenfelter Collection, Charles E. Young Research Library, Department of Special Collections, UCLA.)

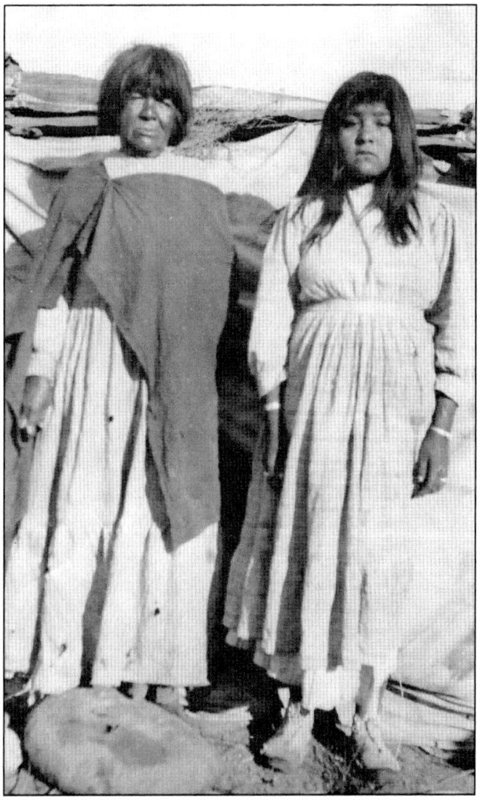

These *c.* 1905 portraits show a Mohave woman and girl and a woman and a man from the Fort Mohave area, midway between present-day Topock and Bullhead City, Arizona. (Courtesy Cline Library, Special Collections, Northern Arizona University.)

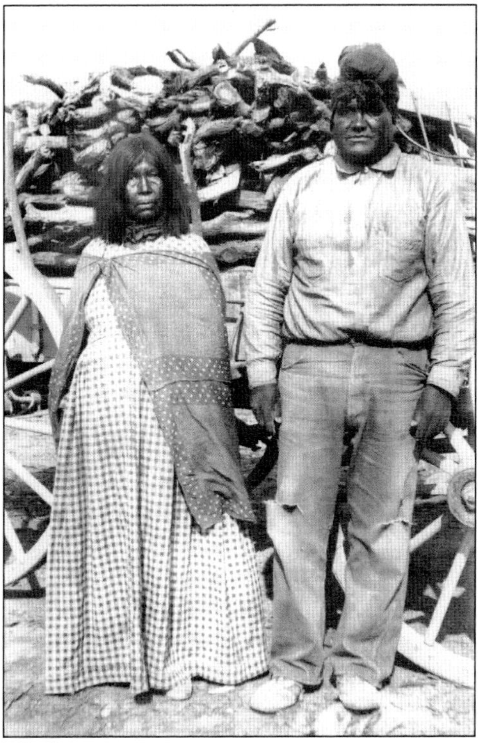

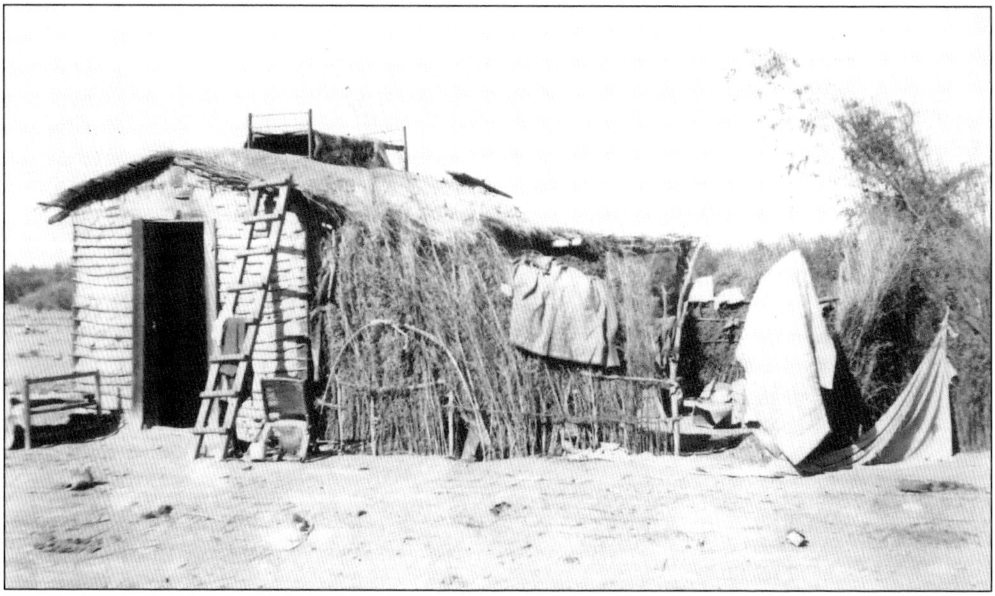

Jedediah Smith observed that the Mohaves did "not live in villages but are rather scattered over the country generally wherever they find the most favorable situations." He described their summer dwellings as lodges "about 3 feet high" and "made of forks and poles covered with grass weeds and dirt flat on the top." (Courtesy Cline Library, Special Collections, Northern Arizona University.)

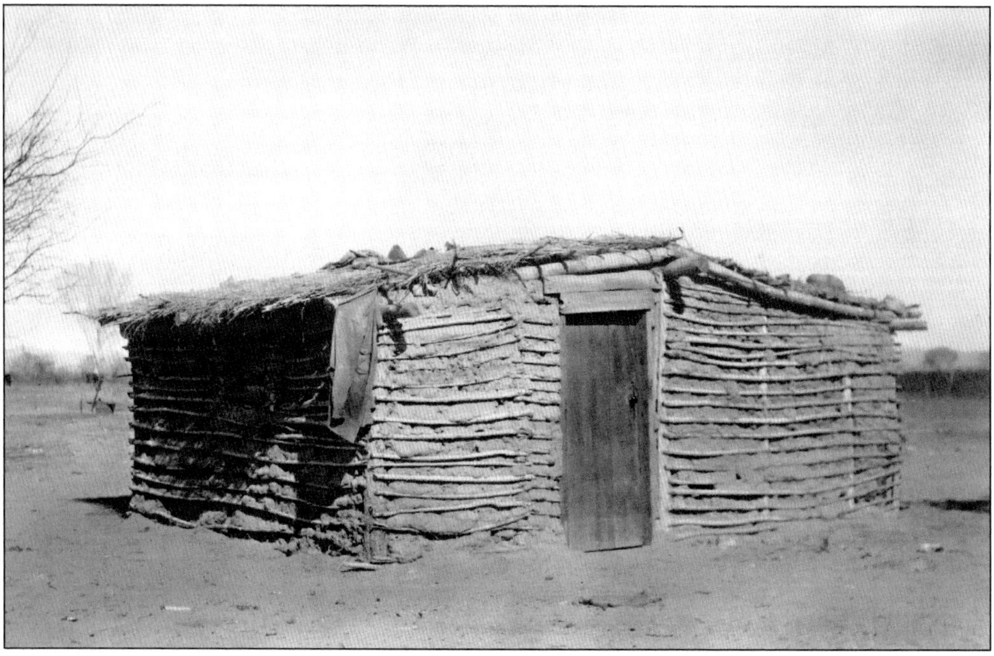

The winter lodges, Smith continued, were "generally small" and "made in the woods but fronting to the south and where the trees are not sufficiently high to keep out the sun. As the rainy season approaches they throw dirt on the roof to give it a slope to carry off the water and secure the sides with dirt leaving only a small aperture for a door." (Courtesy Cline Library, Special Collections, Northern Arizona University.)

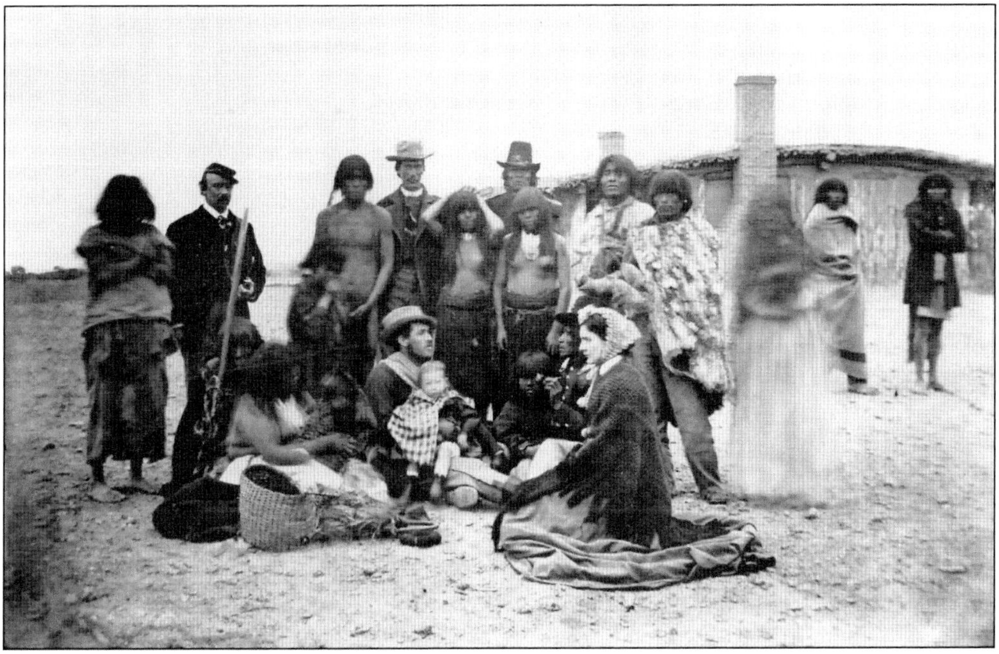

Groups of Mohaves and military personnel gather at Fort Mohave in 1867. In 1859, Lt. Col. William Hoffman organized a force of over 600 troops and, accompanied by a steamboat, marched up the Colorado River from Fort Yuma in order to subdue the Indians. (Courtesy Cline Library, Special Collections, Northern Arizona University.)

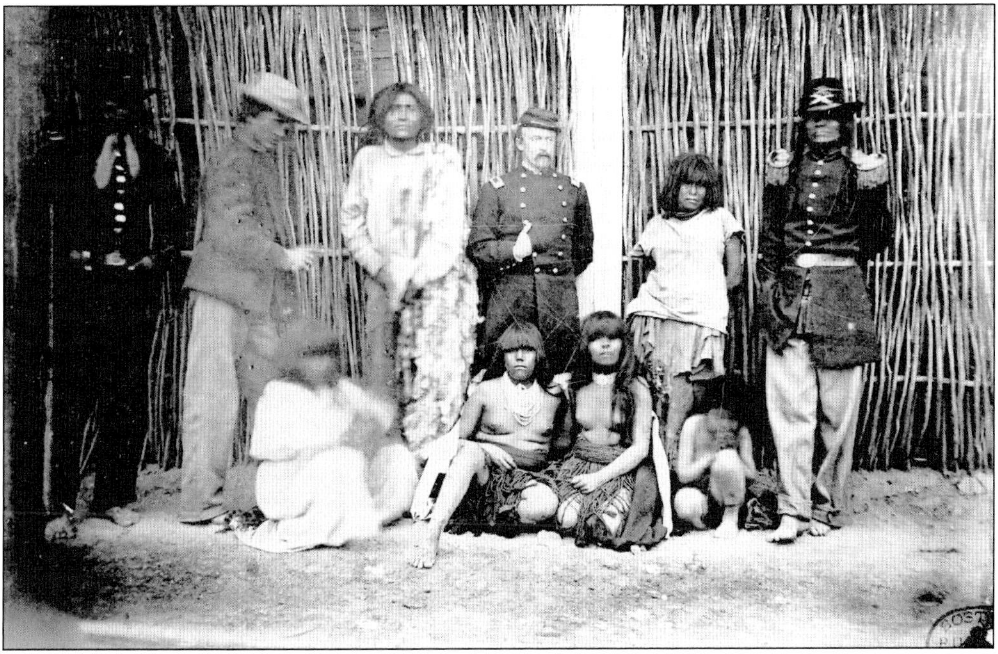

Overwhelming the Mohaves without a fight, Hoffman directed Maj. Lewis Armistead to build "Camp Colorado" on the site of their traditional homelands. A few days later, it was renamed Fort Mohave. In 1880, the government established a reservation at Fort Mohave. (Courtesy Cline Library, Special Collections, Northern Arizona University.)

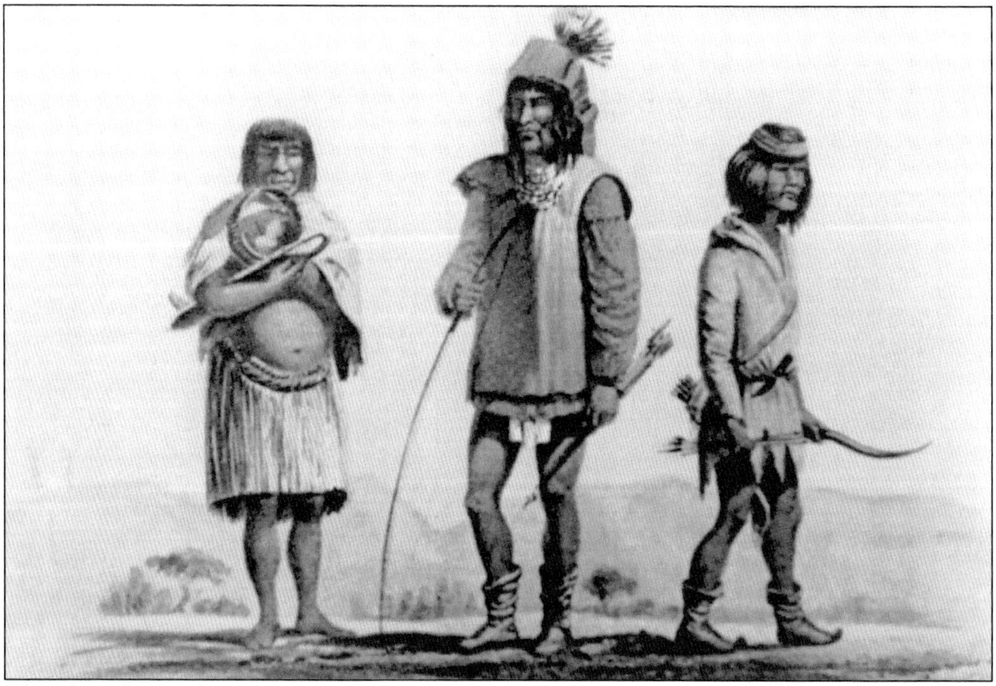

The Chemehuevis ("Nu-Wu") speak Shoshonean, which is in the Uto–Aztecan group of languages. They most likely descended from the Paiutes, who roamed throughout the Great Basin and eventually down the Colorado River valley. The Chemehuevis lived in small groups and spent most of their time gathering wild plants, fishing, and hunting small game. Because they had to travel long distances on food-finding missions, the Chemehuevis had no time for war. Notwithstanding minor skirmishes from 1865 to 1867, the Chemehuevis were friendly with their neighbors, the Mohaves, and assimilated much of their culture. Joseph Ives visited the Chemehuevis during his expedition up the Colorado River in 1858, when this drawing was made by Möllhausen. (Richard E. Lingenfelter Collection, Charles E. Young Research Library, Department of Special Collections, UCLA.)

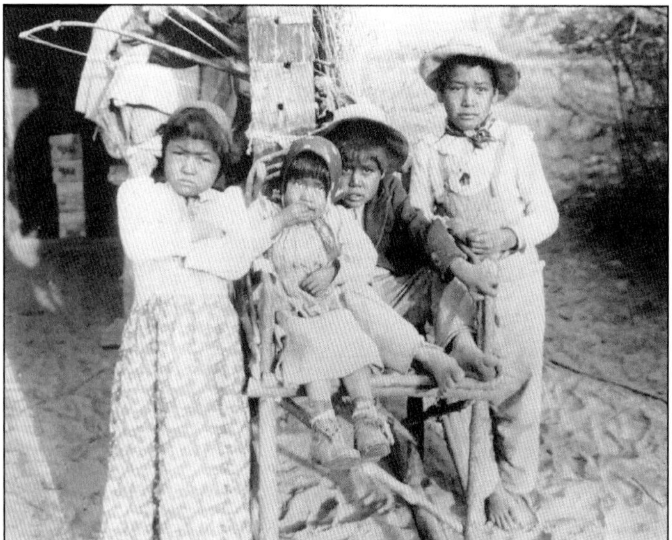

The Chemehuevis gathered wild plants such as were pinon nuts, agave, and mesquite beans. The wild game they hunted were the smaller desert dwellers, though occasionally they feasted on upland deer and the indigenous bighorn sheep. Note the bow and arrows hanging from the rafters in this 1890s photograph of a group of Chemehuevi children in front of their summer home. (Courtesy David Chavez.)

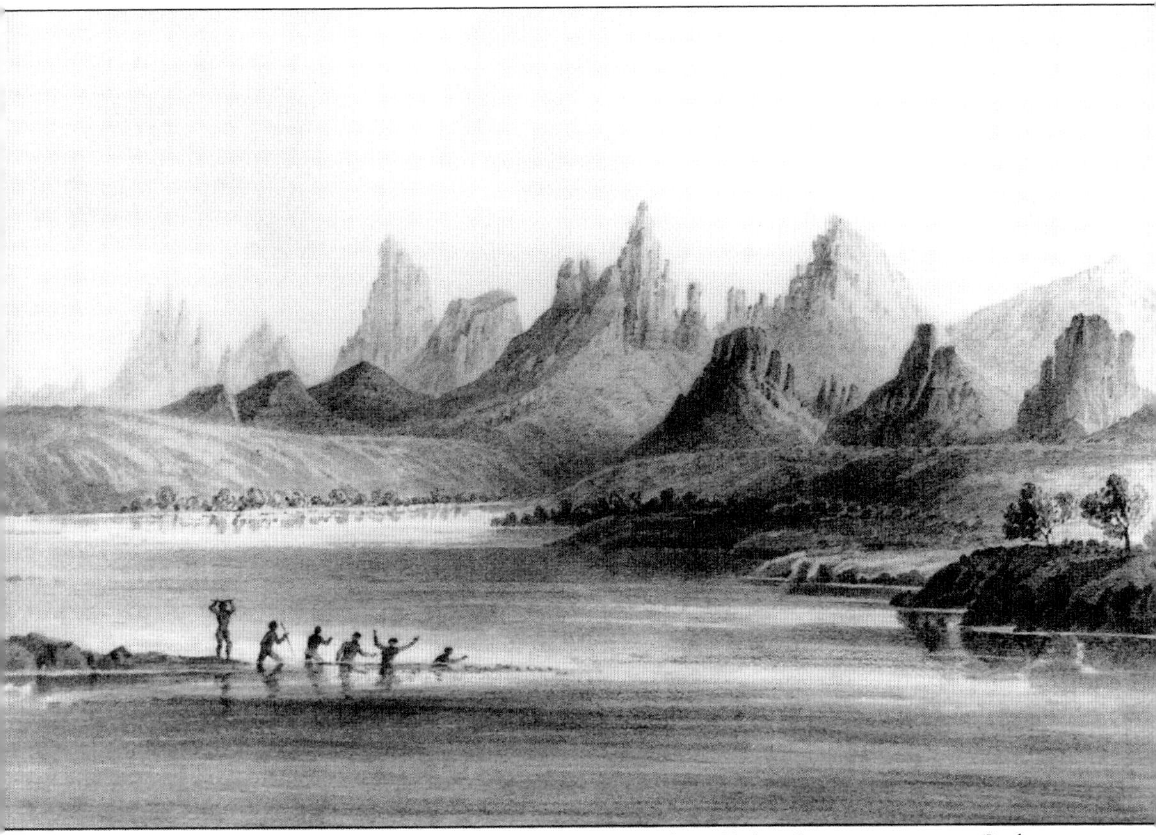

In 1865, the government created the Colorado River Indian Tribes Reservation near Parker, which the Chemehuevis share with the Mohaves, Hopis, and Navajos. In 1907, the American government created the 36,000-acre Chemehuevi Valley Reservation on their own homeland, across the river from present-day Lake Havasu City, not far from the scene of this Möllhausen lithograph just below the "Needles" peaks. Lt. Joseph Ives actually named the peaks known as the Needles. (Richard E. Lingenfelter Collection, Charles E. Young Research Library, Department of Special Collections, UCLA.)

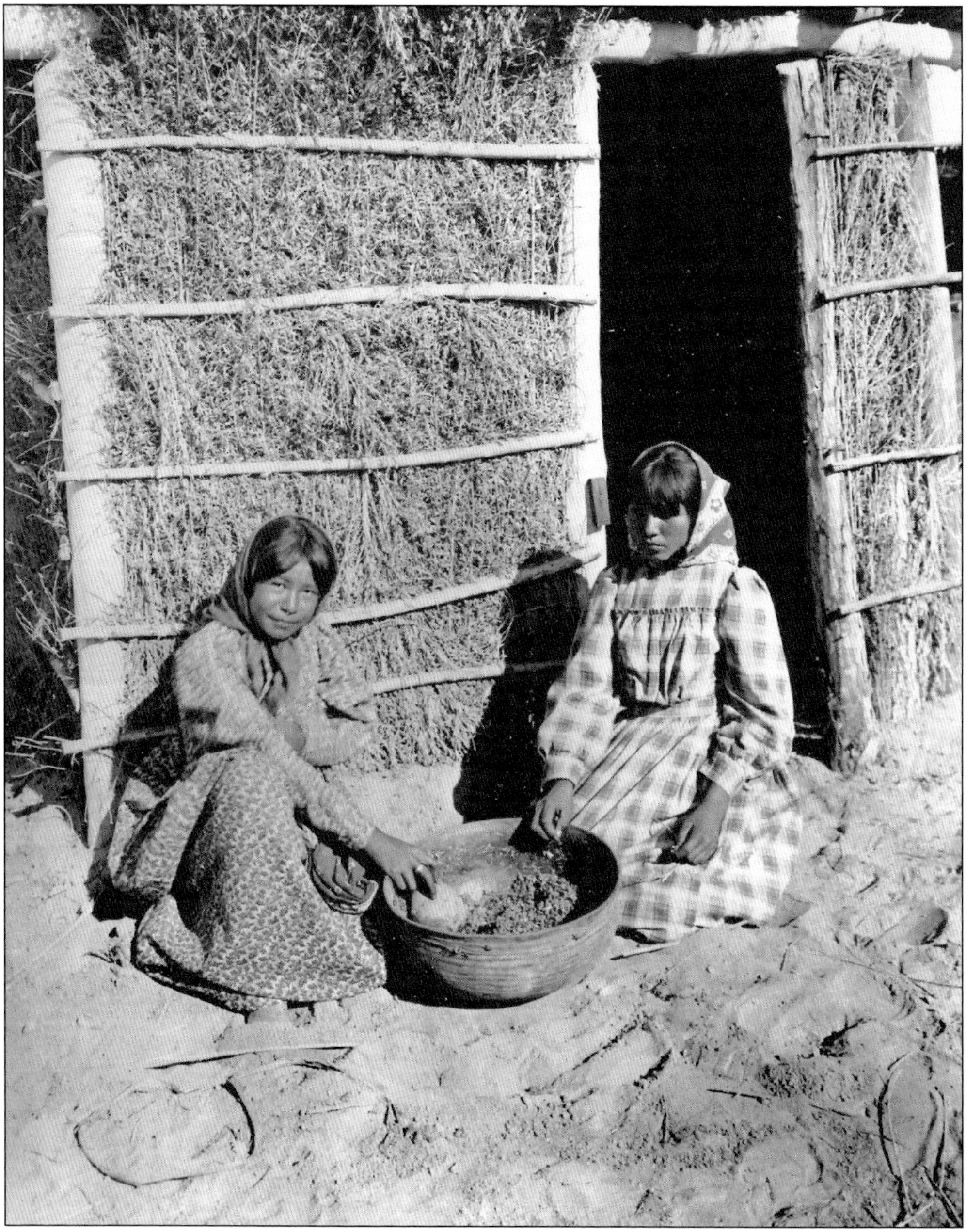

Despite their nomadic nature, there is evidence that the Chemehuevis developed significant sedentary skills. Some traits—earth-covered houses, clay pottery, flood-plain farming, the cultivation of corn and beans, for instance—were no doubt adopted from the Mohaves. In his report, Joseph Ives noted that the Chemehuevis had "baskets and earthen bowls of corn and beans." (Courtesy David Chavez.)

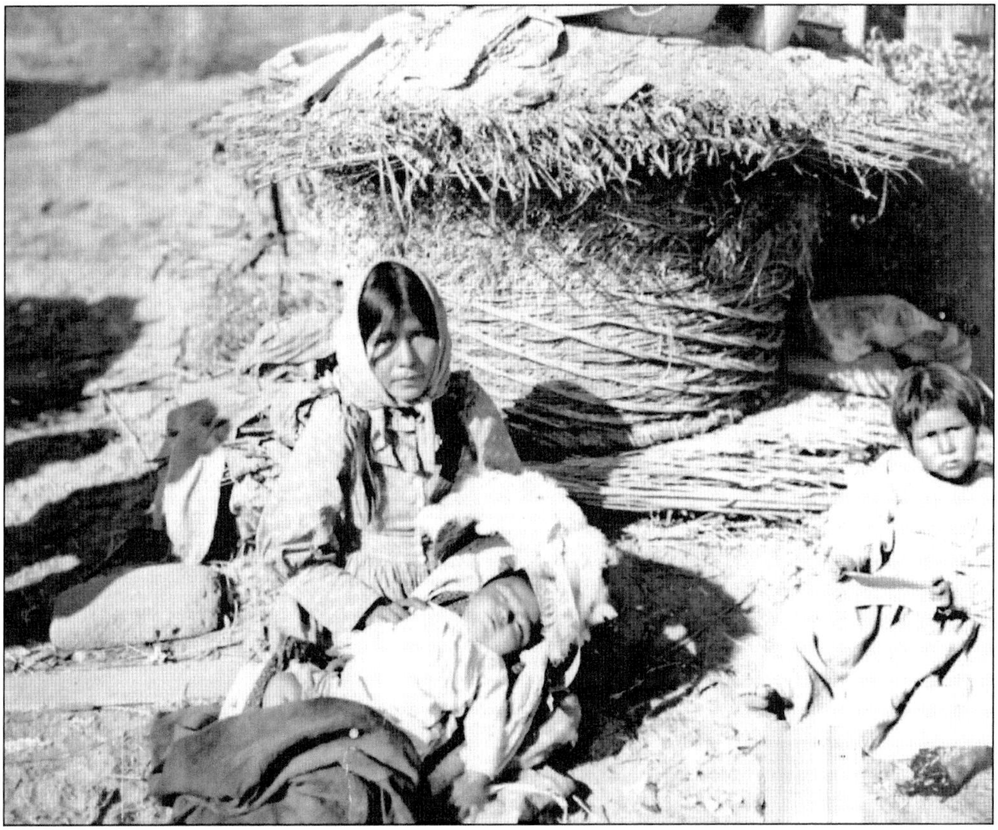

These 1890s images show the large baskets made of arrow weed and willow that were used as granaries for storing corn, beans, and dried squash. In front of one of the large baskets (above), a Chemehuevi mother sits holding her baby in a cradle board made of mesquite and willow. The fact that the hood of the cradle is decorated with eagle feathers indicates that the baby is a boy. (Courtesy David Chavez.)

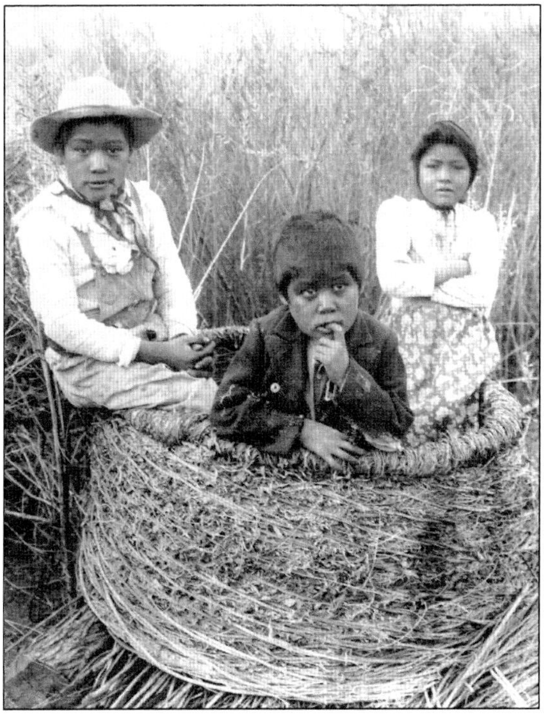

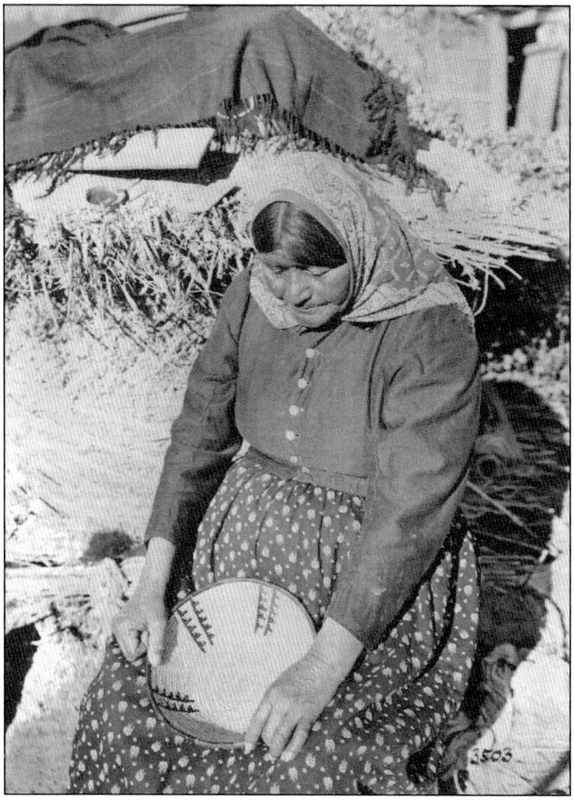

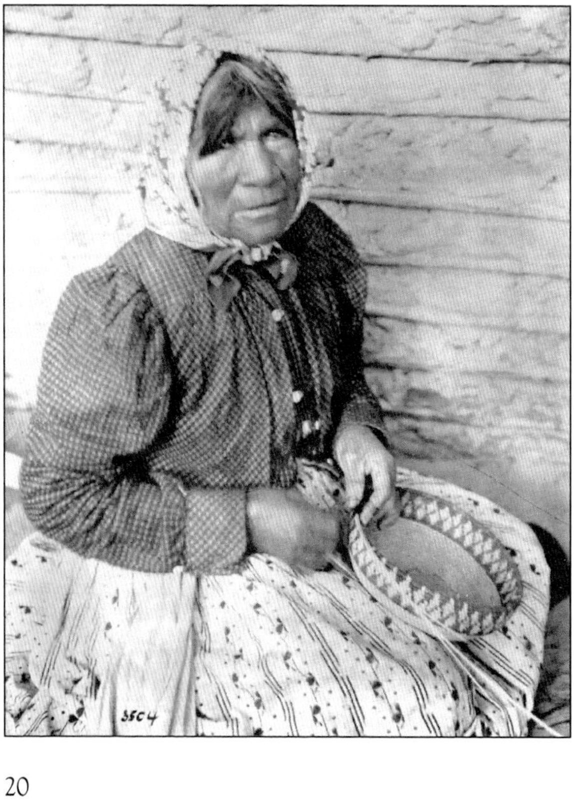

Smaller baskets were made of split willow and juncos for a variety of uses, including decorative. They ranged in size from a quarter-inch to over 20 inches in diameter. These weavers are wearing calico-like dresses and bandannas, now considered to be traditional attire for Chemehuevi women. (Courtesy David Chavez.)

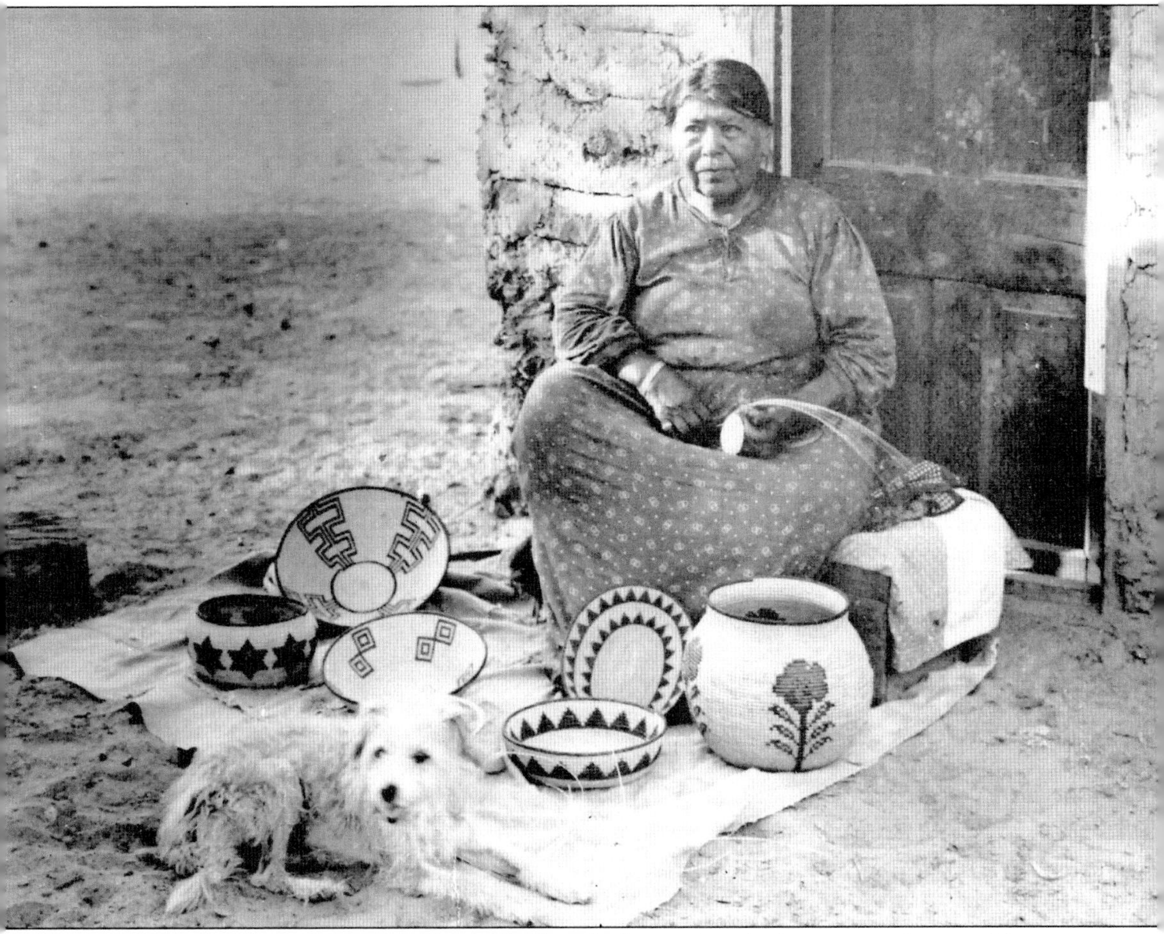

Even today, the Chemehuevis are famous for their basketry, though the art is in danger of dying out. In this photograph, Mary Laird, renowned basket maker, begins a coil for a willow basket. At her feet are some of her finished wares. Note the varied designs woven into the baskets with devil's claw. (Courtesy David Chavez.)

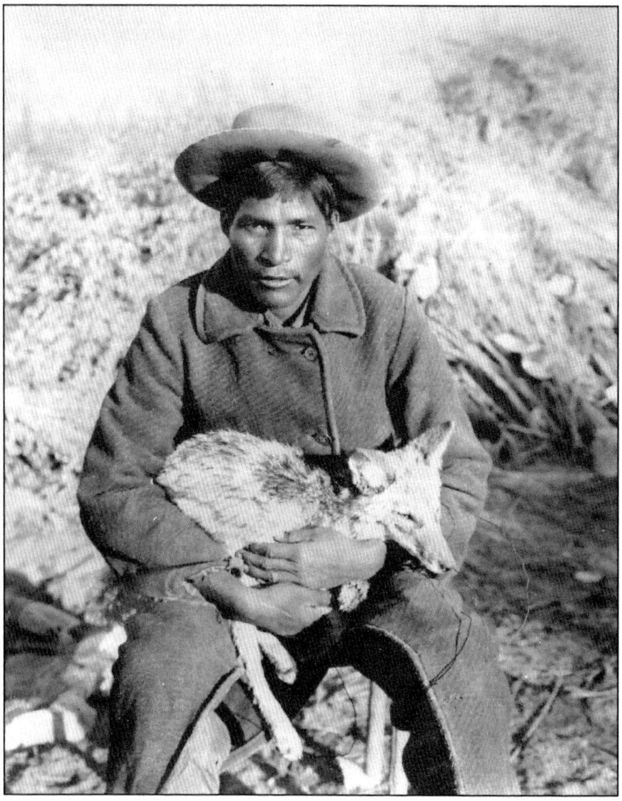

Stories about the coyote, a well-known figure in Chemehuevi mythology, were passed along from generation to generation, setting standards for human behavior. Among other aspects of the Chemehuevi culture adopted from the Mohaves were ideas about the power of dreams, hunting rituals, and funereal ceremonies such as the "Cry," associated with singing and song cycles. (Courtesy David Chavez.)

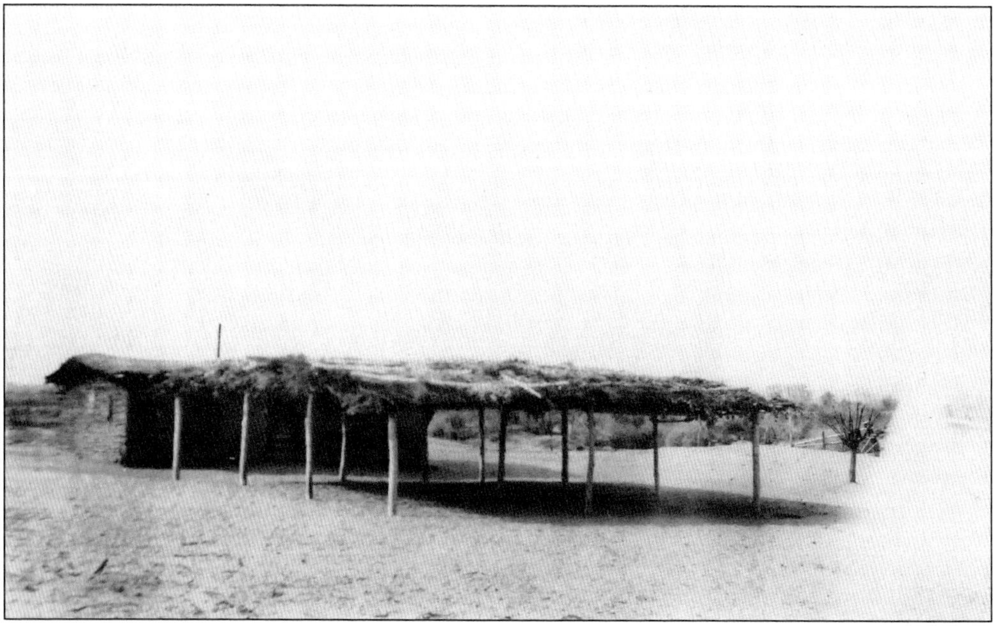

The Cry ceremony was conducted in a lodge similar to this one. (Courtesy Cline Library, Special Collections, Northern Arizona University.)

Two

EARLY EXPLORERS

Juan de Oñate first named the Colorado River "Buena Esperanza" ("Good Hope") in 1640, when he explored the river north—perhaps as far as present-day Needles, California—and then back again south to the mouth of the river at the Gulf of California in Mexico.

Over 130 years later, Fray Francisco Garces renamed the river "Colorado" (a Spanish word for "red") in 1776, when he and his guide Tarabal pushed north along the river in search of possible sites for Franciscan missions. When he reached present-day Needles, California, Garces turned west and headed for the Pacific along a trade route pointed out to him by the Mohaves.

There were a number of other adventurers in the area going after the fur trade. James Ohio Pattie and Ewing Young had their misadventure with the Mohaves in 1826, followed by Jedediah Strong Smith in 1826 and 1827—the latter trip marred by a skirmish with the Mohaves initiated by the same Pattie and Young. Peter Skene Ogden, the mountain man from the Northwest Territories of Washington, Oregon, and Idaho, worked his way down the Colorado from Needles and back in 1829. The trapper Antoine Leroux rafted down the Colorado from the Virgin River in 1837. All of these ventured past the present site of Lake Havasu City.

In 1851, the first official mapping and surveying expedition of the Colorado was led by Capt. Lorenzo Sitgreaves, who was accompanied by Antoine Leroux. According to *The History of Mohave County to 1912* by Dan W. Messersmith, Sitgreaves's orders were to "pursue the Colorado to its junction with the Gulf of California, taking those observations which will enable you accurately to delineate its course." Following the place names in his journal, his journey can be traced from Union Pass, west of present-day Kingman, and down the east side of the river south to where Yuma is situated today. Seeking a bridge site for a railroad, Lt. Amiel W. Whipple was commissioned to survey a reverse route in 1853, journeying up the Colorado north from the mouth of the Bill Williams River to a point near Needles—at Topock, Arizona, some 20 miles north of Lake Havasu City—where the crossing is currently located.

In 1857, Lt. Joseph Christmas Ives was commissioned to survey the Colorado River in order to determine its suitability for steamboat navigation. Although preempted by rival George Alonzo Johnson—who had already made it on the *General Jesup* to Pyramid Canyon, just above the present site of Davis Dam—Ives on the *Explorer* made it as far as Explorer Rock, some 40 miles further, which he determined to be the head of navigation on the Colorado River.

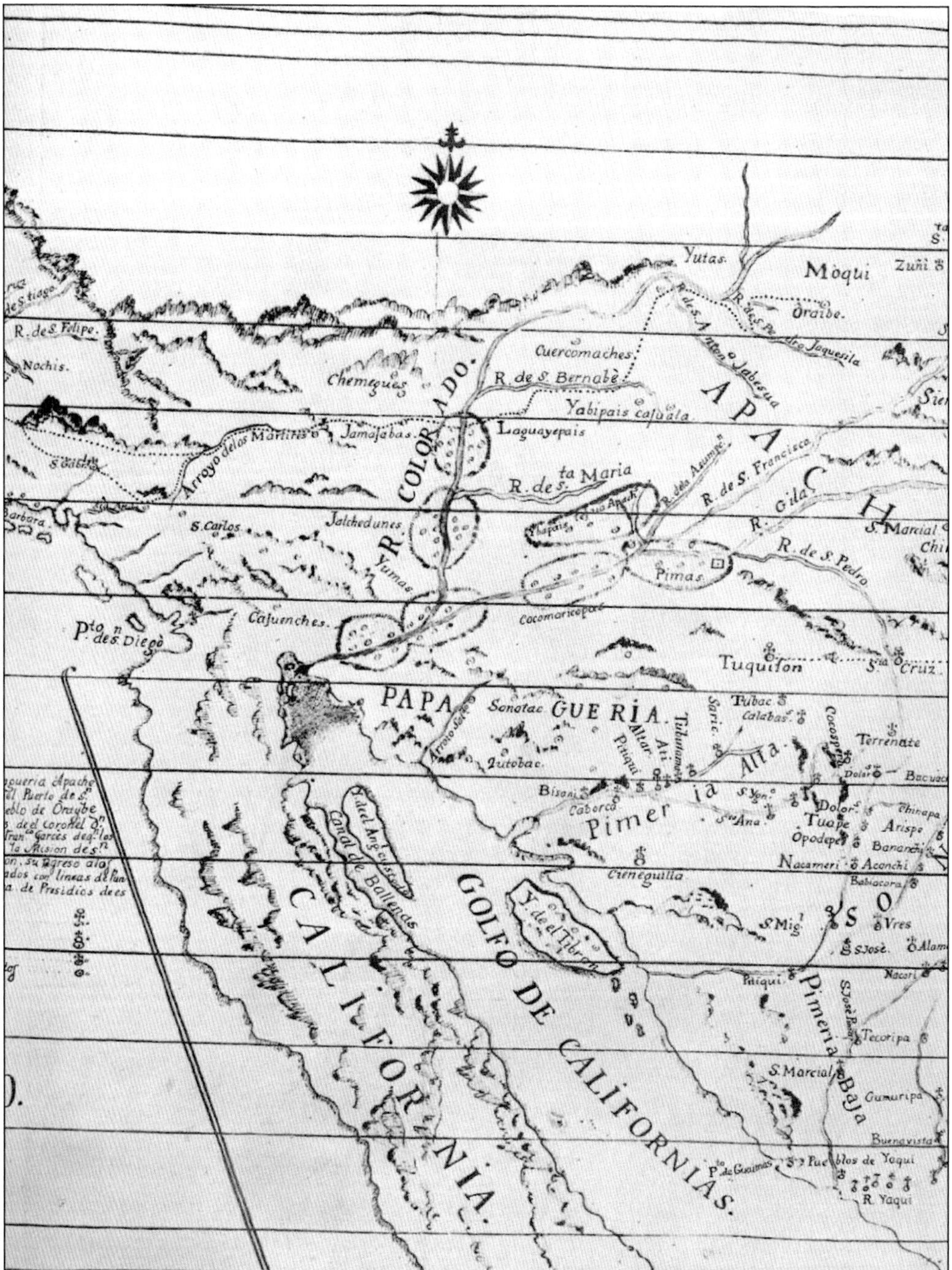

This map from *A Record of Travels in Arizona and California, 1775–1776* by Francisco Garces traces the route he took up the Rio Colorado on his way to California in 1776. (Courtesy Lake Havasu Museum of History.)

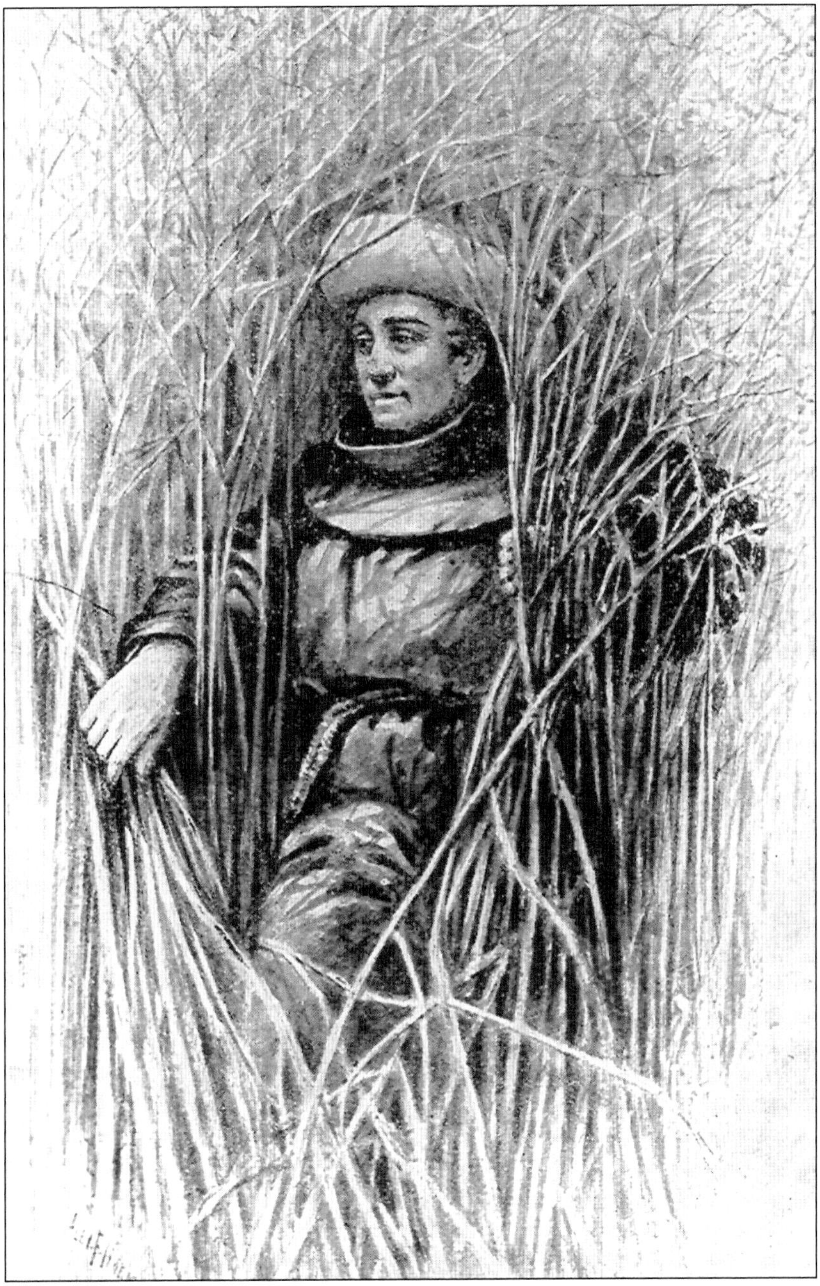

Garces was so well-received by the Mohaves in the present-day Needles area that Father Font, who accompanied him, remarked that "he appears to be but an Indian himself. He sits with them in the circle, or at night around the fire, with his legs crossed, talking with them with much serenity and deliberation" (*On the Trail of a Spanish Pioneer* by Elliot Coues, editor). Moreover, Garces shares their meals "with great gusto and says that they are good for the stomach and very fine." "In short," Font concluded, "God has created him . . . solely for the purpose of seeking out these unhappy, ignorant, and rustic people." Although he got along well with the Mohaves, when Garces traveled east to visit the Hopis ("Moqui") along a route also indicated on the map he was driven out of their village. (Courtesy Sharlot Hall Museum, Prescott, Arizona.)

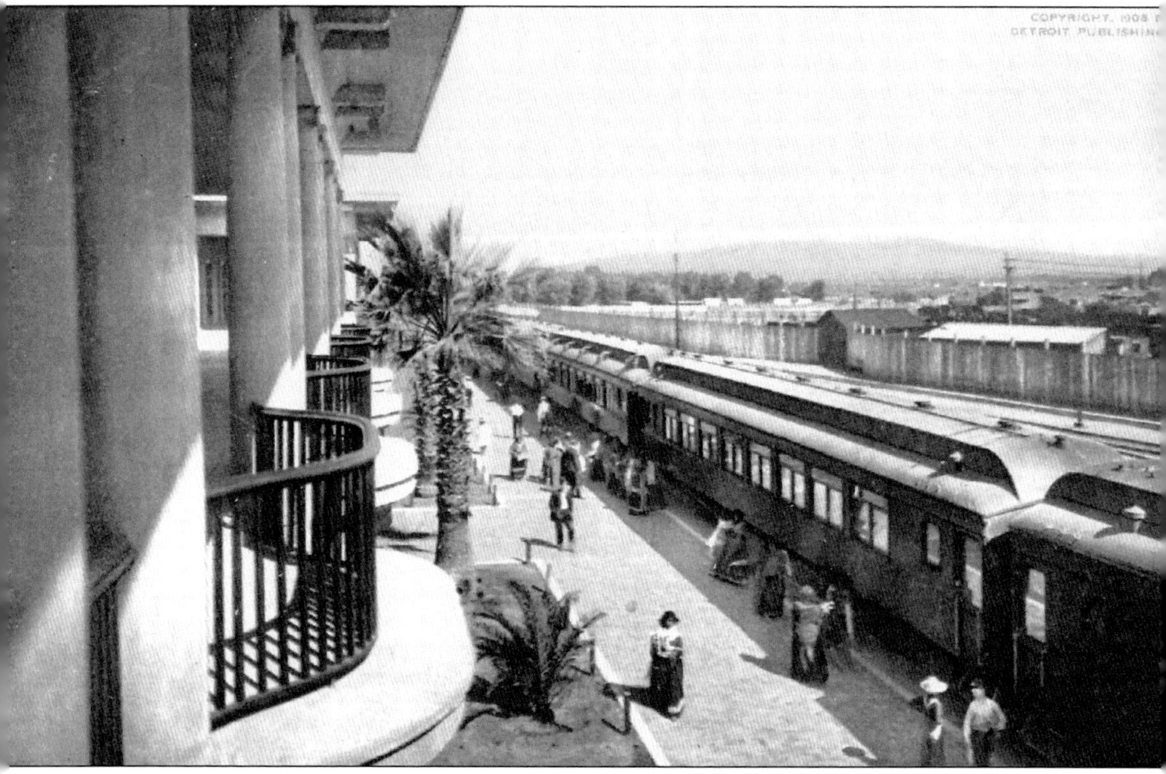

Father Garces remains revered in the area by virtue of the El Garces Hotel, shown here in 1916. Named after Garces, the hotel is located across from the Atchison, Topeka & Santa Fe railroad station in Needles. The El Garces, now in ruins but slated for historic renovation, was one of a series of popular Harvey Houses along the railroad line. (Courtesy Cline Library, Special Collections, Northern Arizona University.)

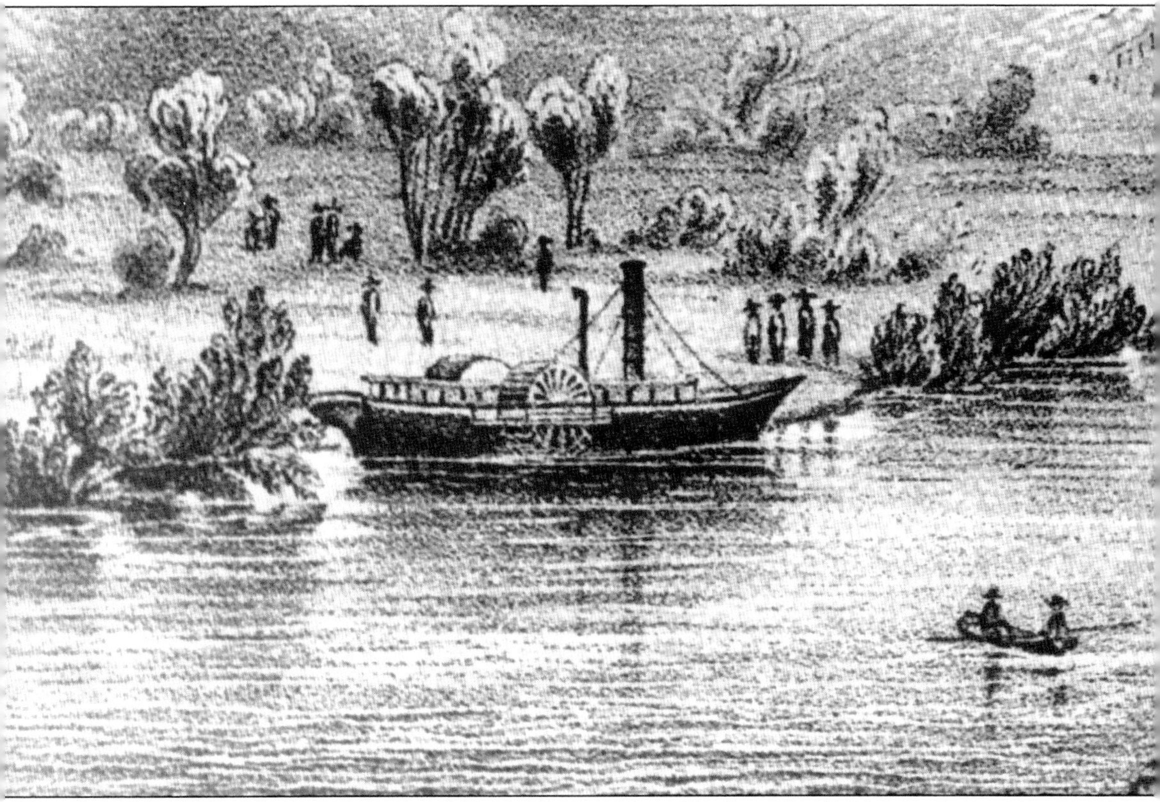

The *General Jesup* was the first steamboat to navigate the Colorado River all the way up to a point some eight miles above present-day Davis Dam. Put into service in 1854 by George Alonzo Johnson of the Colorado Steam Navigation Company, the *General Jesup* was one of two side-wheelers on the river. It was 104 feet long, 17 feet wide at the beam, and could carry 50 tons of freight, drawing 30 inches of water. In 1856, Johnson talked the California legislature into sponsoring an expedition up the Colorado River. After also persuading Secretary of War Jefferson Davis to ask Congress to fund it, Johnson was passed over as captain of the expedition—a distinction given to Lt. Joseph Christmas Ives instead. Nevertheless, Johnson decided to launch his own expedition on the *General Jesup* and made his way 300 miles north on the river, unbeknownst to Ives, until his supplies ran out and he had to return to Fort Yuma. (Richard E. Lingenfelter Collection, Charles E. Young Research Library, Department of Special Collections, UCLA.)

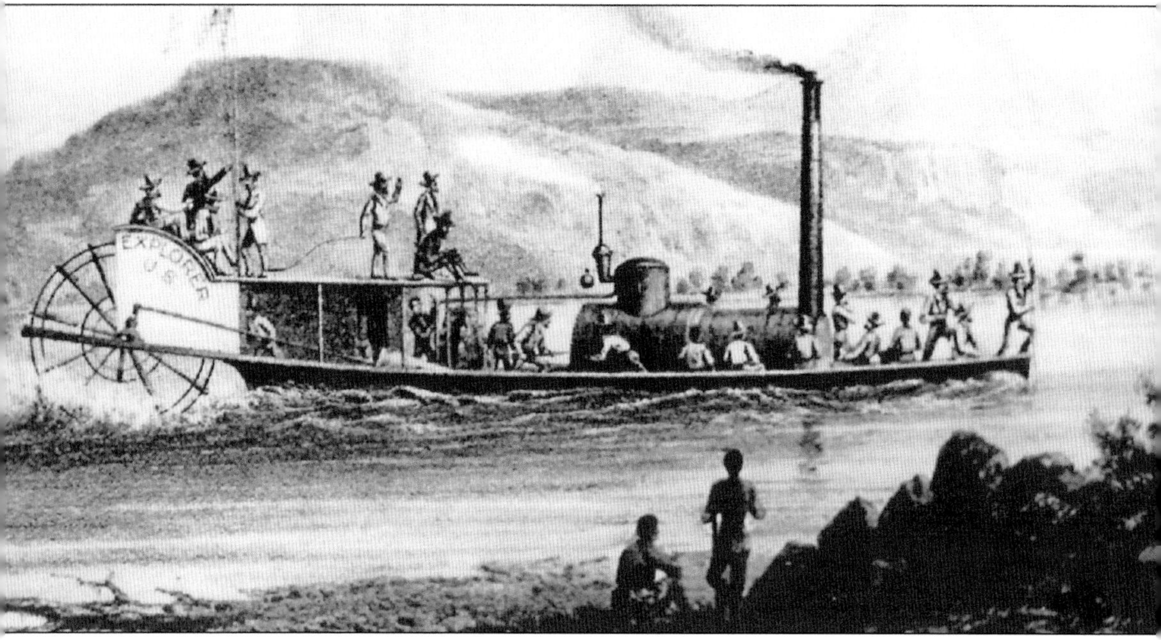

In 1857, the *Explorer*, commanded by Joseph Ives (though actually piloted by Capt. David C. Robinson), was launched from Fort Yuma on the first official government expedition to survey the Colorado River. The *Explorer* was a little steel-hulled stern-wheeler, only 54 feet long and 13 feet wide at the beam, but drew three feet of water when fully loaded. Because of her deep draft—the weight of the engine and oversized boiler, the cabin behind the engine, and a howitzer on the bow leaving her with only six inches of freeboard—the *Explorer* had a difficult time getting up the river. Early on, she bogged down on a sandbar. Upstream she struck a rock, christened by Ives as Explorer Rock, and after repairs was forced to retreat back to Fort Yuma. (Richard E. Lingenfelter Collection, Charles E. Young Research Library, Department of Special Collections, UCLA.)

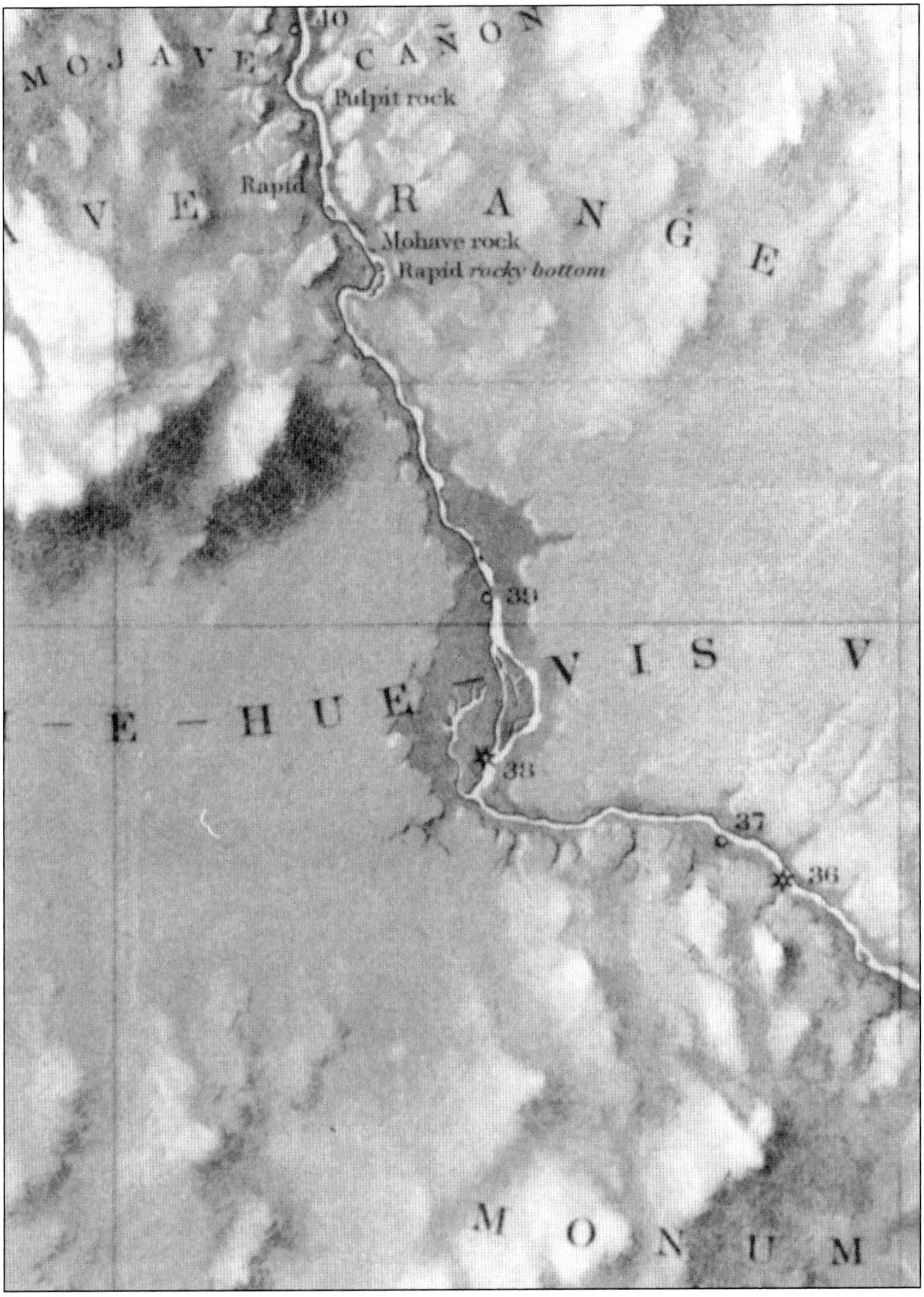

This map of the Chemehuevi Valley—entitled "Explorations and Surveys, War Department, Map No. 1, Rio Colorado of the West explored by 1st Lt. Joseph C. Ives, Top. Eng., 1858"—shows where Ives made his camps on his way up the river. Campsite number 38 was later named Chemehuevi Landing, directly across the river from what is now Lake Havasu City. (Richard E. Lingenfelter Collection, Charles E. Young Research Library, Department of Special Collections, UCLA.)

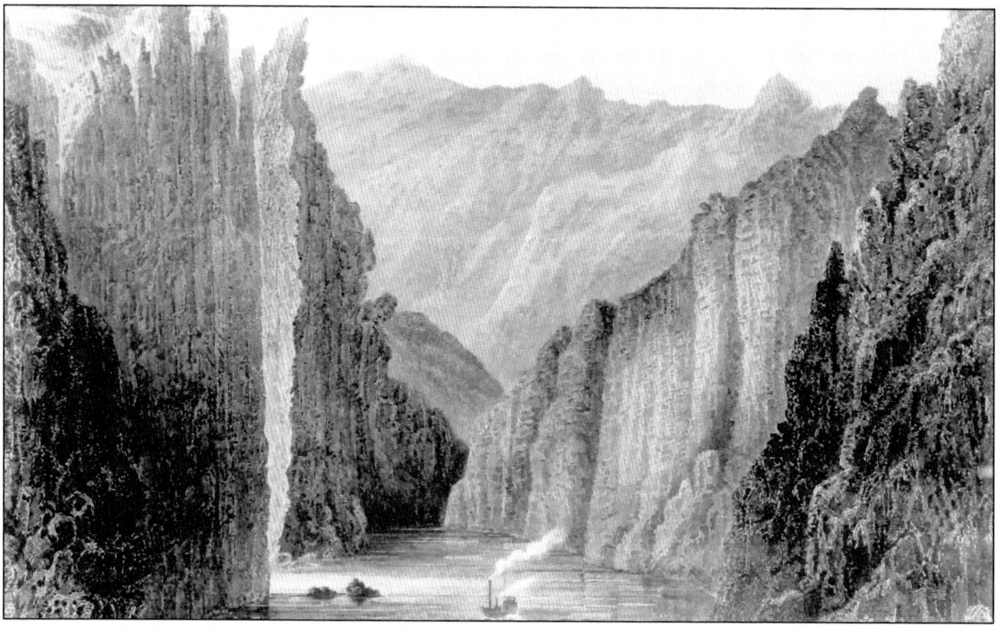

Also identified on the Ives map is Mohave Canyon, now known as Topock Gorge, located just above the Chemehuevi Valley. Mohave Canyon is illustrated here by a Baldwin Möllhausen lithograph of a sketch made on the Ives expedition, who perhaps was overdramatizing the steepness of the canyon walls. (Richard E. Lingenfelter Collection, Charles E. Young Research Library, Department of Special Collections, UCLA.)

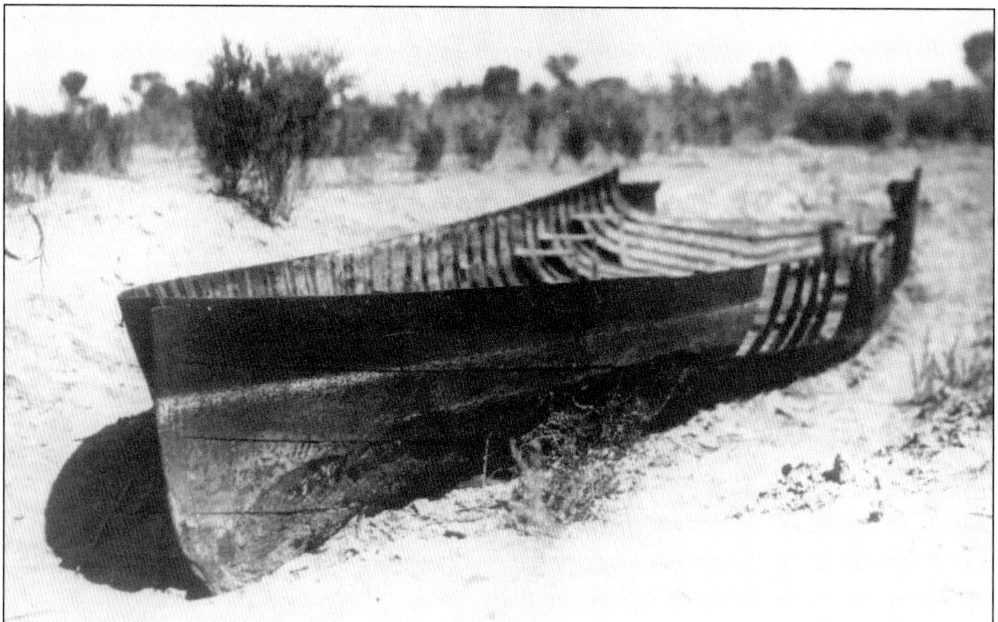

In Yuma, stripped of her machinery, the *Explorer* was employed as a barge until breaking loose from her moorings in 1864 and drifting into a slough, where she was presumed sunk. Her rusted and rotted out remains were found in one of the dry channels in the Colorado River delta below Yuma in 1929. (Courtesy Arizona Historical Society, Southern Arizona Division.)

Three

STEAMBOATS ON THE COLORADO RIVER

The first steamboat on the Colorado River was the *Uncle Sam*, launched in 1852 by James Turnbull, who had been awarded a contract to supply goods to Fort Yuma. But the *Uncle Sam* sank, and the contract was given to George Alonzo Johnson. In 1854, Johnson purchased a side-wheeler, the *General Jesup*, but because of problems with rapids and sandbars on the river, Johnson turned to stern-wheelers, bringing the *Colorado* into service in 1855.

The *Colorado* was captained by Isaac Polhamus Jr., who went on to pilot several other steamers in Johnson's fleet, including the *Cocopah II* in 1867, and the *Mohave II* in 1876, the only two-piper on the river. By that time, Johnson's business, the Colorado Steam Navigation Company, had grown to 10 steamers and a half-dozen barges, all under the charge of Captain Polhamus. Second in command was Capt. John Alexander Mellon.

Steamboat travel on the Colorado was always an adventure. Even boats drawing very little water— some as little as two feet—were frequently victimized by the ever-shifting sandbars. Sometimes the only way to negotiate the sandbars was by turning the boat around and digging through with the paddle wheel on the stern, a technique devised by Captain Mellon. At low tide, hands on deck often had to go overboard and pull the boats out. At high tide, it was difficult to steer the boats through the rough waters in the narrow canyons.

Life on board was an adventure as well. In *Vanished Arizona*, Martha Summerhayes remarked that her trip upriver on the *Gila*, piloted by Melon in 1874, was hot. "We had staterooms," she writes, "but could not remain in them long at a time, on account of the intense heat." At night, passengers were forced to take their straw bedding out on the deck. Even the dining room was hot. "The metal handles on the knives were uncomfortably warm to the touch and . . . the wooden arms of the chairs felt as if they were slowly igniting." The fare itself was meager: "fresh biscuits without butter, very salty boiled beef, and some canned vegetables." Drinking water was kept in canteens "covered in flannel and dipped in water" and hung from the rails in the shade, making the water "a trifle cooler than the air."

By the time of his retirement in 1904, Captain Polhamus had spent nearly 50 years on the river, servicing ports from Fort Yuma to Fort Mohave on a regular basis. Although much of the commerce had to do with transporting troops and supplies between the forts, stops were made for scattered ranches and mining settlements all along the way. One of the stops frequented by Polhamus was Liverpool Landing, near the present site of Lake Havasu City. Polhamus and others had small ranches in the nearby Chemehuevi Valley. Liverpool Landing and Chemehuevi Landing were the closest stops to Fort Mohave.

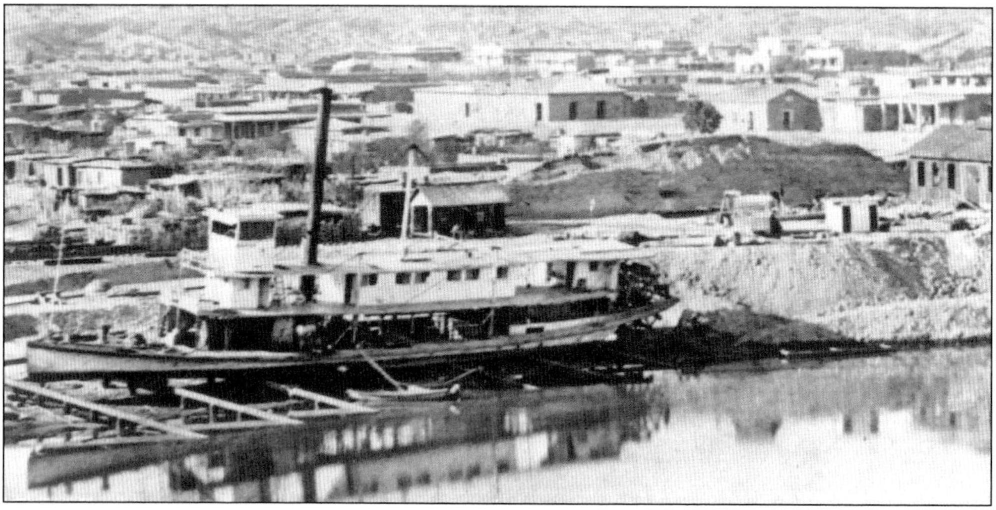

The *Colorado*, launched in 1855, was the first stern-wheeler put into service. It was 120 feet long and could carry 60 tons on less than two feet of water. The *Colorado* was the first steamboat on the river captained by Isaac Polhamus, who had just come west. Learning his trade on the relatively peaceful Hudson and Sacramento Rivers, Polhamus refused to run the *Colorado* north through the rough waters of the Mohave Canyon (Topock Gorge), 60 miles below Fort Mohave, until ordered to do so by the post commander, Major Armistead. After its retirement in 1862, the engine works of the *Colorado* were fitted onto the *Colorado II*. The *Colorado II*—145 feet long, 29 feet wide, and with a capacity for 179 tons of freight—ran until 1882. (Above courtesy Arizona State Library, Archives and Public Records, Archives Division, Phoenix; below courtesy Sharlot Hall Museum, Prescott, Arizona.)

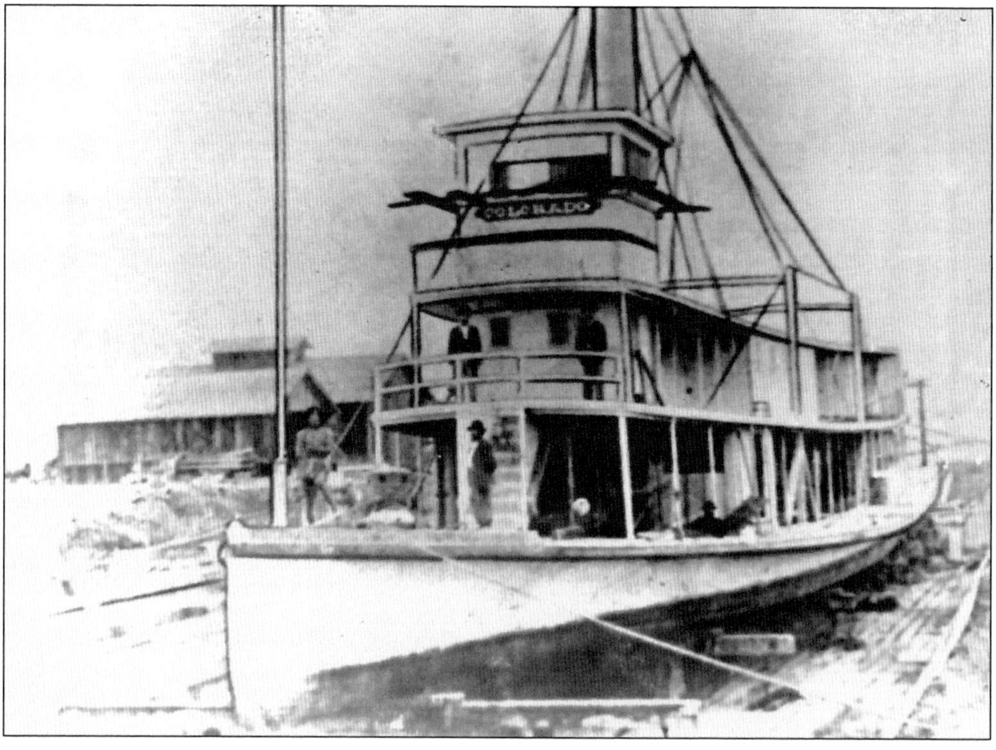

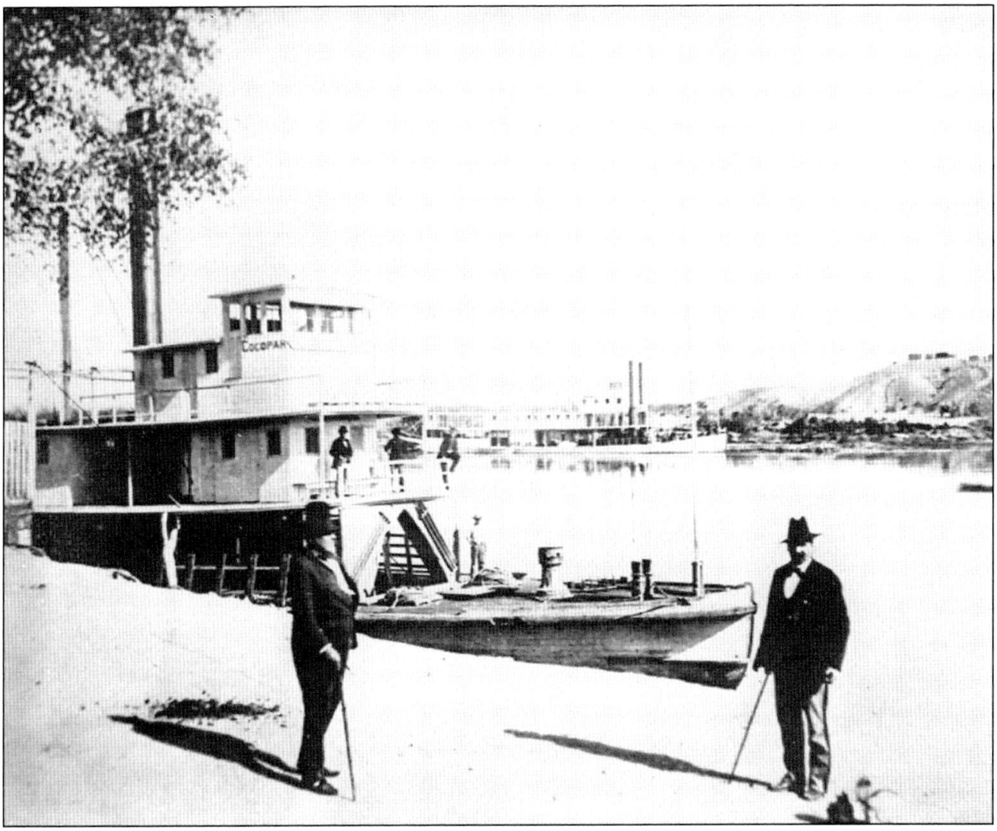

Launched in 1867, the *Cocopah II* was 147.5 feet long, 29 feet wide, and could carry 120 tons of freight on less than 20 inches of water. Isaac Polhamus also captained this boat. In 1881, the *Cocopah II* was dismantled. (Courtesy Sharlot Hall Museum, Prescott, Arizona.)

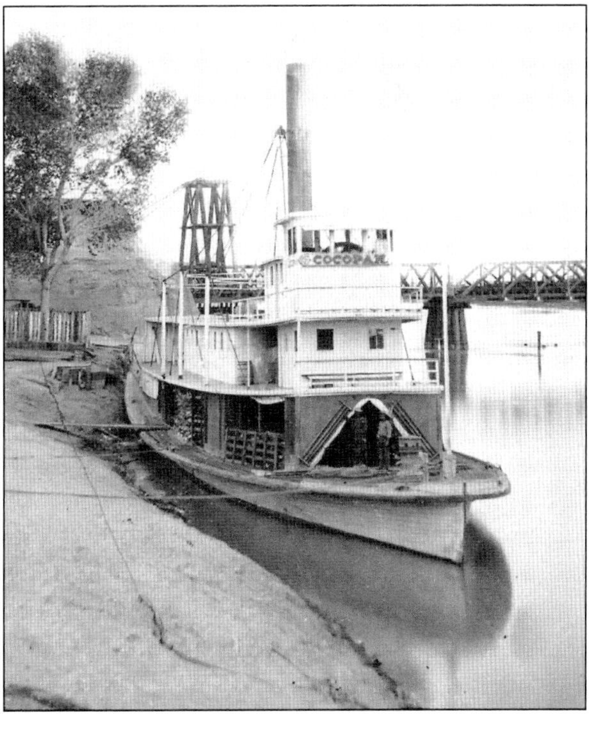

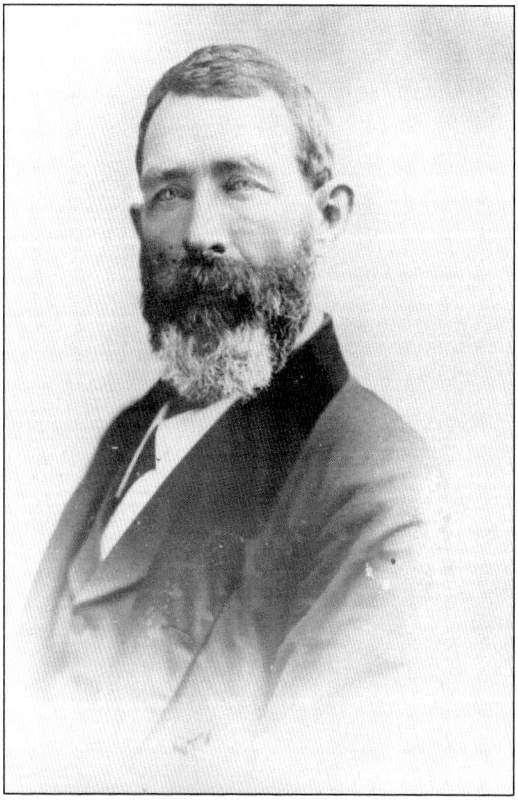

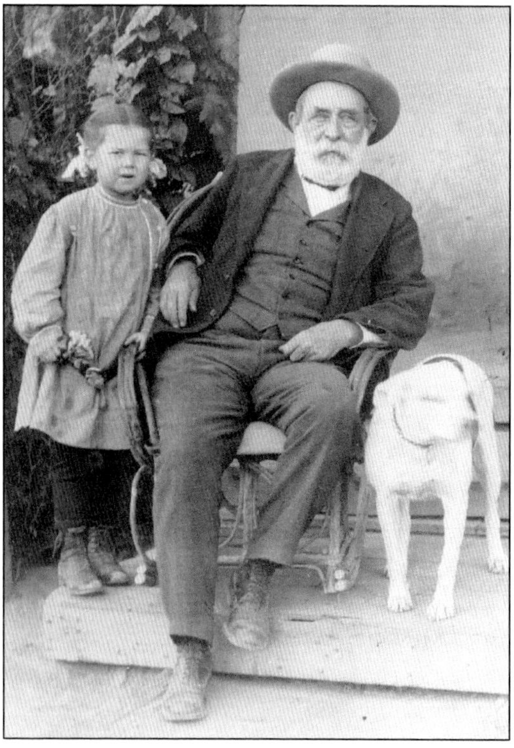

Isaac Polhamus Jr. ultimately became known as the "Dean of the Colorado River." In 1859, George A. Johnson turned over the Colorado Steam Navigation Company to Polhamus. Polhamus continued as superintendent—even after 1877 when the business was sold to the Southern Pacific Railroad—until 1886, when he and Jack Mellon bought the company. Polhamus and Mellon owned the company until 1904, when finally, at the age of 76 and after nearly 50 years on the river, Polhamus retired. Polhamus was closely associated with the area around Lake Havasu City, as his ranch in the Chemehuevi Valley was located only three miles north of Liverpool Landing. (Above courtesy Arizona Collection, Arizona State University Libraries; below courtesy Arizona Historical Society, Southern Arizona Division.)

Capt. John Alexander "Jack" Mellon was another famous steamboat captain on the Colorado River. Mellon came from New Brunswick to the river in 1864 to work for Thomas E. Trueworthy's Union Line, in chief competition with George Johnson's Colorado Steam Navigation line. Shortly after arriving, Mellon joined Johnson's line, becoming second in command, and worked the river for over 40 years. The railroad station where the cantilevered bridge was built across the Colorado River by Atlantic & Pacific in 1890 (at present-day Topock, Arizona) was first named after Capt. Jack Mellon, though it was misspelled as "Mellen." (Richard E. Lingenfelter Collection, Charles E. Young Research Library, Department of Special Collections, UCLA.)

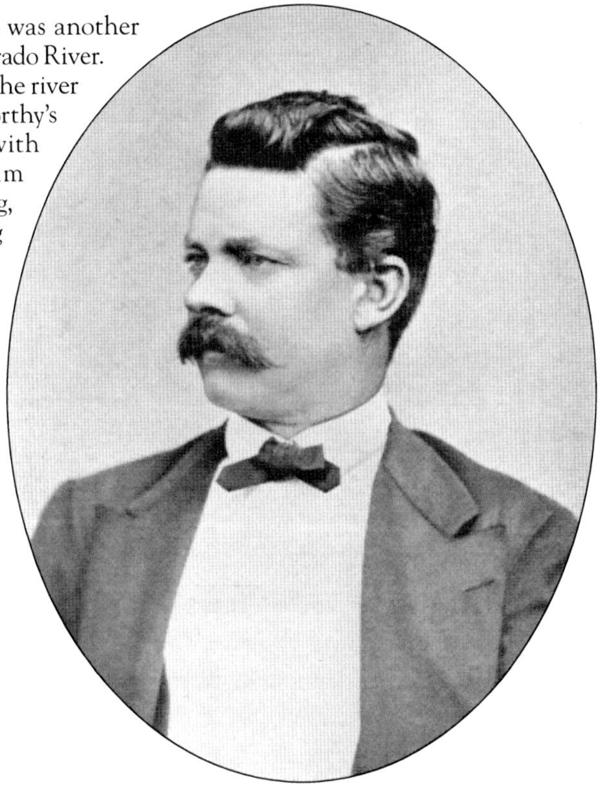

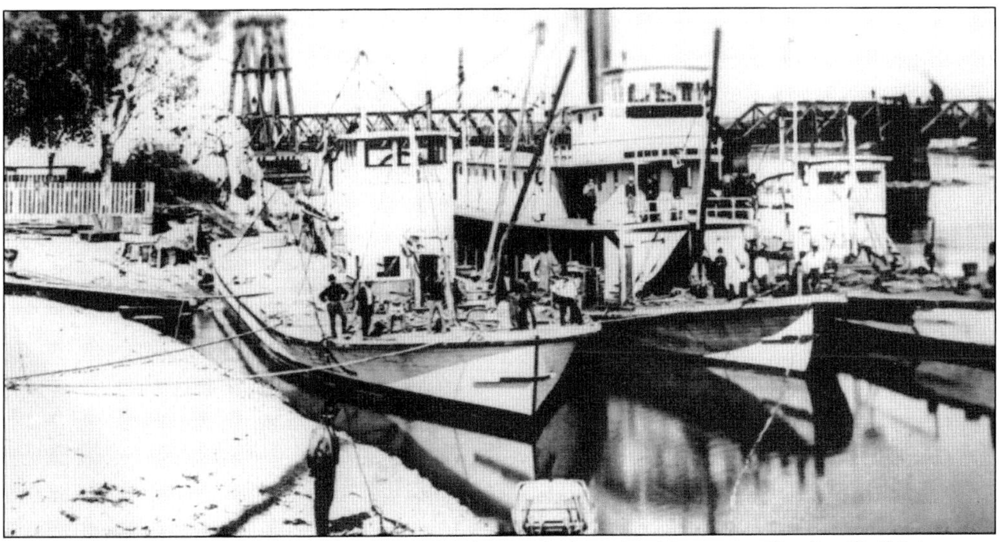

At the port in Yuma, three steamers are tied up side by side. (Courtesy Sharlot Hall Museum, Prescott, Arizona.)

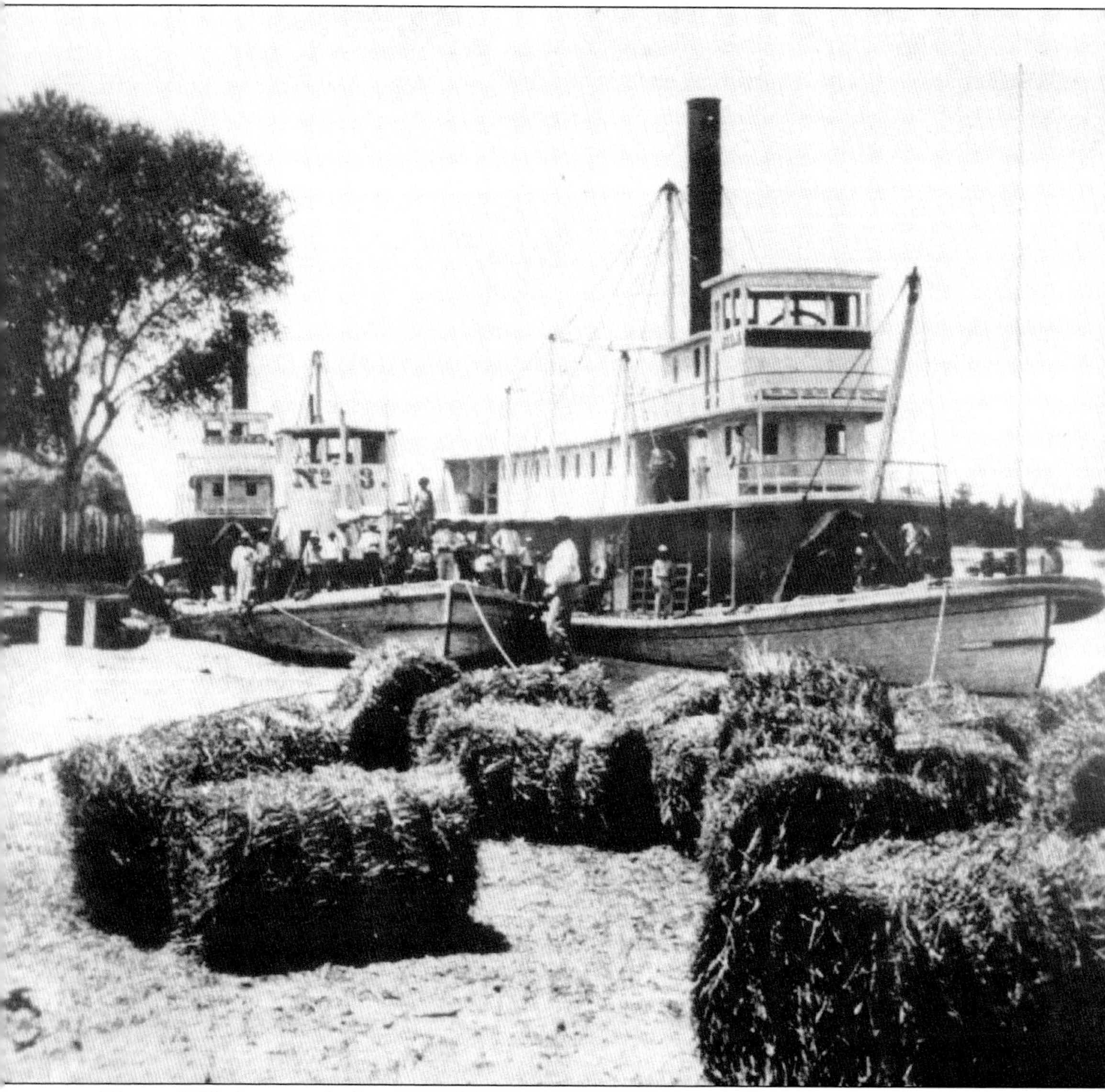

This *c.* 1876 photograph shows the *Gila*, Barge 3, and the *Cocopah* tied up at the port in Yuma. (Courtesy Sharlot Hall Museum, Prescott, Arizona.)

Launched in 1873 and first piloted by Jack Mellon, the *Gila*—149 feet long, 31 feet wide at the beam, displacing 236 tons, and drawing 16.5 inches of water—was the most durable boat on the river, hauling freight and passengers for more than 25 years. Rebuilt as the *Cochan*, she ran for another 10 years, until the river was finally closed to navigation. From 1879 to 1887, the *Gila* saw service under charter for gold mines in Eldorado Canyon in Nevada and salt mines at the mouth of the Virgin River in Utah. (Right courtesy Sharlot Hall Museum, Prescott, Arizona; below courtesy Arizona State Library, Archives and Public Records, Archives Division, Phoenix.)

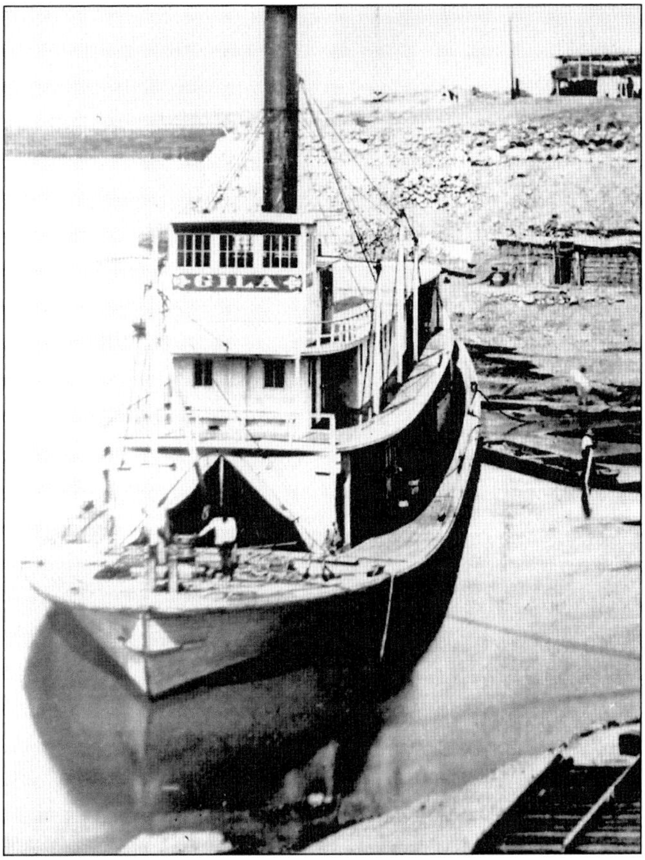

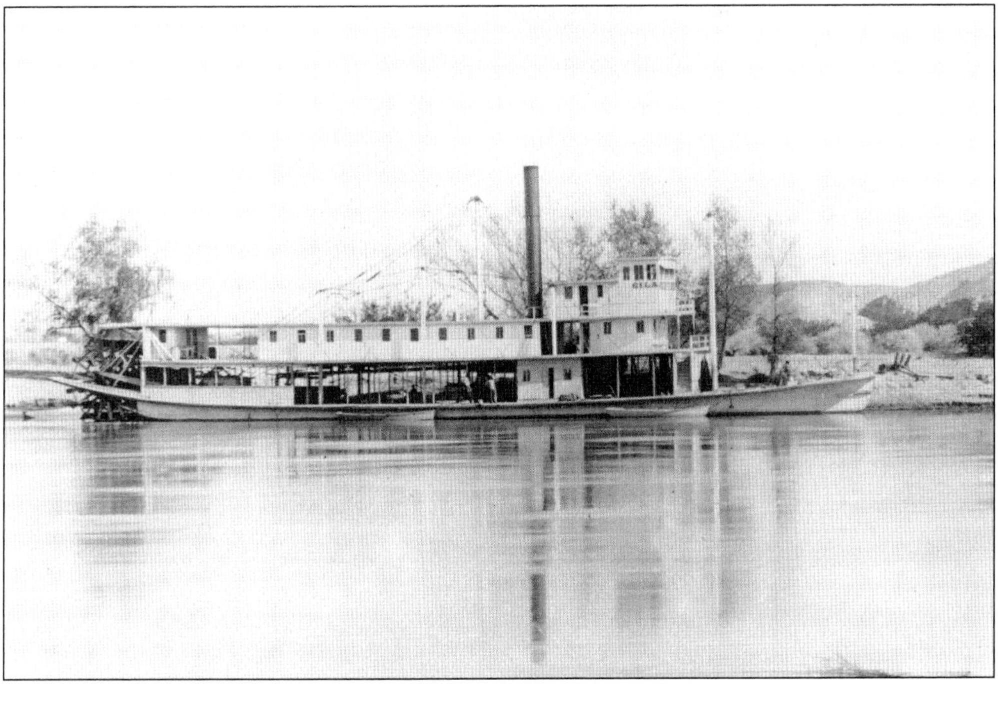

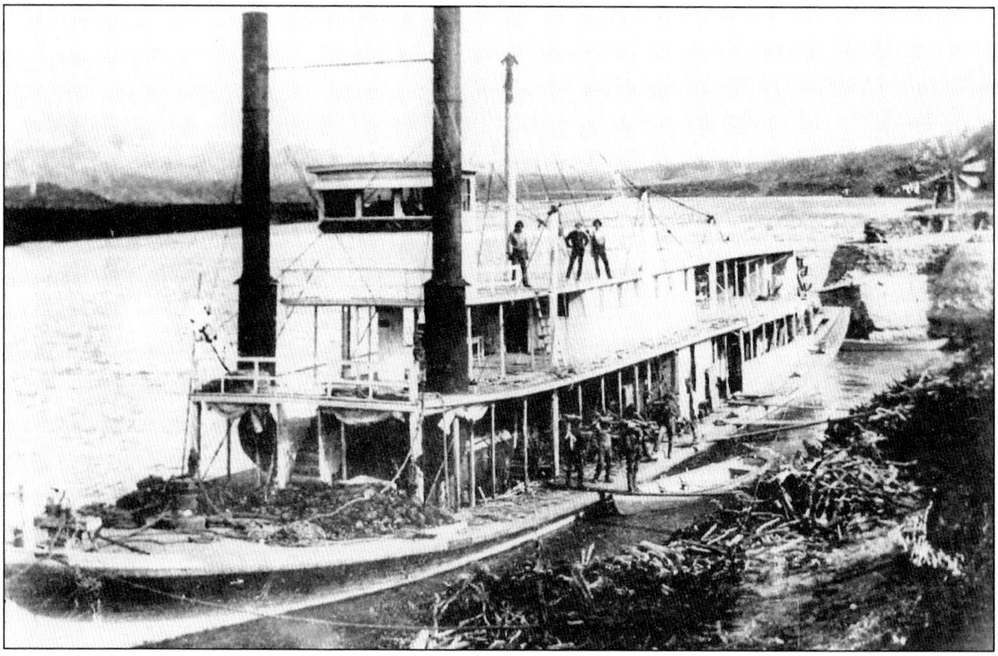

Launched in 1876, the *Mohave II* was the largest steamboat to ever run the river. Displacing 188 tons and drawing only a foot of water, the steamboat was 149.5 feet long and 31.5 feet at the beam. Because of her shallow draft, the captain was able to take her all the way up to the Virgin River. Advertised as "palatial" and "magnificent," the *Mohave II* was also a pleasure boat that made trips into the Gulf of California. The *Mohave II* was retired in 1900. (Courtesy Lake Havasu Museum of History.)

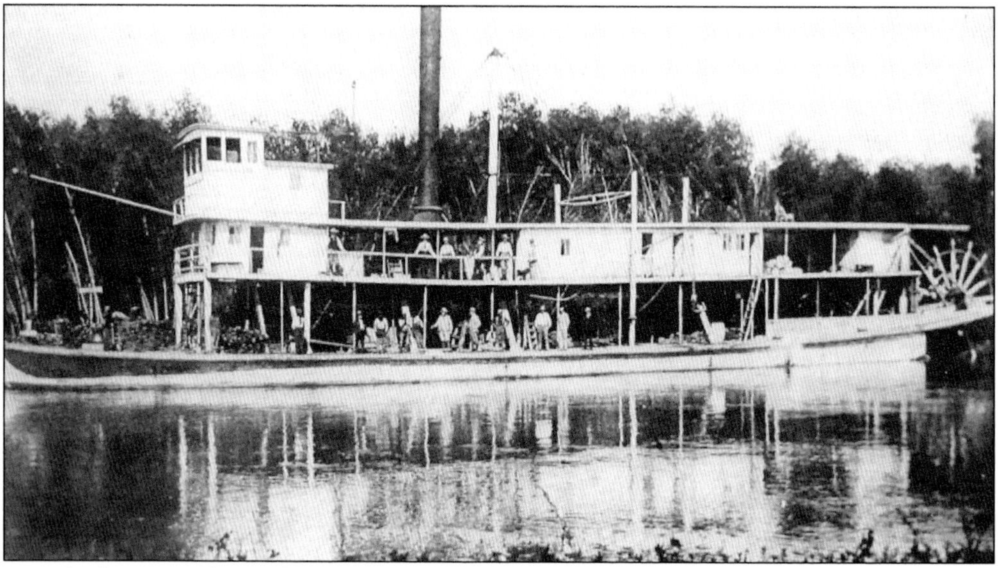

Launched in 1899, the *Cochan* (known as the *Gila* before rebuilt) was 135 feet long, 31 feet wide at the beam, and could carry 125 tons of freight, drawing less than two feet of water. "She's not much for beauty," said Mellon, "but she can wax the sandbars" (*Steamboats on the Colorado River* by Richard E. Lingenfelter.) (Courtesy Mohave Museum of History and Art, No. 807.)

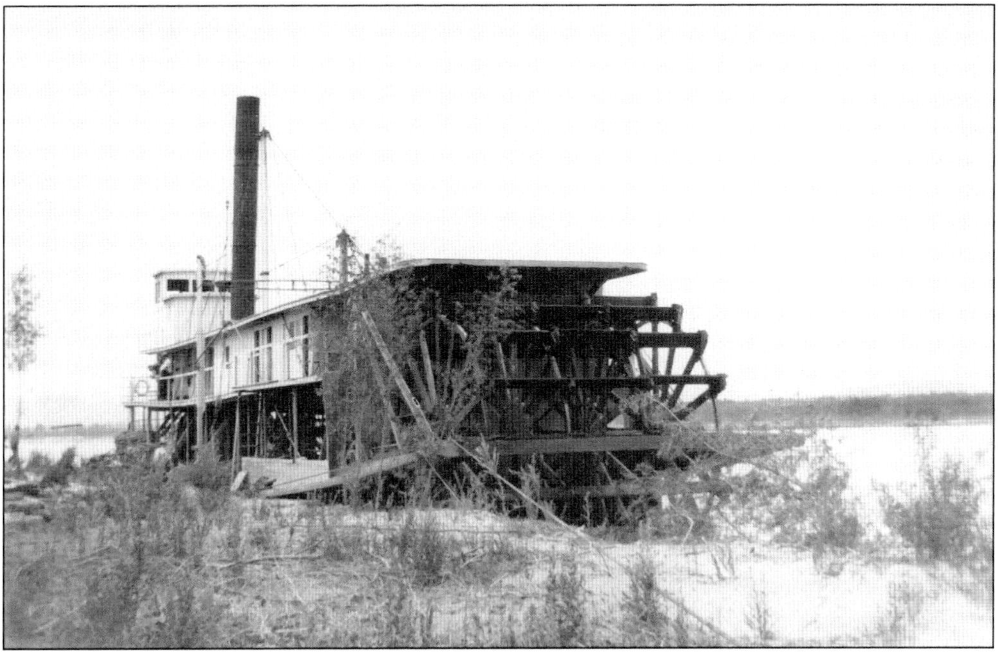

Until 1905, the *Cochan* ran up and down the Colorado River, servicing the mines at Searchlight, Nevada. Back in Yuma, the *Cochan* continued to find work until dismantled in 1910. (Above courtesy Arizona Historical Society, Southern Arizona Division; below courtesy Lake Havasu Museum of History.)

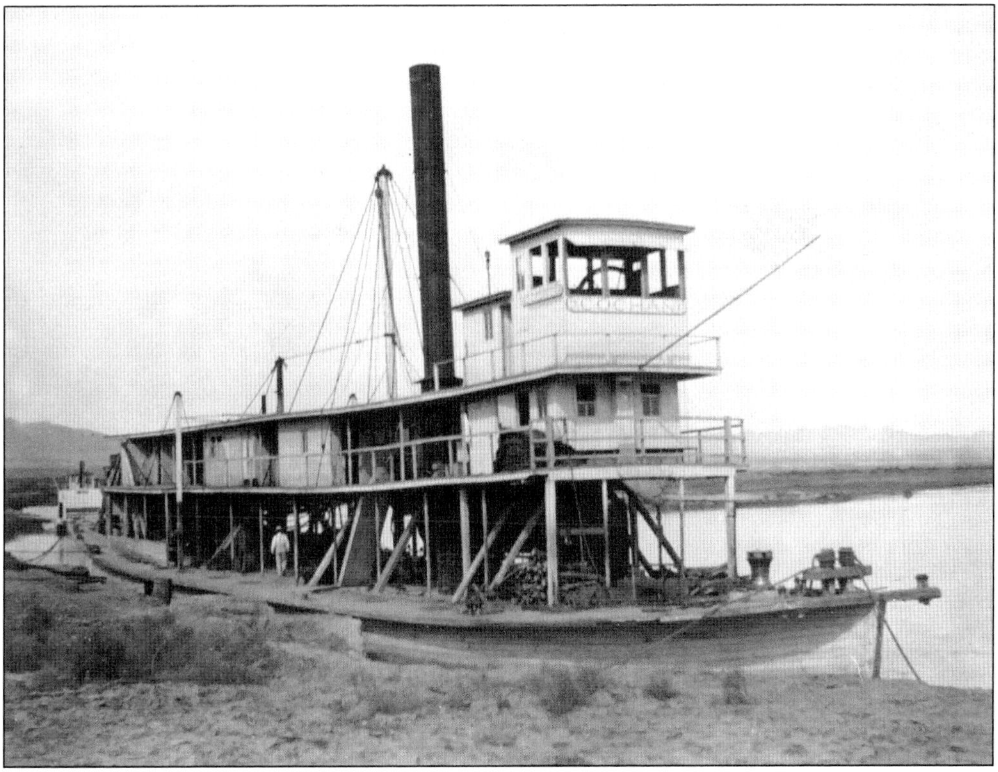

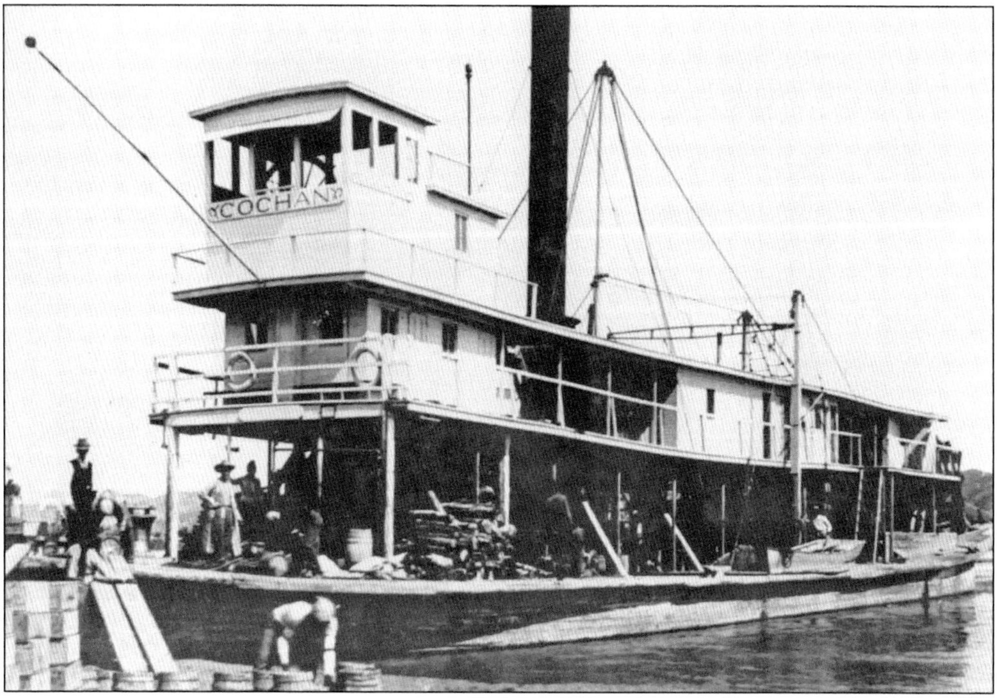

Prior to a trip up the Colorado, the *Cochan* is seen here in the process of being loaded with passengers and freight. (Courtesy Arizona Historical Society, Southern Arizona Division.)

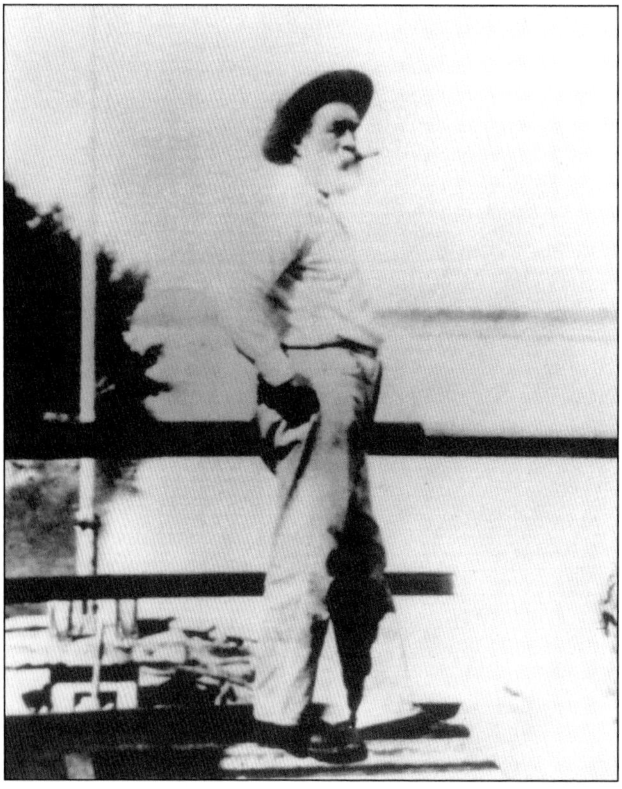

Steamboating on the Colorado River essentially ended in 1909 with the completion of the Laguna Dam, some 14 miles above Yuma. Isaac Polhamus (shown here), the river's most famous captain, however, survived until 1922, passing away at the age of 94. Jack Mellon survived until 1924, passing away at the age of 83. (Courtesy Arizona State Library, Archives and Public Records, Archives Division, Phoenix, #97-7823.)

Four

Mining in the Lake Havasu City Area

A number of placer mines were scattered up and down the Colorado River in the middle of the 19th century. In fact, it was rumored that placers above Yuma had been worked by the Spanish a hundred years earlier. But when John Thomas Moss discovered silver in 1861, the rush was on! After playing out his silver mine in Eldorado Canyon on the west side of the river, Moss prospected the hills on the east side of the river, discovering gold north of Fort Mohave in 1864, and working his way down to the Hualapai Mountains, south of what is now Kingman.

Soon after, it was reported that the Chemehuevi Mountains (now known as the Mohaves), just above Lake Havasu City, were rich in silver and gold. A newspaper article in the *Mohave County Miner* at the turn of the century described the western slopes of the Chemehuevis as "one vast bed of gold bearing wash." "Many thousands of dollars have been dry-washed out of the gulches," it was reported, "and the whole district is sprinkled with gold from numerous gold fissures." The highest peak in the Chemehuevis is named after A. G. Crossman, a placer miner in the area, sometimes referred to in the news as the "Gold King of the Chemehuevis."

Newspapers, such as the *Mohave County Miner,* are replete with tales of the mines and the miners, the rediscovery of the Lost Dutchman, for instance, published in 1902. "Dick Cleve brought to Kingman 400 lbs. of rich gold ore Tuesday from the deposit in the Chemehuevis," began the account. "Dick was meandering along and saw a rattler wiggling among a pile of brown rocks, and seized a rock to fire at the snake when he found it so heavy that instead of throwing it . . . pronounced it gold."

One of the most successful mines in the area was Jackson McCracken's silver lode, discovered in 1873. Silver from the McCracken and Signal mines was milled at nearby Greenwood City on Big Sandy Creek in the southeast part of the county. Greenwood City was connected by road to Liverpool Landing near Lake Havasu City.

Liverpool Landing (sometimes called "Godman") was an important port for shipping ore and supplies for mines located in the Lake Havasu City area. According to one source (*Lake Havasu City* by Roman Malach), Liverpool Landing, located near Windsor Beach, is noted on the 1879 Smith map of Arizona; on Hinton's map of 1886, on the General Land Office map of 1892, and on the U.S. Geological Survey map of 1911. The name of the landing may have referred to the destination city where the ores were shipped, as may have been the case with Pittsburg Landing, located on Pittsburg Flat (now Thompson Bay on Lake Havasu), though the spelling of Pittsburgh, the city, is different. Both communities at Liverpool Landing and Pittsburg Landing are now buried beneath the flood waters of the lake.

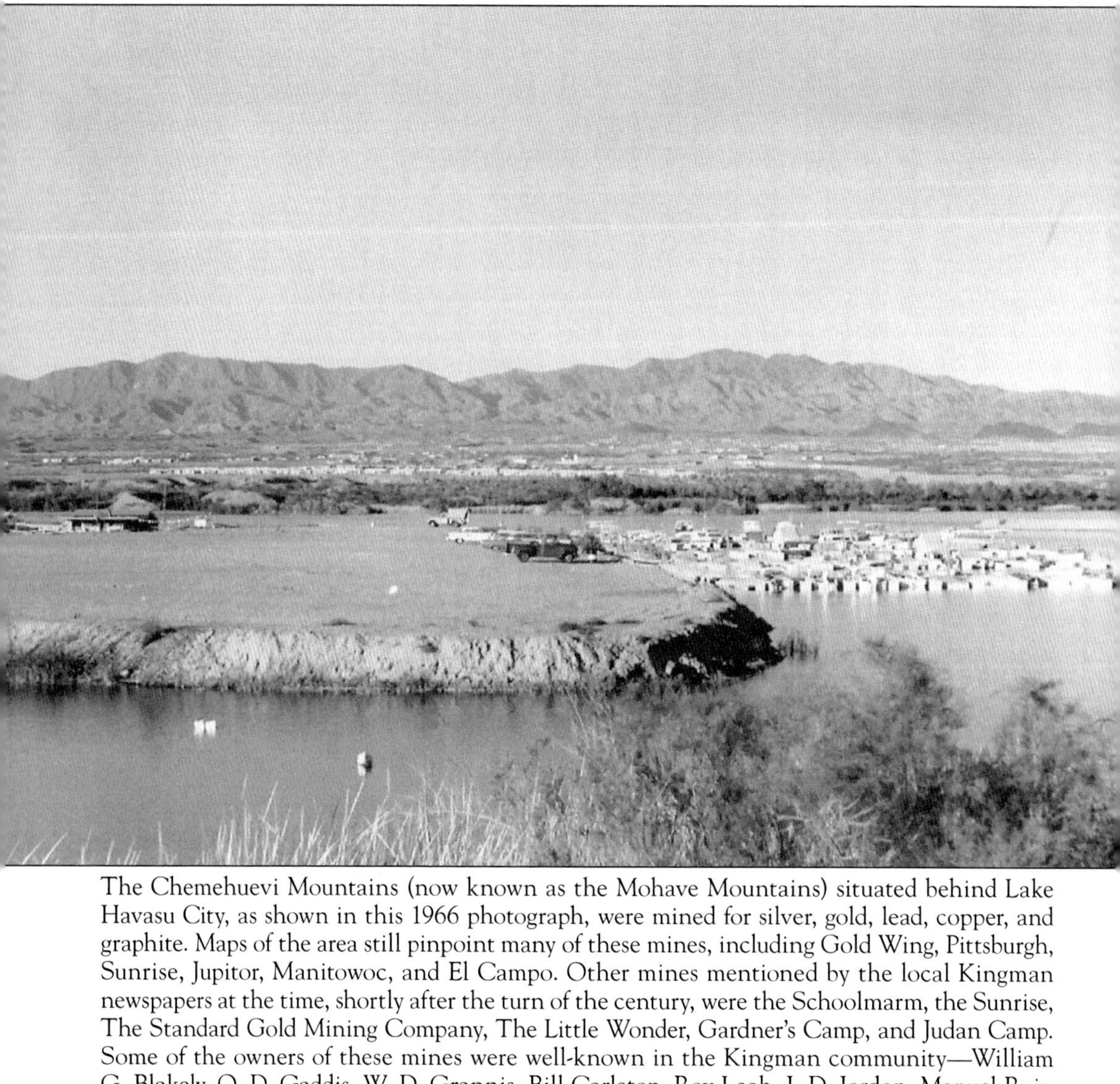

The Chemehuevi Mountains (now known as the Mohave Mountains) situated behind Lake Havasu City, as shown in this 1966 photograph, were mined for silver, gold, lead, copper, and graphite. Maps of the area still pinpoint many of these mines, including Gold Wing, Pittsburgh, Sunrise, Jupitor, Manitowoc, and El Campo. Other mines mentioned by the local Kingman newspapers at the time, shortly after the turn of the century, were the Schoolmarm, the Sunrise, The Standard Gold Mining Company, The Little Wonder, Gardner's Camp, and Judan Camp. Some of the owners of these mines were well-known in the Kingman community—William G. Blakely, O. D. Gaddis, W. D. Grannis, Bill Carleton, Roy Leah, J. D. Jordon, Manuel Ruiz, Recorder Feeney, Ernst Saloman, Otto Saloman, George W. Jones, Dennis Kelleher, Elmer Ziegler, Joe Brittan, George Grosscup, and Jack Simpson among them. Kingman was the nearest town of size with an assay office. As late as 1934, the Arizona Bureau of Mines reported the Best Bet, Susan, Santa Claus, and Dutch Flat mines still operating in the Chemehuevis. (Courtesy Lake Havasu Museum of History.)

One of the first gold mining operations to work lode deposits in the Chemehuevis was the Sunrise mine, located near the top of Crossman Peak, assessment work beginning there in 1890. Walter Scott and Clay E. Smith, owners of the Sunrise, hired the former Atlantic & Pacific railroad crew boss, John Reardon, to drive a shaft at the Sunrise in 1894. (Courtesy Mohave Museum of History and Art, No. 5804.)

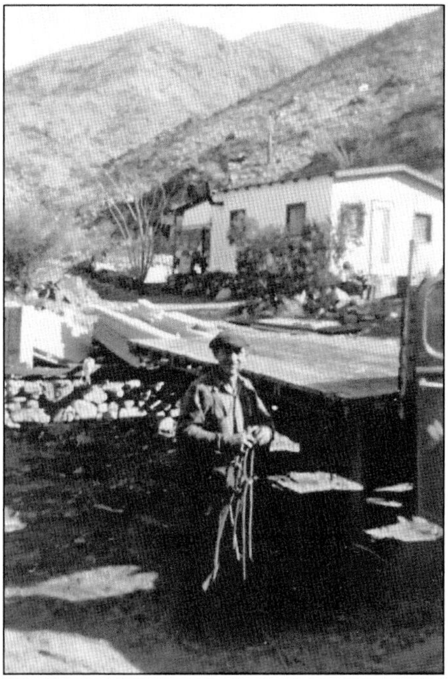

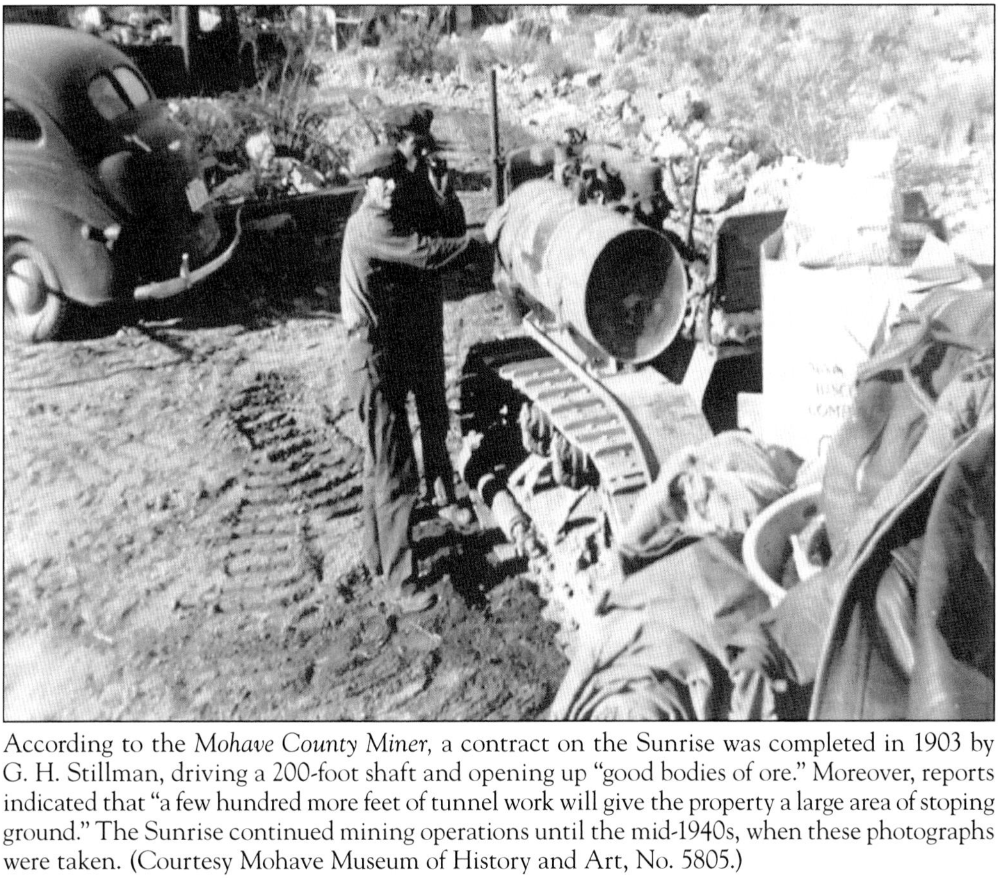

According to the *Mohave County Miner,* a contract on the Sunrise was completed in 1903 by G. H. Stillman, driving a 200-foot shaft and opening up "good bodies of ore." Moreover, reports indicated that "a few hundred more feet of tunnel work will give the property a large area of stoping ground." The Sunrise continued mining operations until the mid-1940s, when these photographs were taken. (Courtesy Mohave Museum of History and Art, No. 5805.)

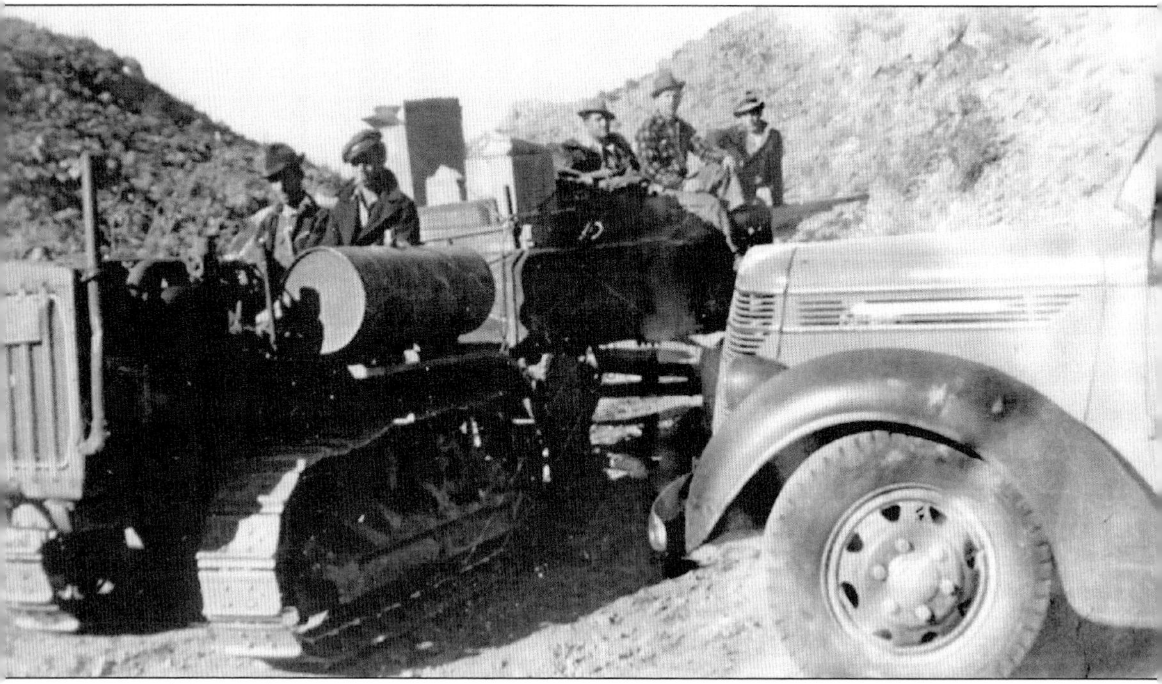

From left to right, "Press" Moon (driver), N. R. Dunton, and workers Belding, Mike Place, and Parley Ingram pose with equipment at the Sunrise mine in the 1940s. (Courtesy Mohave Museum of History and Art, No. 5806.)

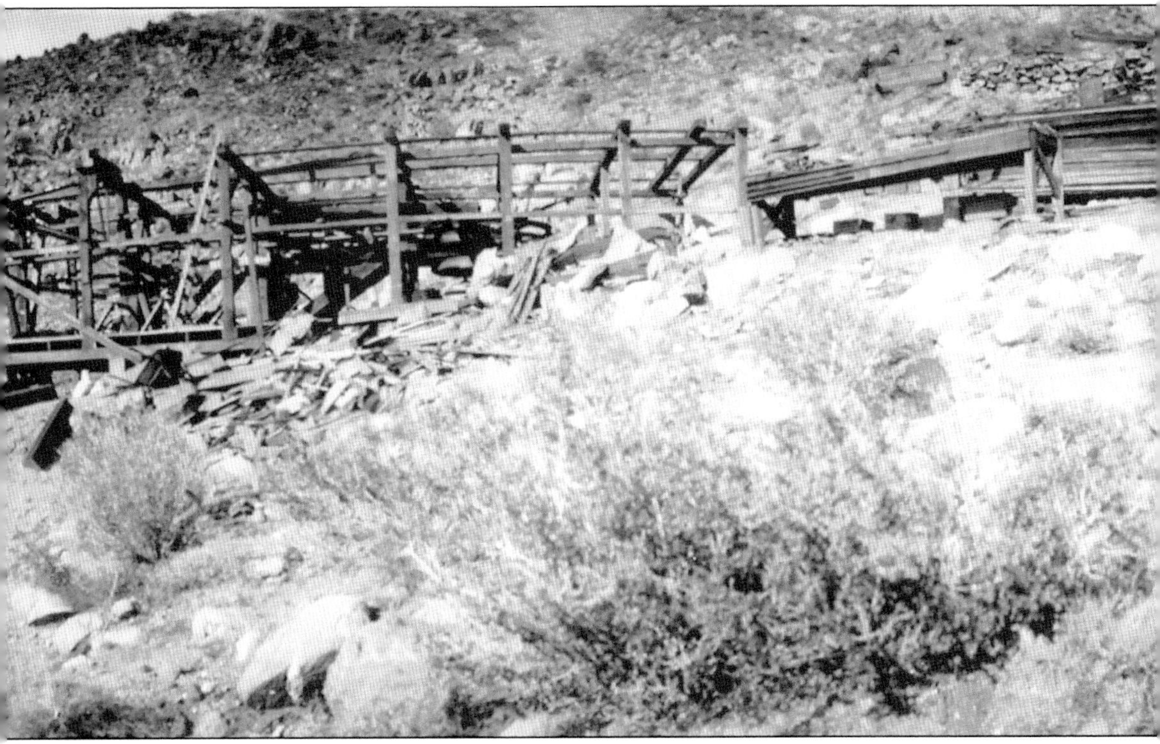

Gold Wing camp (ruins shown above) sprung up in the 1930s in the Gold Wing Mining District, a region of Franconia Wash, some 20 miles southeast of Topock and about five miles from the Colorado River. At one time, the camp consisted of three cabins and eight tents, with a population of 75 working the placer mines in the district. In the mid-1930s, gold production, coarse grains of gold panned or scraped from dry gravels and cemented together by lime carbonate, was reported (at as much as $35 an ounce) to amount to $1,200. The Gold Wing mine once operated a three-stamp mill near the Colorado River. (Courtesy Mohave Museum of History and Art, No. 3150.)

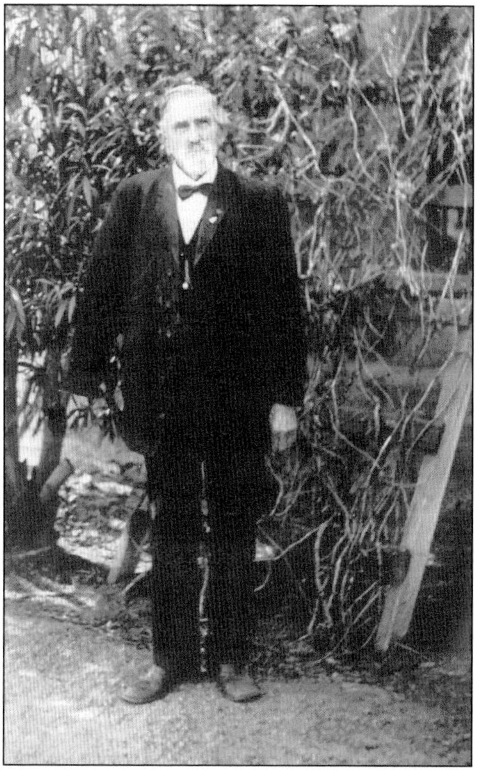

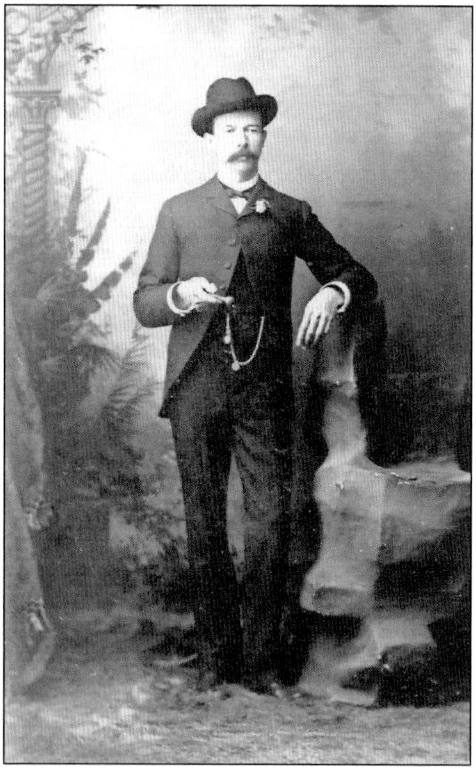

Kingman judge William G. Blakely (above) and postmaster O. D. Gaddis (below) were the owners of the most famous mine in the Chemehuevis, the Lost Dutchman. Located on the south face of Crossman Peak, the Lost Dutchman in 1913 boasted gold ore assayed at $39.27 an ounce for a recovery of $35 a ton. Even the tailings were running at $16 a ton. A 65-foot deep tunnel had uncovered a 12-inch vein of gold at the Lost Dutchman. The mine got its name as a result of an 1870 claim by a miner who, returning from an assay trip to San Francisco, died from heat prostration on his way to the mine, taking with him to the grave its exact location. Years later, the mine was rediscovered by Dick Cleve and John Blakely and renamed the Rattlesnake. (Courtesy Mohave Museum of History and Art, Nos. 6708 and 8150.)

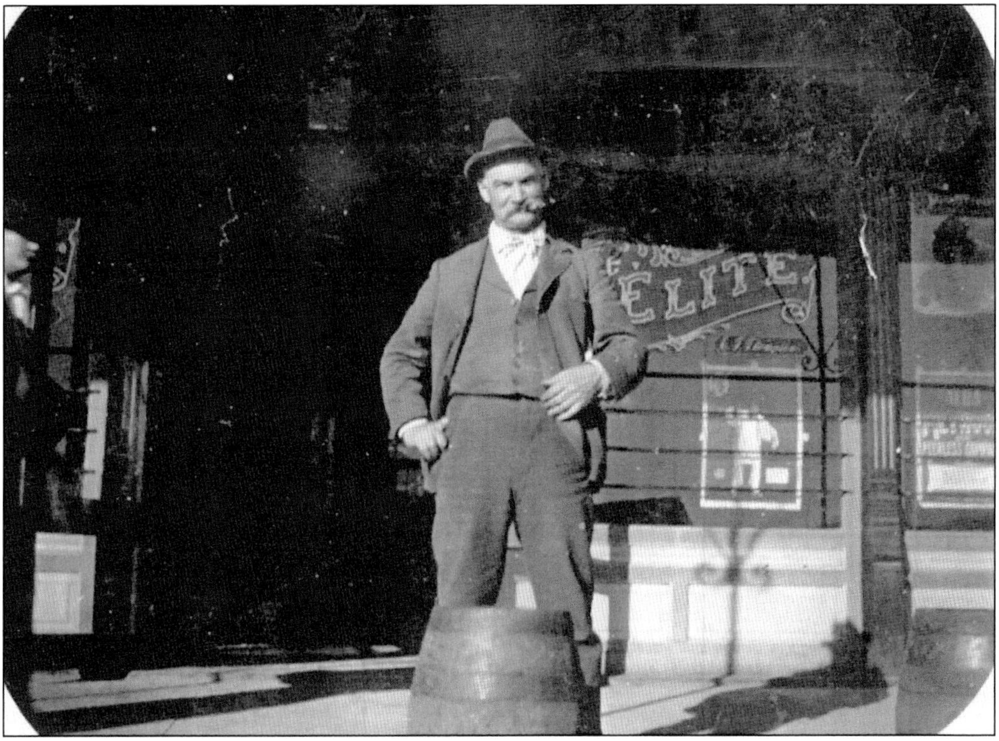

In 1903, John Kolar (pictured above), a blacksmith in Kingman, and Henry P. Ewing (pictured below, third from left) took over the silver and gold mine in the Chemehuevis known as the Pittsburgh, formerly owned by Cass Hite and Billy Hutt. In 1892, Hite and Hutt had driven a shaft down 20 feet and discovered a vein of ore three feet wide and 80 feet long, assessed at $250 per ton. (Courtesy Mohave Museum of History and Art, No. 4083.)

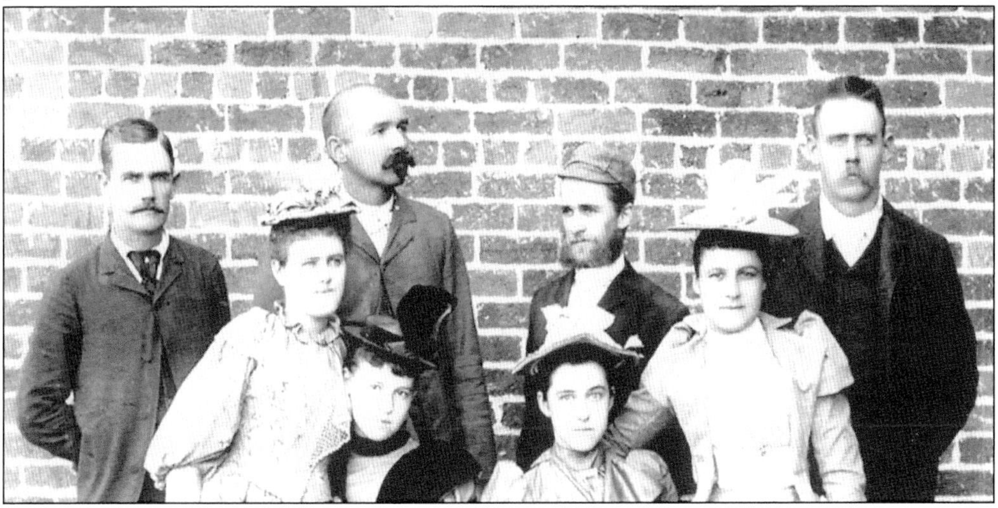

Kolar and Ewing made extensive improvements to the Pittsburgh, which the *Mohave County Miner* reported had "considerable rich ore in the stopes" with an even "better showing" at the bottom of the shaft. It is speculated that ore from the Pittsburgh mine was shipped out of Pittsburg Landing, below Thompson Bay on the south side of the Pittsburg peninsula in Lake Havasu City. (Courtesy Mohave Museum of History and Art, No. 6963.)

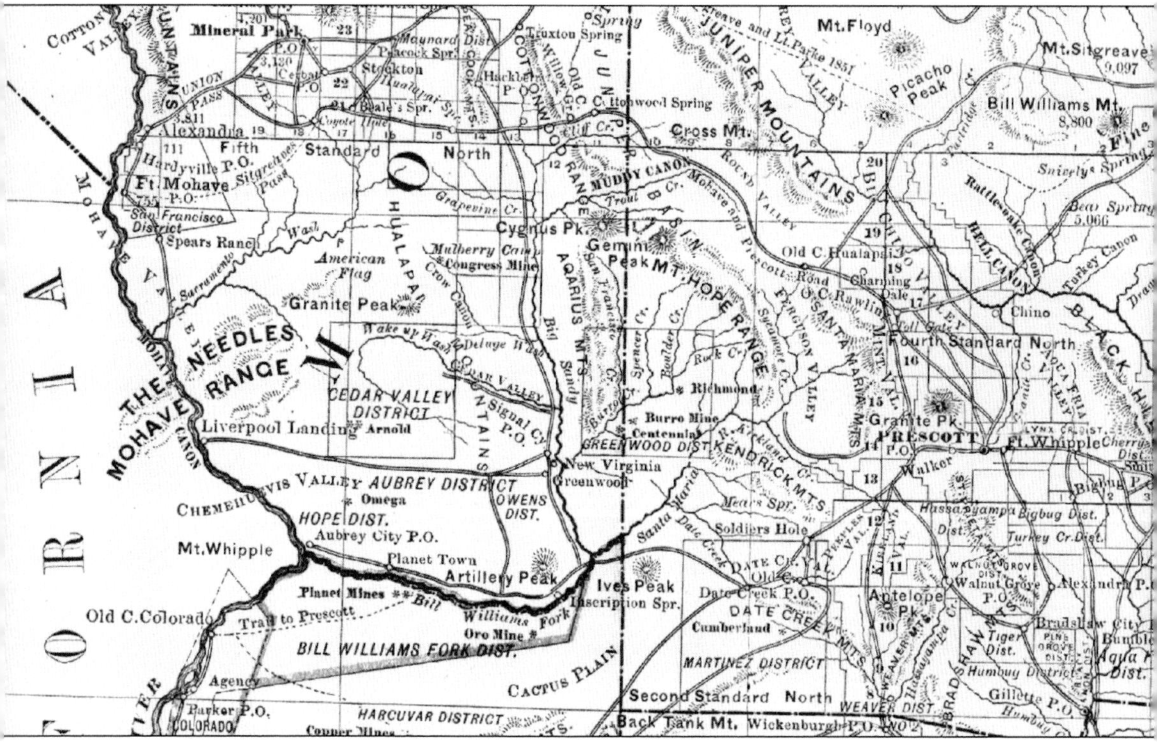

Clearly visible on this 1890 Rand McNally map is the road connecting the McCracken mine, Signal, and Greenwood City to Liverpool Landing on the Colorado River, just below "The Needles" and the "Mohave Range" labels on the map, near the site where Windsor Beach State Park in Lake Havasu City is now located. (Richard E. Lingenfelter Collection, Charles E. Young Research Library, Department of Special Collections, UCLA.)

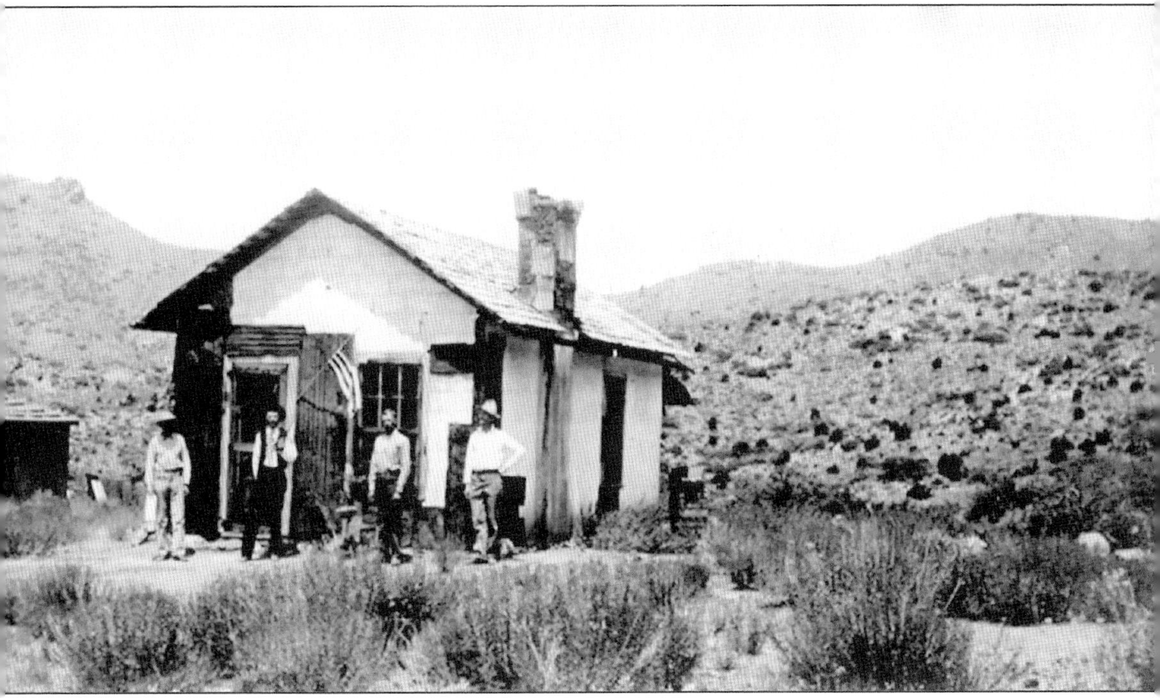

Frank (or Jackson) McCracken (far right) stands in front of a building in the town of McCracken, Arizona, on the Fourth of July, sometime after the date when the McCracken mine was first discovered, August 17, 1874. By 1877, McCracken was said to have been the best equipped silver mine in Arizona. It also produced lead and copper. (Courtesy Mohave Museum of History and Art, Nos. 4506 and 7035.)

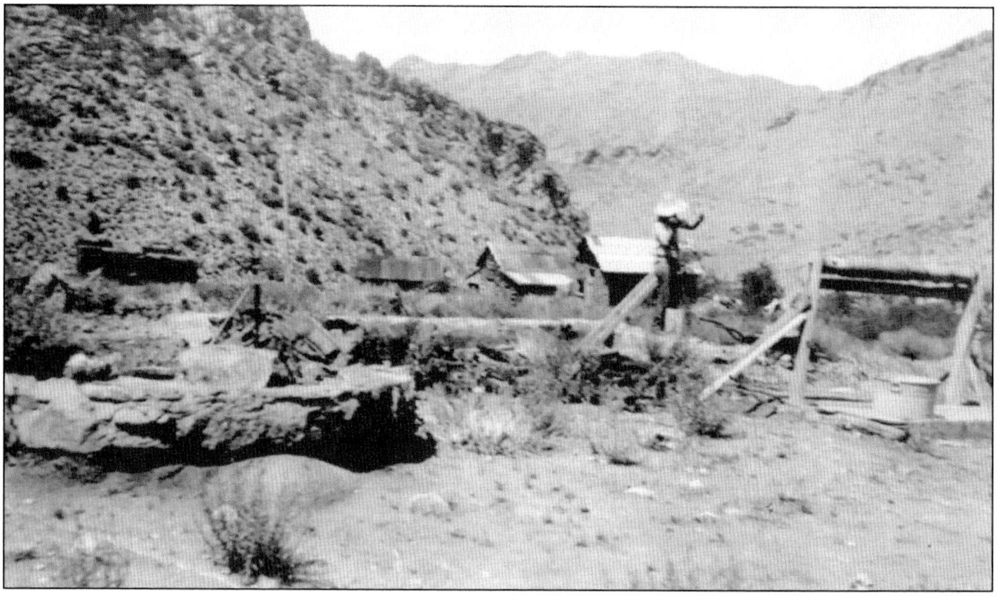

The town of McCracken was located in the Owens Mining District in southeastern Mohave County near Wikieup, Arizona. The district was named for "Chloride Jack" Owen, who along with Jack McCracken discovered the McCracken mine. (Courtesy Mohave Museum of History and Art, No. 4497.)

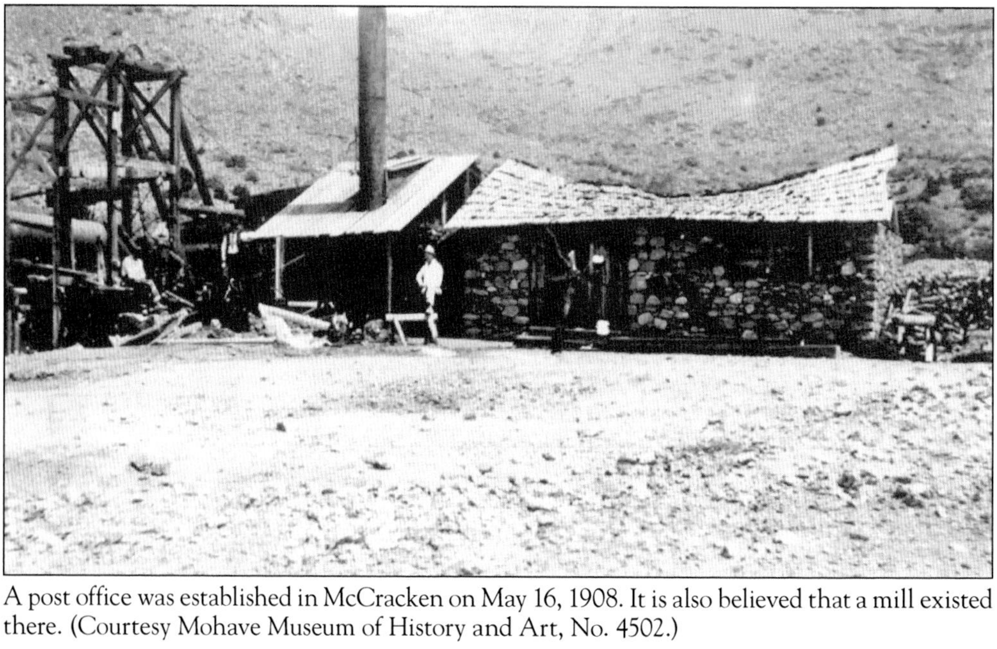

A post office was established in McCracken on May 16, 1908. It is also believed that a mill existed there. (Courtesy Mohave Museum of History and Art, No. 4502.)

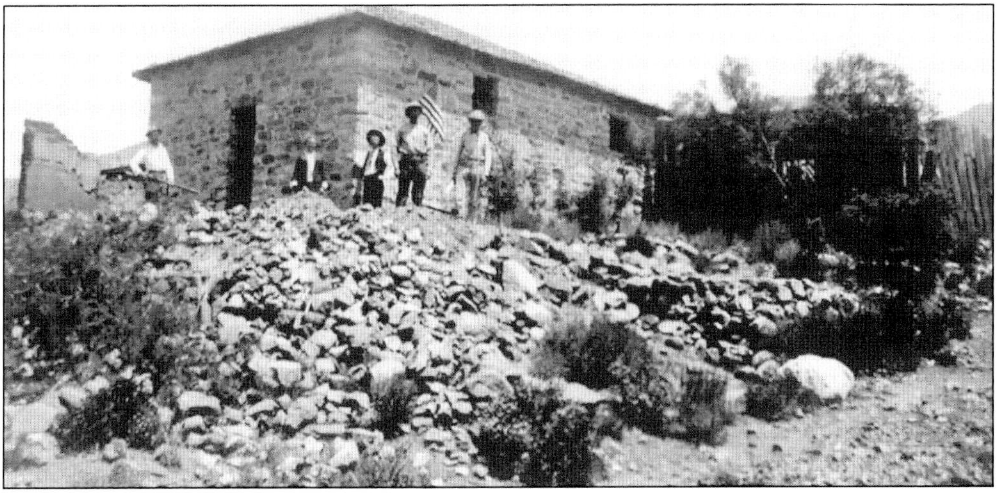

Mr. McCracken (far right) is standing with others in front of a stone building located on the top of McCracken Peak in the town of McCracken. (Courtesy Mohave Museum of History and Art, No. 4495.)

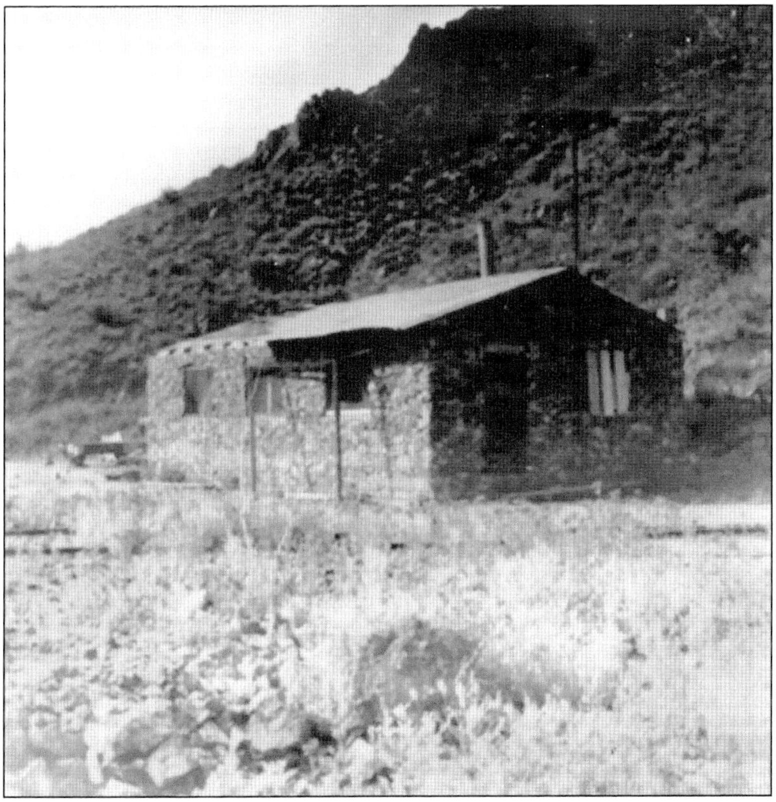

This stone building was the only structure still standing in the town of McCracken when this photograph was taken in 1974. (Courtesy Mohave Museum of History and Art, No. 2438.)

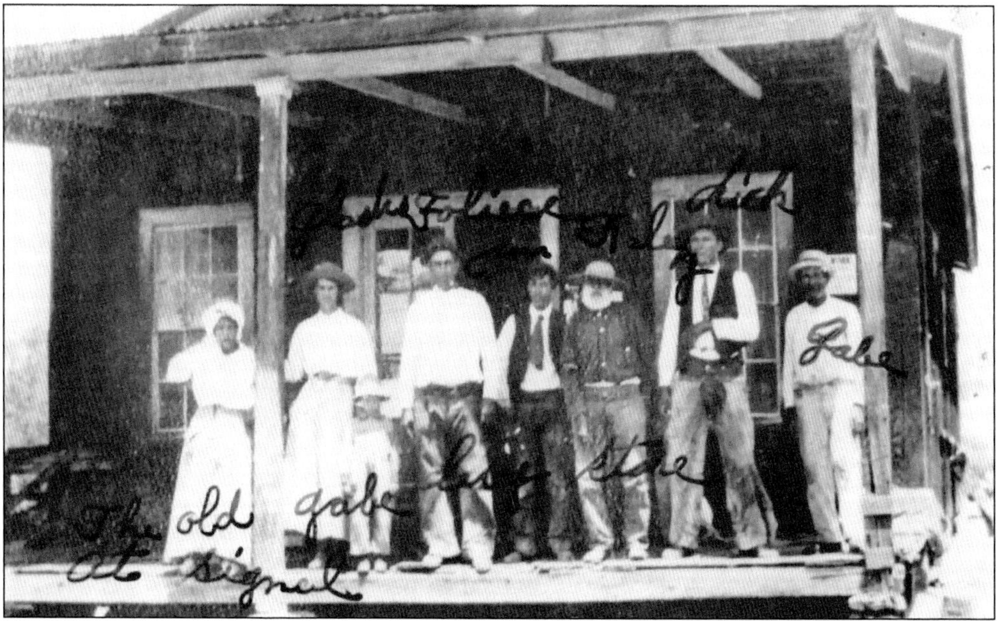

Gabriel Levy, "Uncle Gabe" (far right), stands on the porch of his store in Signal, Arizona, *c.* 1920. The Signal mine, for which the town was named, was discovered in 1874, the same year as the nearby McCracken mine. A post office operated in the town of Signal from October 15, 1877, until May 14, 1932. (Courtesy Mohave Museum of History and Art, No 9595.)

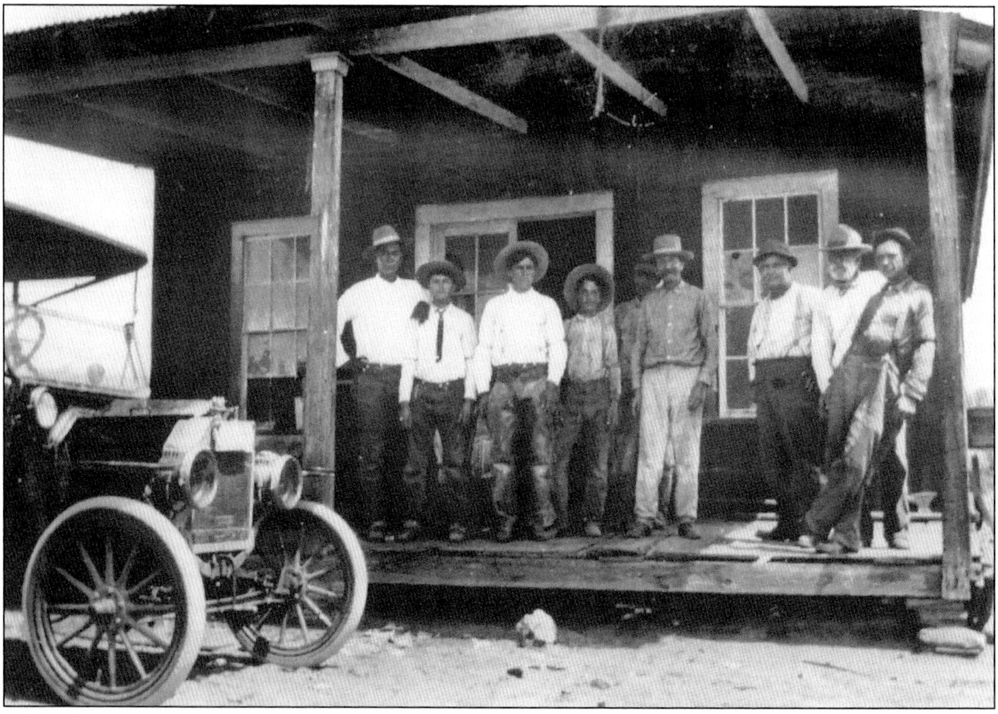

This photograph of the Gabe Levy store in Signal was believed to have been taken in the early 1930s. Gabe Levy died in 1932. (Courtesy Mohave Museum of History and Art, No. 8753.)

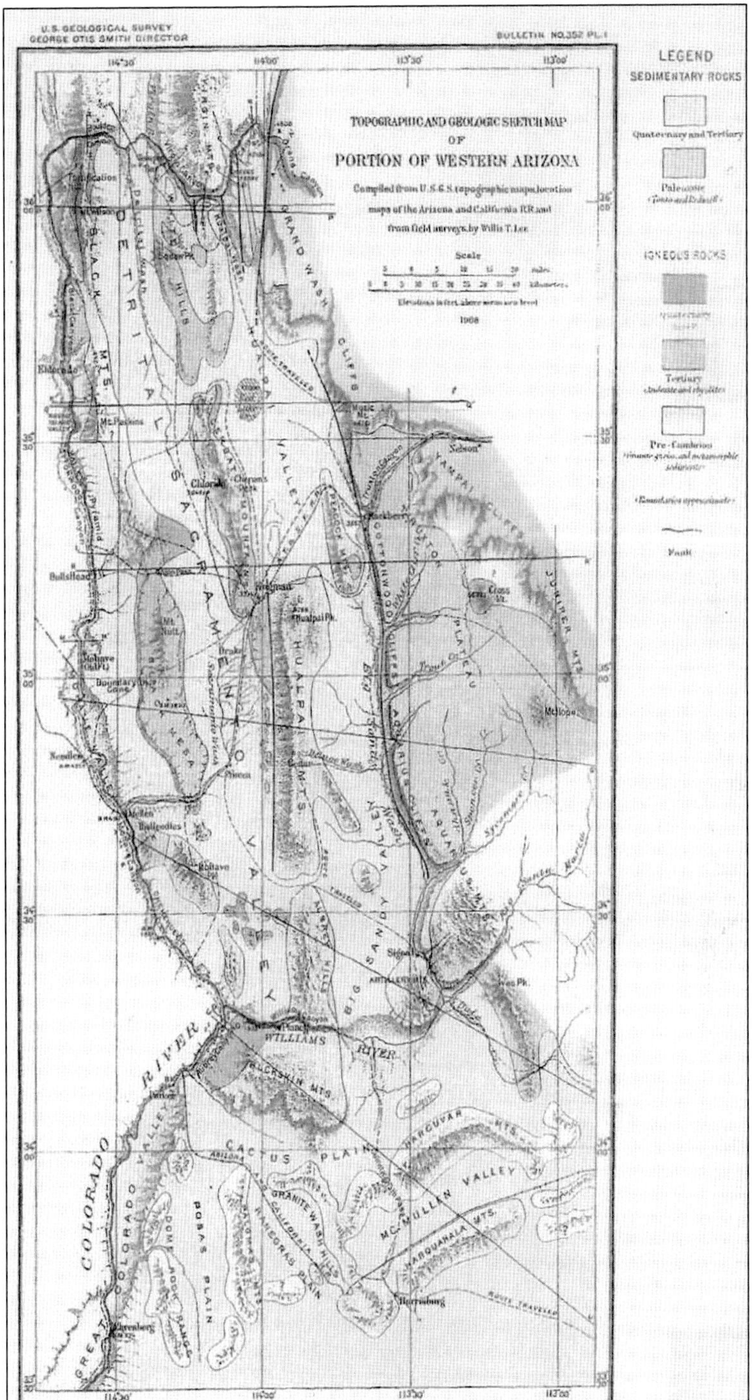

This U.S. Geological Survey map of 1908 identifies mining areas east of the Colorado River, close to Liverpool Landing (midway between the railroad bridge at Topock and the Bill Williams River), which served as a steamboat shipping port for ores and supplies. The Chemehuevi Mountains and Pittsburg Point are clearly delineated on this map. (Courtesy Lake Havasu Museum of History.)

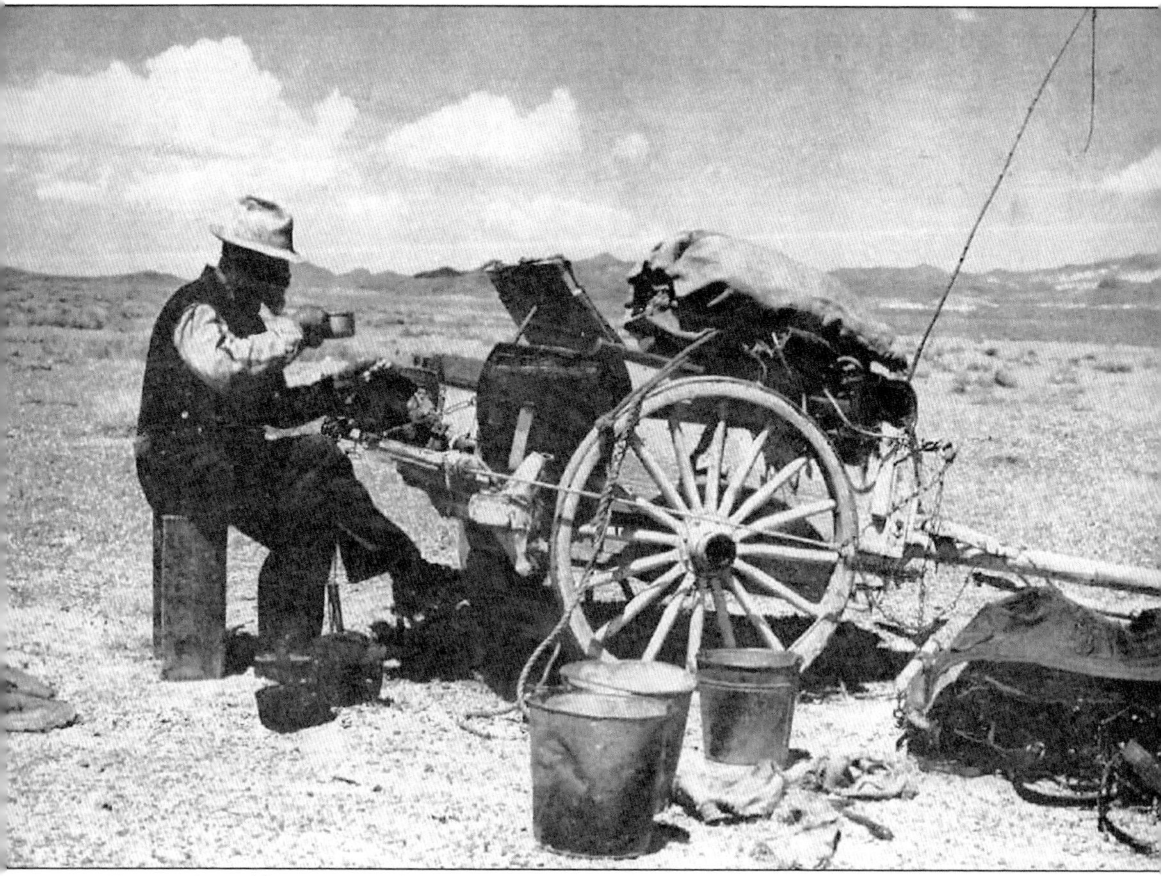

Even today, old miners or "desert rats" comb the mountains and arroyos for silver and gold, as glorified in this 1954 photograph of a prospector taking a break to enjoy his lunch. (Courtesy Lake Havasu Museum of History.)

Five

Parker Dam and Lake Havasu

Although steamboat commerce on the river continued after the coming of the railroads, hauling freight between the railroad bridges at Topock and Parker, it essentially ended when the Laguna Dam above Yuma was built in 1909. And though mines and mills continued operating into the mid-1930s—the Best Bet mine and the Gold Wing mine, for instance, as well as the 50-ton floating mill just north of Lake Havasu City—mining on the river ended as well. Many of the mines and the mills, along with the communities established at Chemehuevi, Liverpool, and Pittsburg landings, were buried beneath the flood waters of Lake Havasu, created by the building of Parker Dam.

In the early 1930s, concern for the water supply in Los Angeles led to the formation of the Metropolitan Water District of Southern California, the building of the Colorado River Aqueduct, and the construction of Parker Dam. Initial survey work began in 1932 in order to determine the best location and ideal elevation for the dam. All through the summers of 1933–1934, the survey party chief A. E. "Bud" Graham and his crew worked to establish the potential level of the lake and rights-of-way over properties that would be flooded when the dam was finished. "Sometimes we had to hang out over a cliff to get a sighting," said Bud in *A. E. "Bud" Graham* by Gary W. McCarthy. "It was scary and you had to be part mountain goat."

Finally, when the right-of-way work was completed, the contract between the Metropolitan Water District and the U.S. Bureau of Reclamation provided for building a dam 277 feet high above the bedrock and 80 feet above the normal water level of the river. When finished in 1938, the total height of the dam turned out to be 320 feet from the base of its footing, drilled 240 feet into bedrock, making it the deepest dam in the world.

By the time the reservoir behind the dam was filled to capacity, the powerhouse finished, and the pumping stations pushing water up and over the mountains into California, the cost of the project had totaled $13,000,000—all paid for by the Metropolitan Water District.

In 1939, according to the "Aqueduct News" published by the Metropolitan Water District, a Native American couple named the lake behind the dam "Havasu," a Mohave word for blue-green water. Visiting the dam one day, the 103-year-old man, Haranai, and his 98-year-old wife, Oach, wanted to know about the "magic" that turned the color of the Colorado River from red to blue.

The whole character of the river was changed as a result of the building of Parker Dam. The dam, however, created in its stead the 45-mile long reservoir known as Lake Havasu, providing the nexus for the founding of Lake Havasu City on its shores.

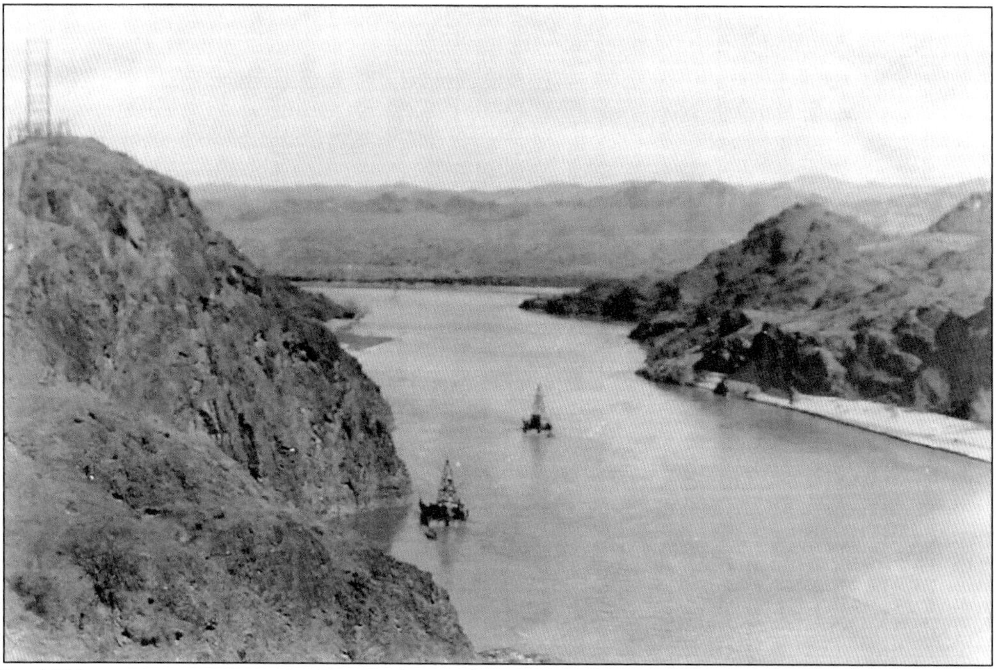

In 1931, young surveyor A. E. "Bud" Graham, then living in Parker, Arizona, but later moving to Lake Havasu City, began scouting a site on the Colorado River for the future Parker Dam. Pictured here is the site about 10 miles above Parker that was ultimately selected. (Courtesy Ruth Graham.)

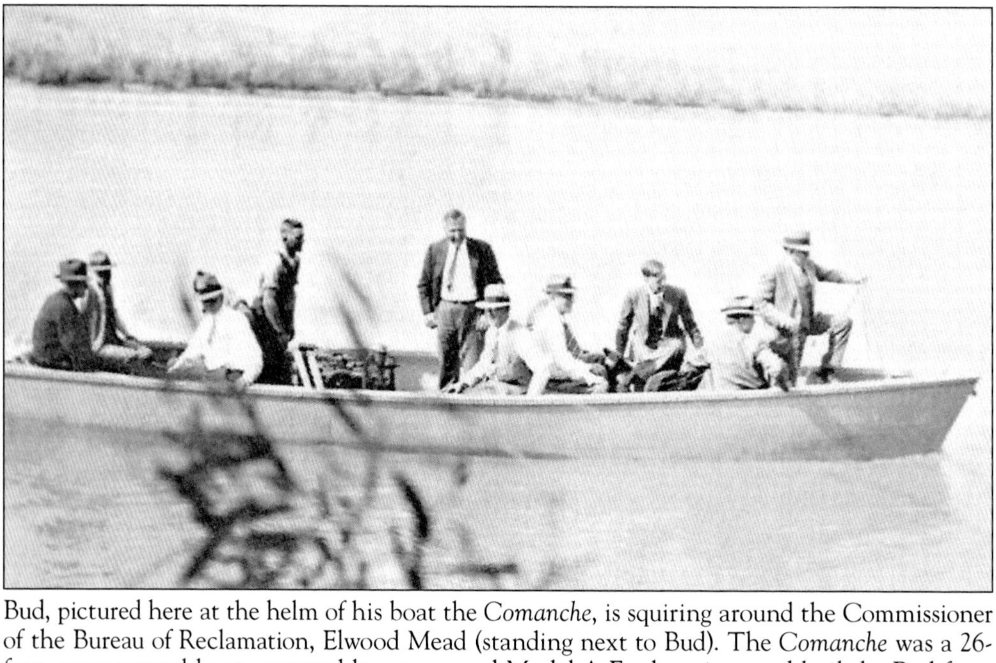

Bud, pictured here at the helm of his boat the *Comanche*, is squiring around the Commissioner of the Bureau of Reclamation, Elwood Mead (standing next to Bud). The *Comanche* was a 26-foot, open-tunnel boat, powered by a scrapped Model-A Ford engine, and built by Bud from salvaged timber that had floated down river from the construction of Hoover Dam. (Courtesy Ruth Graham.)

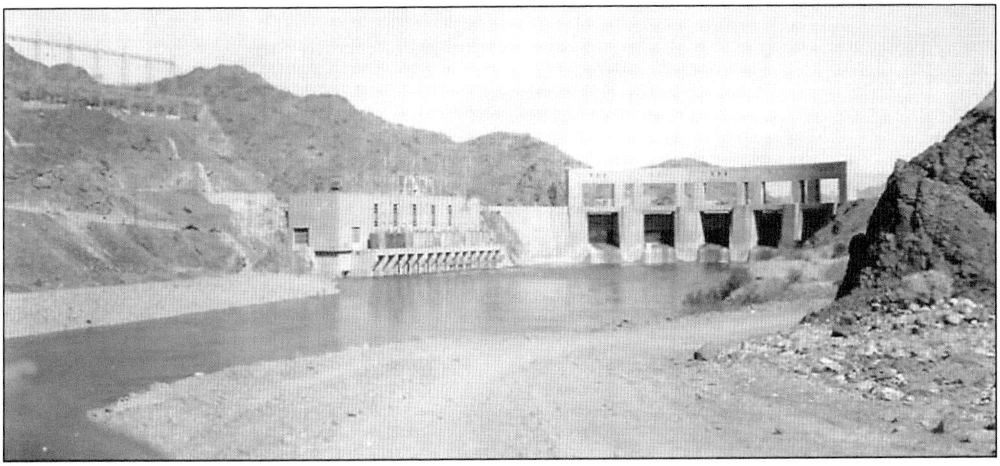

The completion of the Parker Dam in 1938 created the reservoir known as Lake Havasu. It provided not only a major source of water for California and Arizona, but also a major recreation area for residents and visitors in Lake Havasu City. In 1941, water began flowing to Los Angeles and San Diego in California. In 1985, it also began flowing to Phoenix and Tucson in Arizona. (Courtesy Lake Havasu Museum of History.)

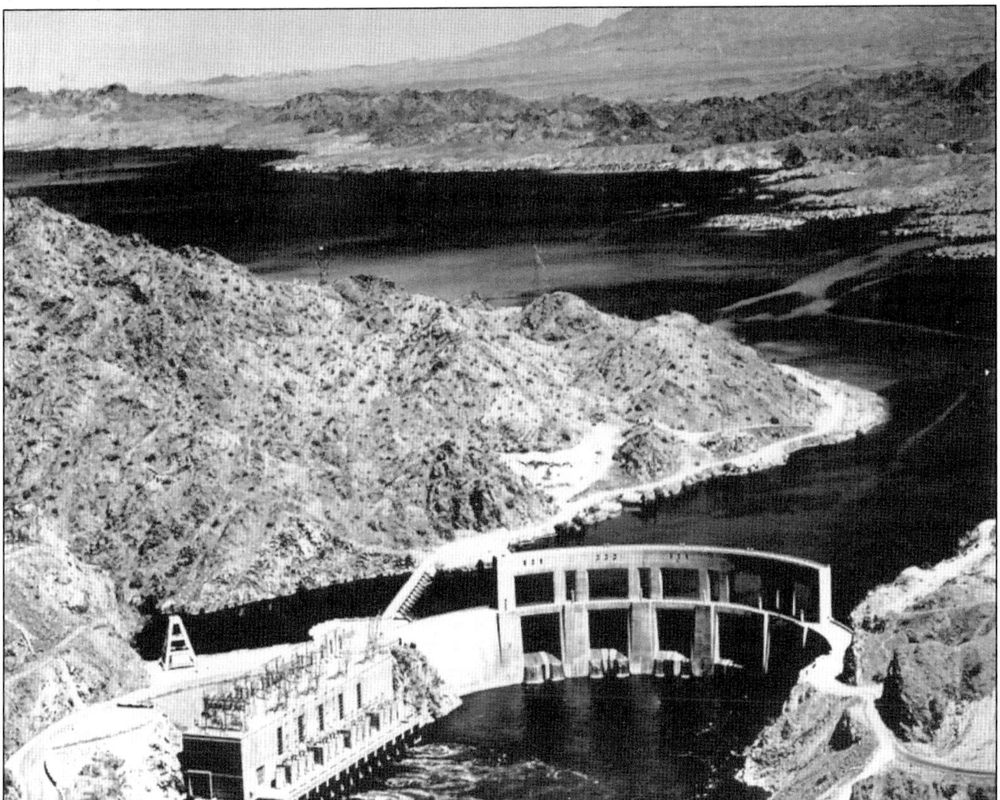

The reservoir itself stores almost 211 billion gallons or 646,200 acre-feet of water, providing an opportunity to enjoy various water sports, including fishing. Conditions are ideal for black and striped bass, crappie, bluegill, catfish, and trout. (Courtesy Mohave Museum of History and Art, No. 2227.)

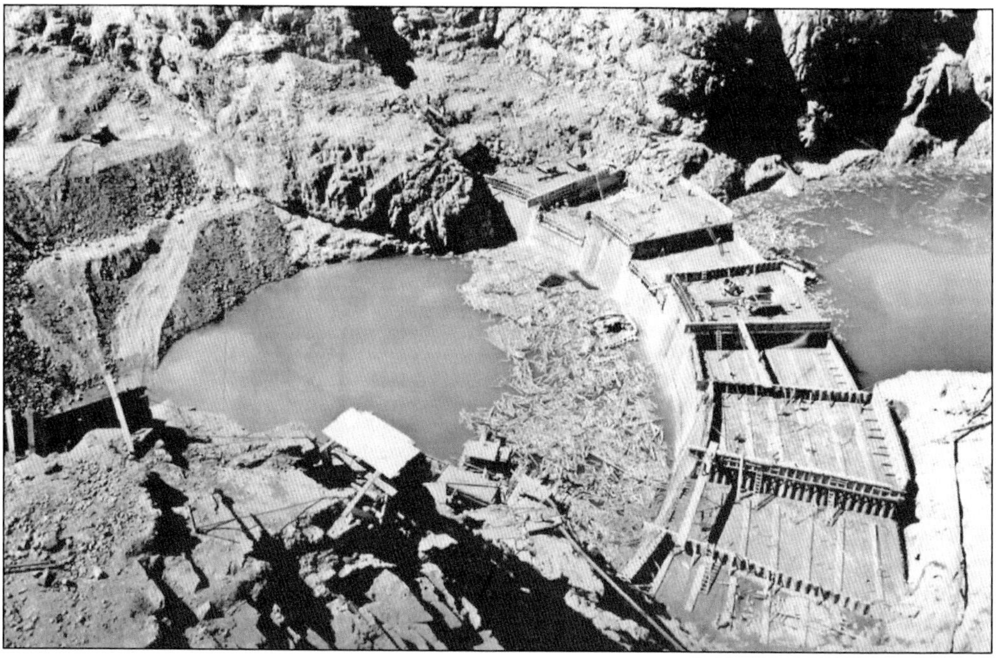

Western Construction News and Highway Builders reported that a contract between the Bureau of Reclamation and the Metropolitan Water District of Southern California (MWD) in 1934 provided for the "design and construction . . . of a dam at the head of the Colorado river aqueduct near Parker, Arizona." (Courtesy Mohave Museum of Art and History, No. 2228.)

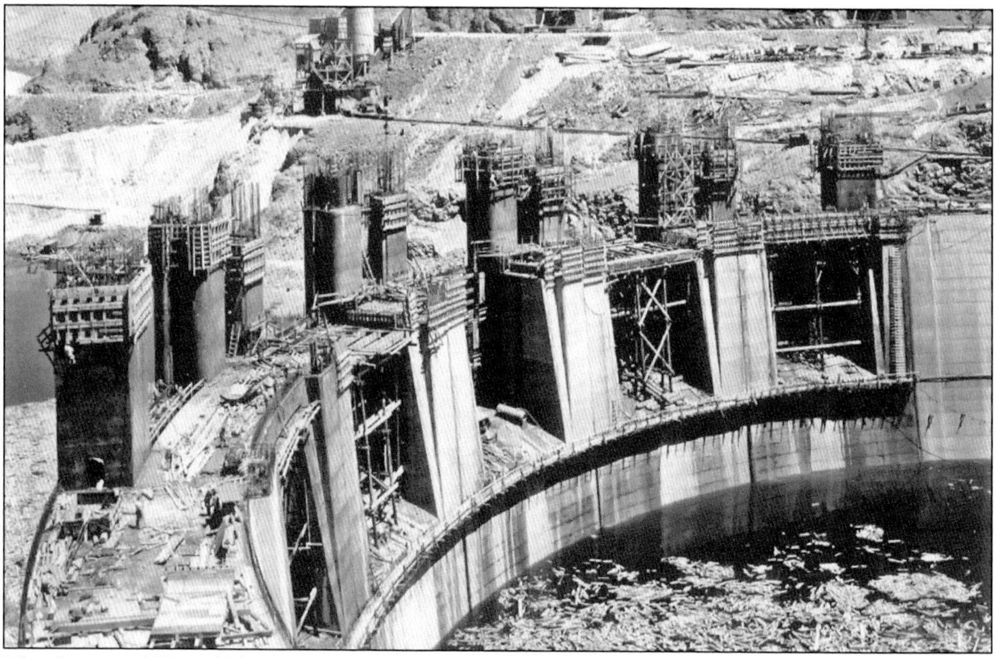

The dam would be of "the concrete-gravity type," the contract continued, "with large stony gates superimposed and will contain 330,000 cu. yd. of concrete. A $2,000,000 PWA loan and grant provides for initial construction of this dam." (Courtesy Mohave Museum of Art and History, No. 2226.)

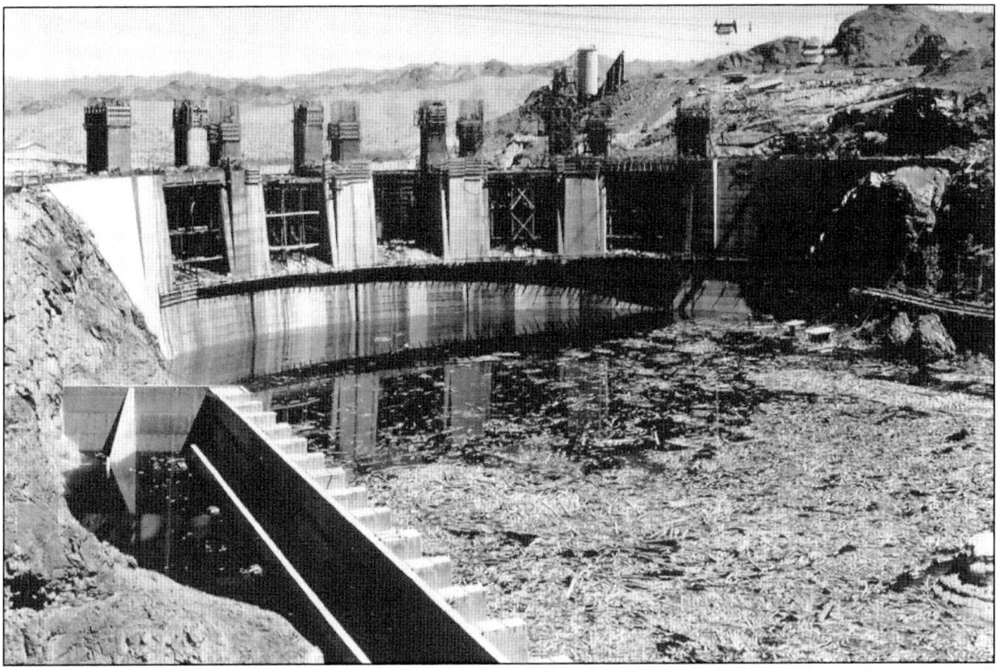

In 1934, during the initial stages in the construction of the Parker Dam, a "grand showdown" over a fair water allotment for Arizona took place between the State of Arizona and the U.S. Department of the Interior. (Courtesy Mohave Museum of Art and History, No. 1499.)

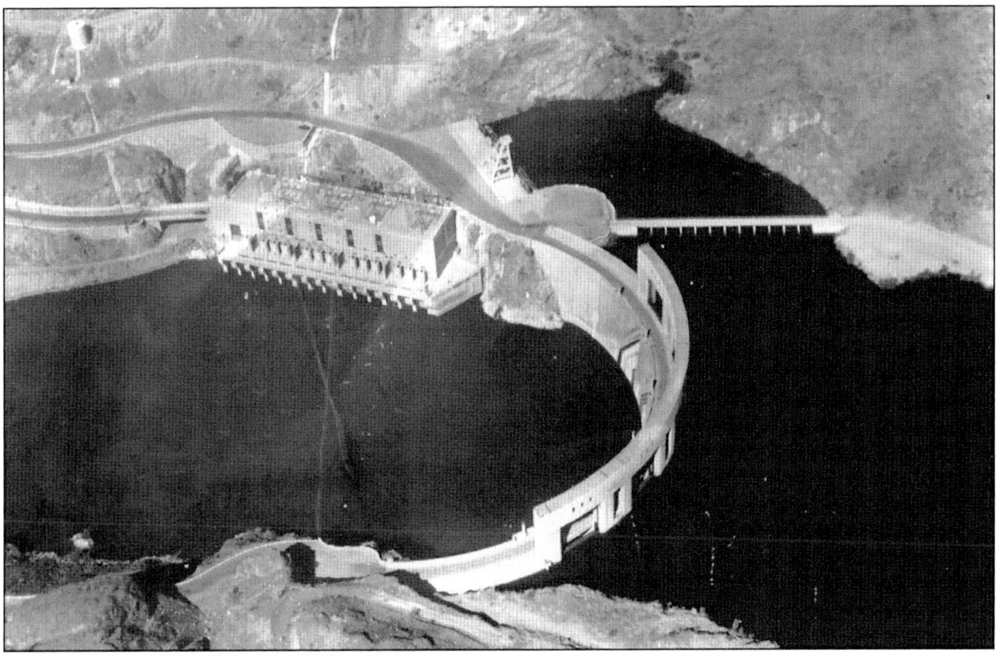

The governor of Arizona, B. B. Moeur, and the state senator from Parker, Nellie Bush, declared martial law and called out the National Guard until the dispute was settled. Ultimately the U.S. Supreme Court stepped in and the state of Arizona was awarded 2.8 million acre-feet of water from the Colorado River. (Courtesy Mohave Museum of Art and History, No. 9222.)

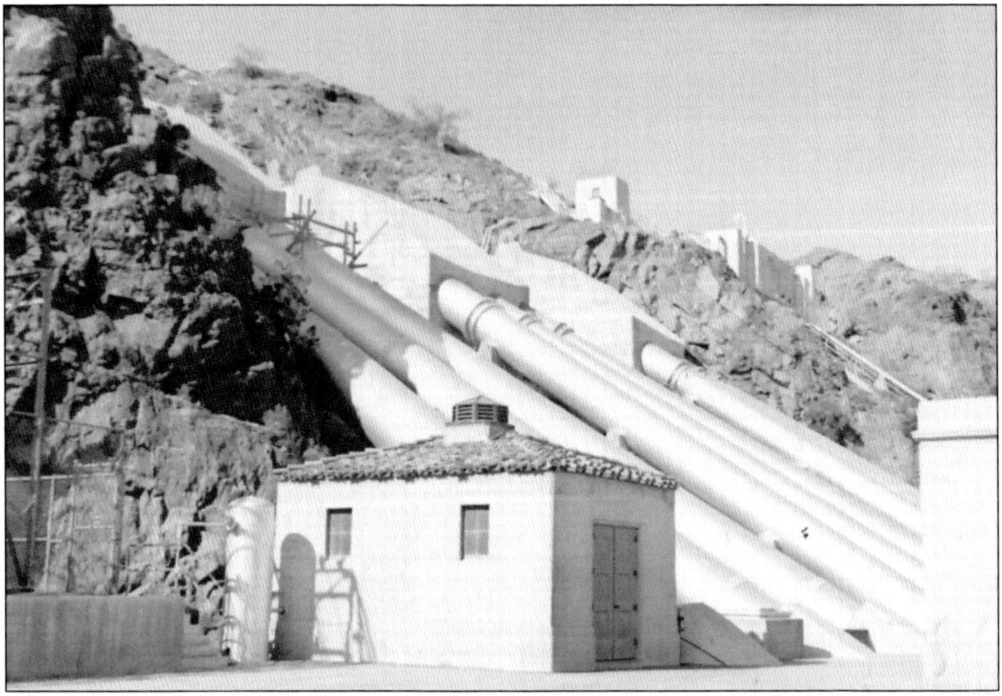

The main purpose of the dam was to provide for the diversion of water to Southern California. In order to do so, the Whitsett pumping station (shown here), two miles upstream from the dam site, has to lift water 291 feet from Lake Havasu to the Gene reservoir located on the other side of the mountains. (Courtesy Ruth Graham.)

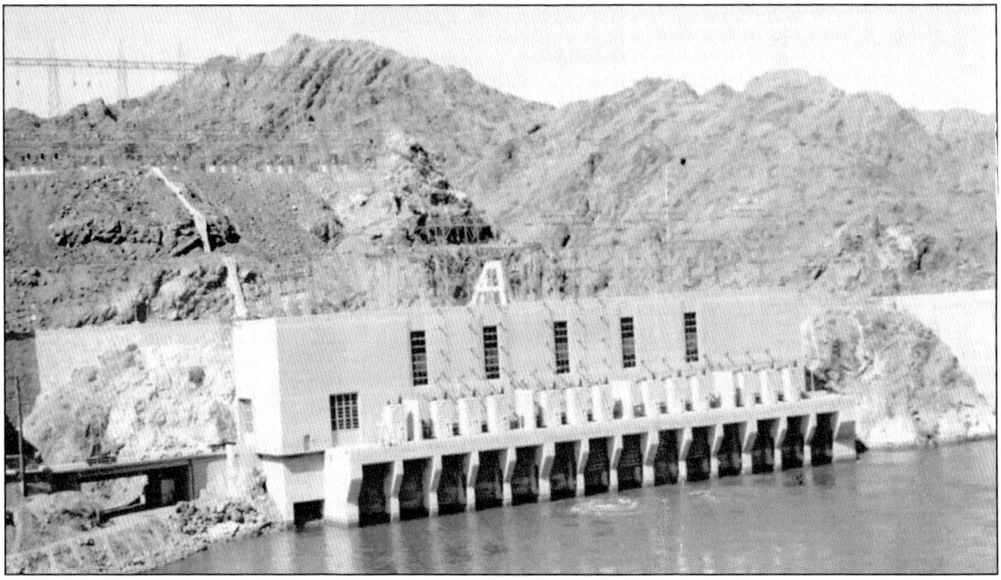

The Parker power plant, located just below the dam, houses four hydroelectric generators, each one producing 30 megawatts of power. Four 22-feet-in-diameter "penstocks" each carry up to 5500 cubic feet of water per second to turn the generators. Of the total 120 megawatts of power generated by the Parker plant, 50 percent is reserved by the MWD to operate the Whitsett pumping station. (Courtesy Ruth Graham.)

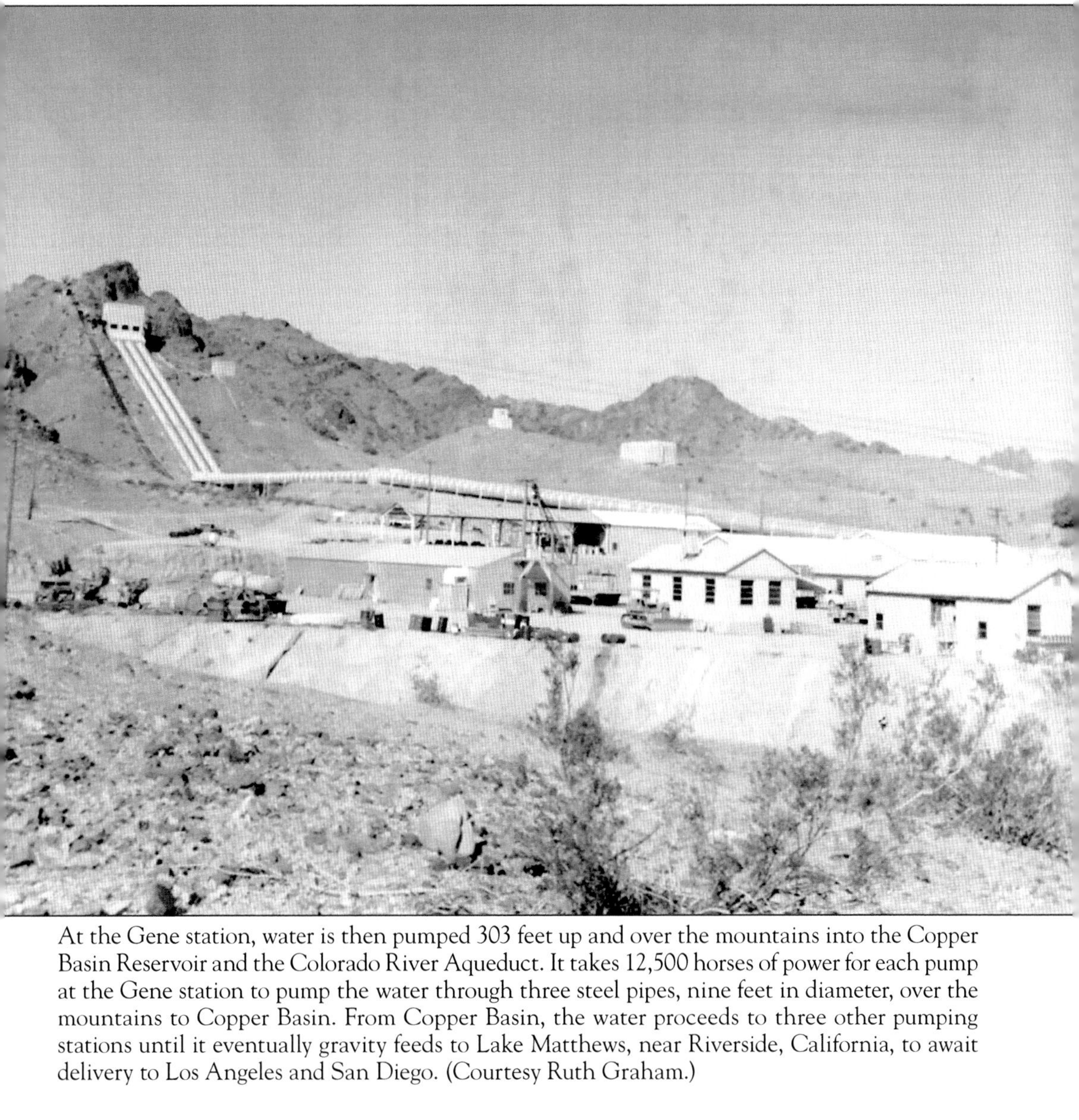

At the Gene station, water is then pumped 303 feet up and over the mountains into the Copper Basin Reservoir and the Colorado River Aqueduct. It takes 12,500 horses of power for each pump at the Gene station to pump the water through three steel pipes, nine feet in diameter, over the mountains to Copper Basin. From Copper Basin, the water proceeds to three other pumping stations until it eventually gravity feeds to Lake Matthews, near Riverside, California, to await delivery to Los Angeles and San Diego. (Courtesy Ruth Graham.)

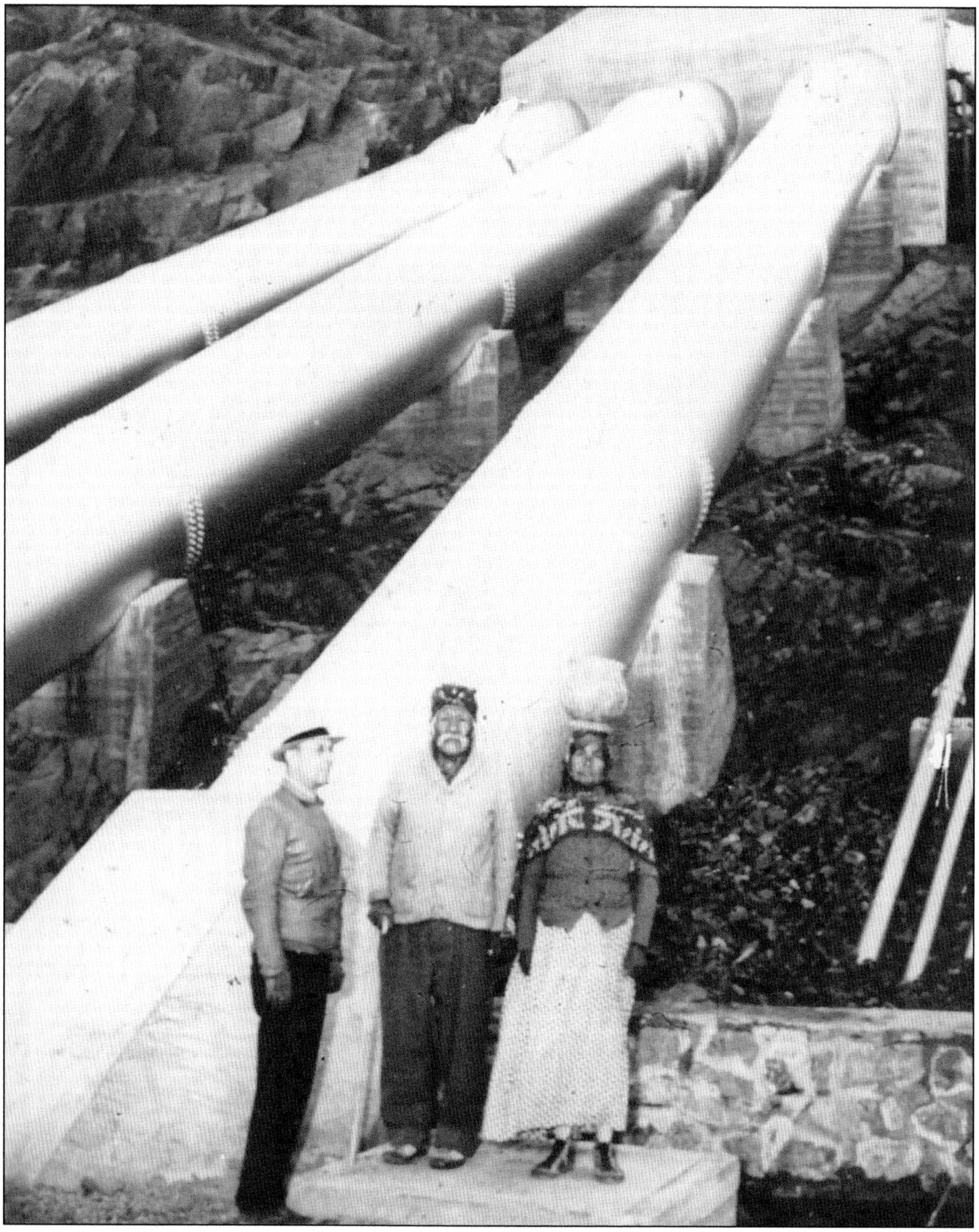

The Mohave couple who named Lake Havasu, Haranai and his wife Oach, stand proudly with a Metropolitan Water District official at the dedication of the Whitsett plant in 1939. The story is that Haranai and Oach weren't as impressed by the dam so much as with the change of the color of the muddy river water from red to blue. (Courtesy Wayne T. Patch.)

Six

SITE SIX

World War II brought the suspension of all mining activity in the Chemehuevi Mountains, as the area became a target for the Kingman Army Air Field's Yucca Aerial Gunnery Range. The emergency landing field for the Kingman contingent, designated as "Site Six," was built on the tip of Pittsburg Point, the peninsula jutting out into Lake Havasu and now part of Lake Havasu City. In 1944, Site Six became a rest and convalescence camp for the Kingman Army Air Field. Officers and pilots who were sent overseas were brought there to recuperate.

In 1946, Vic and Corinne Spratt moved from Needles to Site Six in order to take charge of the facilities there, which then included two air strips, seven barracks buildings, a large covered boat dock, a bar, kitchen, mess hall, and grocery store. Although the war was over, servicemen would still visit there on leave, staying in one of the barracks on army cots and eating at the mess hall. The mess hall served as many as 300 people at a time.

The Spratts had first become acquainted with Pittsburg Point in the 1930s, making the long trip on the winding dirt road from Route 66. In 1941, they actually bought part of the land later occupied at Site Six, planning to build a home there on a hill that slopes down to the waterfront on Catfish Bay. When they went to the county courthouse to claim their land, however, they learned that it had been leased by the U.S. government and was operating as a rehabilitation center for the Army Air Corps. With the aid of a lawyer, the Spratts ultimately regained their land and all the buildings on it and opened Site Six as a fishing resort.

In 1957, "Doc" Young came to the resort with his wife and hired on as a mechanic, electrician, carpenter, and all-around handyman. Mrs. Young took over the barracks and the restaurant. The natural surroundings were still primitive when the Youngs were at Site Six: a grove of salt cedar, herds of wild horses and burros, coyotes, bobcats, and birds. Roadrunners were all over the place. The fishing was great. "We fished any spare time we had," said Doc told the *Lake Havasu City Herald*. "You could always limit out bass in a couple of hours. The biggest one I caught weighed 9½ pounds."

The Spratts continued to own the resort until Robert Paxton McCulloch Sr., looking for an area to test his outboard motors, flew over in 1958 and decided to land. Almost before they realized it, they had sold him most of their holdings. Four ex-servicemen who also owned 3,353 acres on the site had a similar reaction. McCulloch found two of the partners in a state of shock because they had learned that their other two partners had just died in an airplane accident. McCulloch offered them $300,000 and they took it three days later.

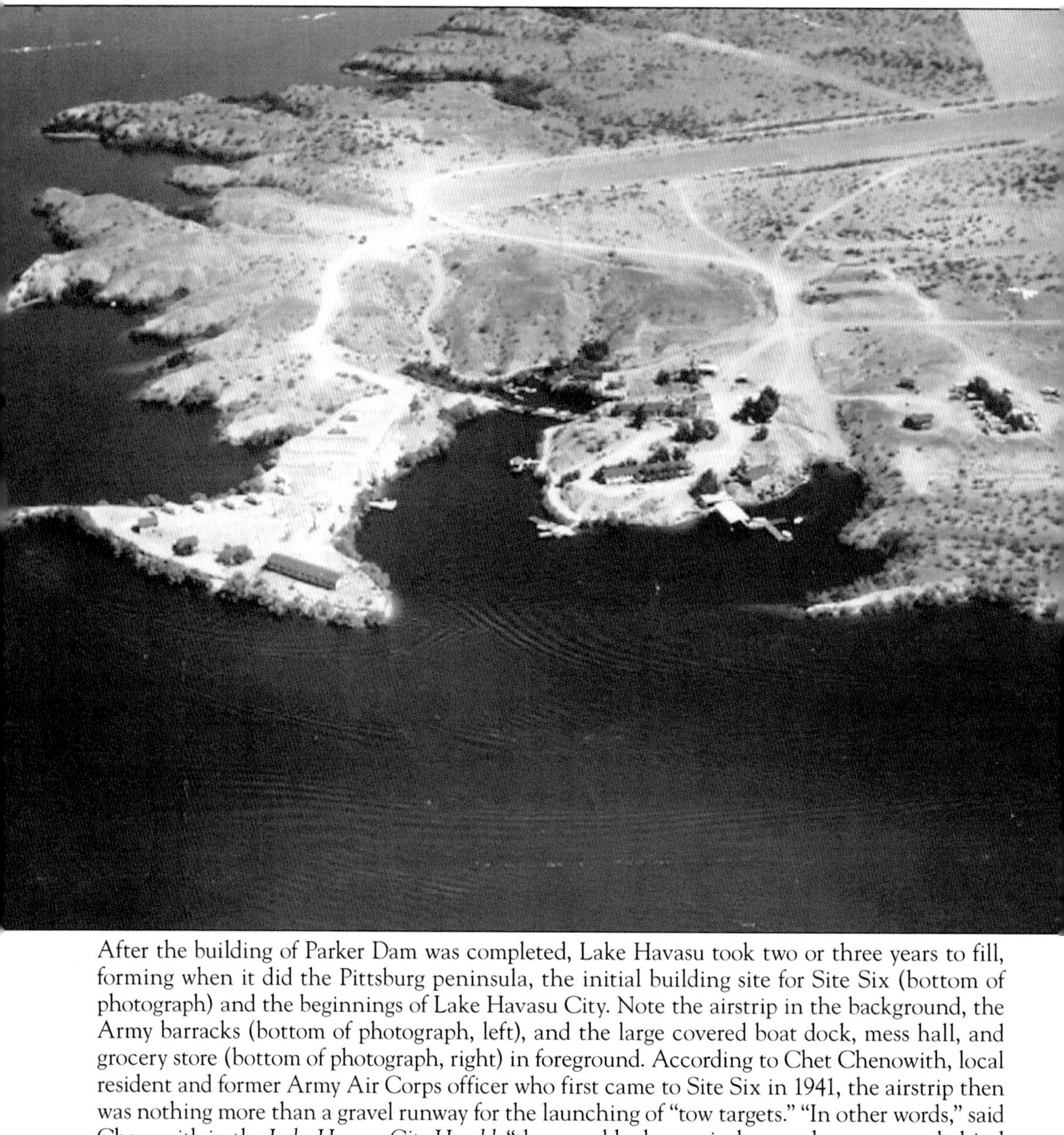

After the building of Parker Dam was completed, Lake Havasu took two or three years to fill, forming when it did the Pittsburg peninsula, the initial building site for Site Six (bottom of photograph) and the beginnings of Lake Havasu City. Note the airstrip in the background, the Army barracks (bottom of photograph, left), and the large covered boat dock, mess hall, and grocery store (bottom of photograph, right) in foreground. According to Chet Chenowith, local resident and former Army Air Corps officer who first came to Site Six in 1941, the airstrip then was nothing more than a gravel runway for the launching of "tow targets." "In other words," said Chenowith in the *Lake Havasu City Herald*, "they would take an airplane and tow a target behind and shoot at it to knock it out of the sky." Apparently, there were seven such sites created. The one on Lake Havasu was number six. (Courtesy Lake Havasu Museum of History.)

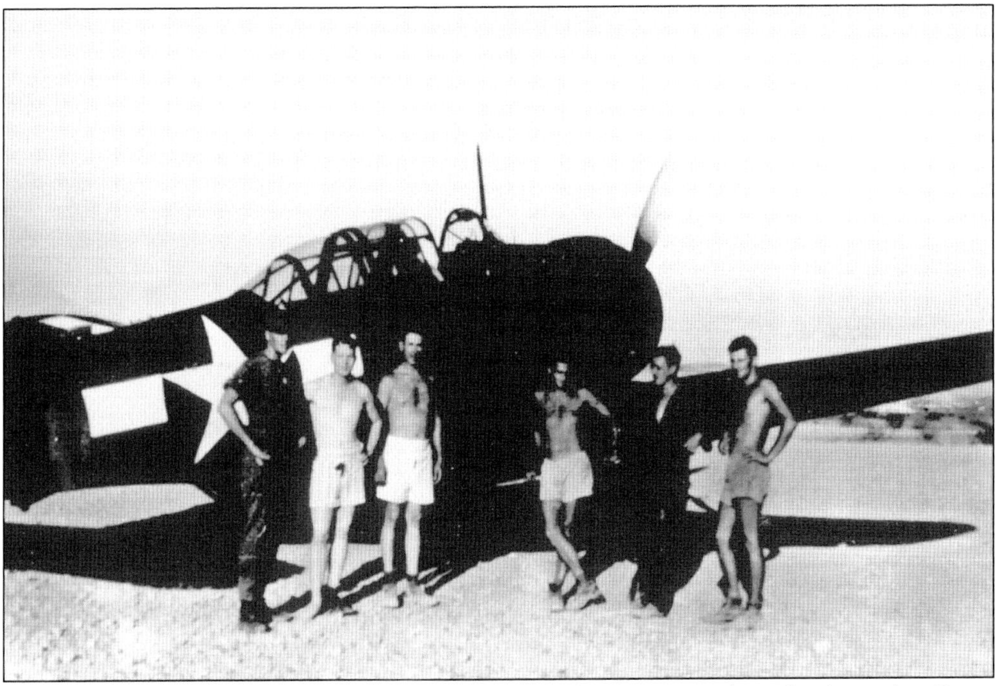

After World War II began, Site Six became a rest and recuperation base for Army Air Corps pilots. (Courtesy Mohave Museum of History and Art, No. 8390.)

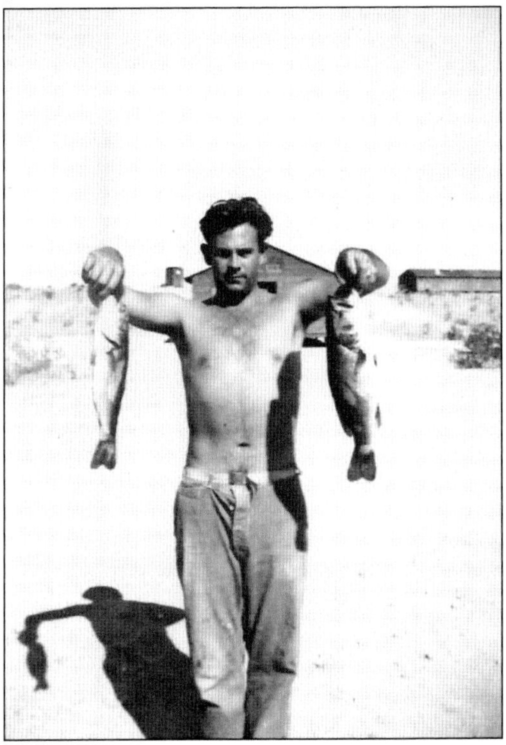

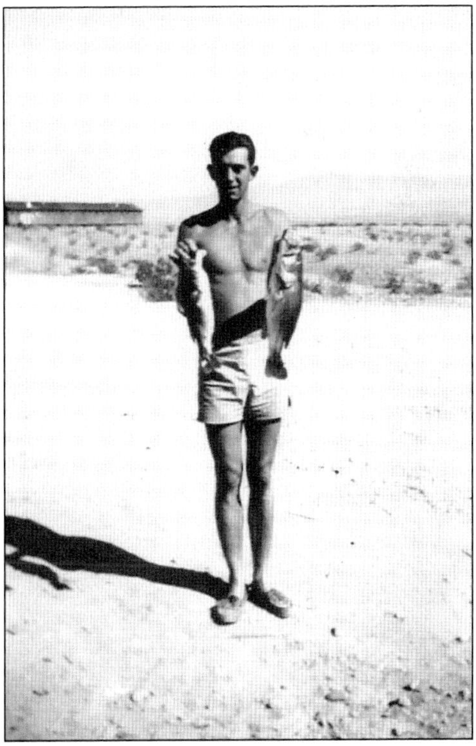

World War II servicemen spent their rest and relaxation time at Site Six fishing. (Courtesy Lake Havasu Museum of History.)

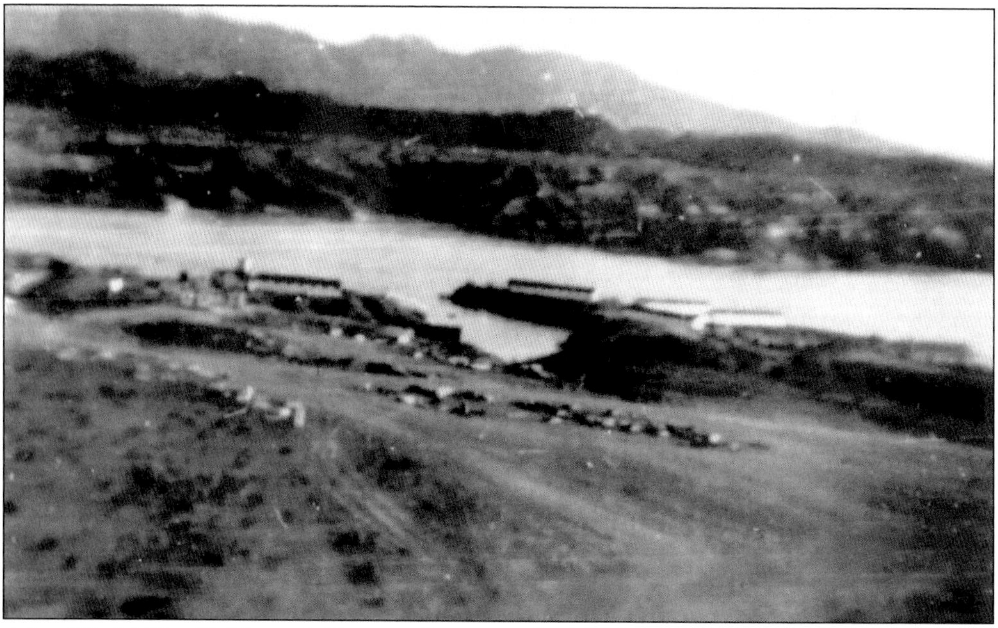

After World War II, Vic and Corinne Spratt took over Site Six and made it into a fishing camp—converting the barracks (above photograph, left, and below photograph, right) into their living quarters, a grocery store, and a restaurant and bar known as the Lake Havasu Air Park Site Six. Access to the resort by road was difficult, so most visitors flew in. (Courtesy Mohave Museum of History and Art, No. 8385.)

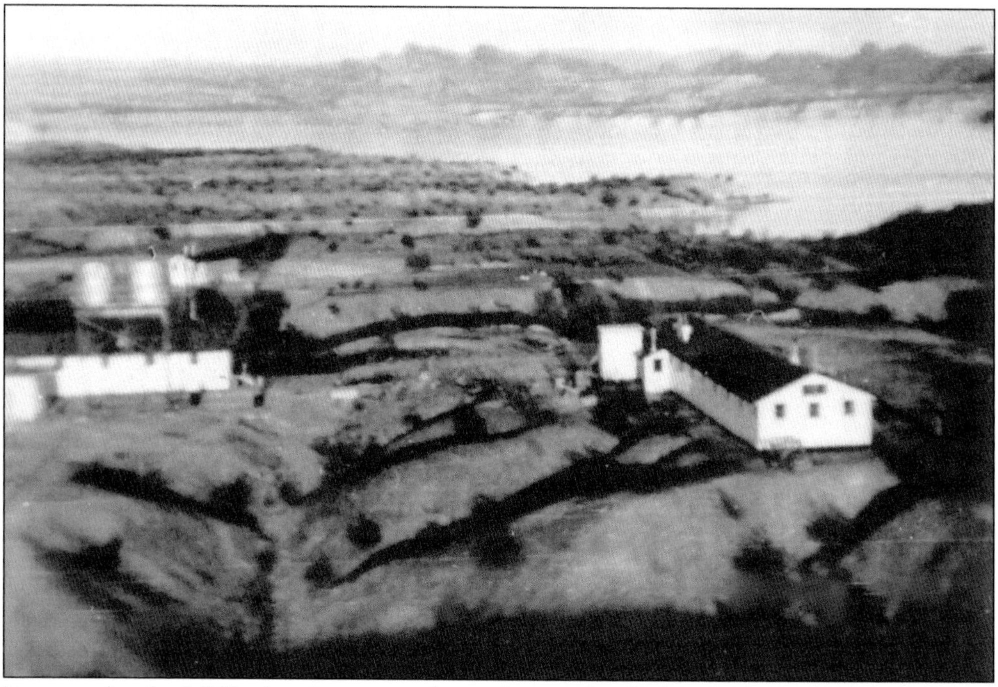

Because they had difficulty obtaining a liquor license for the bar at the air park, the Spratts attached a bottle opener to a long cord so that drinks could be consumed legally beyond the two-foot limits of the premises. (Courtesy Mohave Museum of History and Art, No. 8384.)

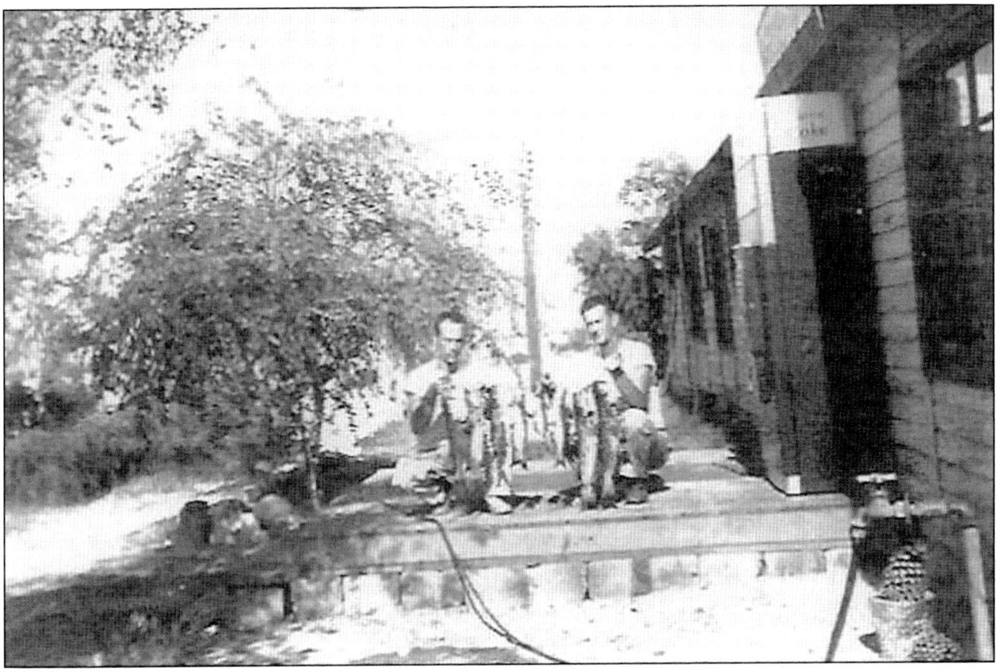

These photographs show the variety of fish caught at the Spratt fishing facility. (Above courtesy Lake Havasu Museum of History; right courtesy Mohave Museum of History and Art, No. 8393.)

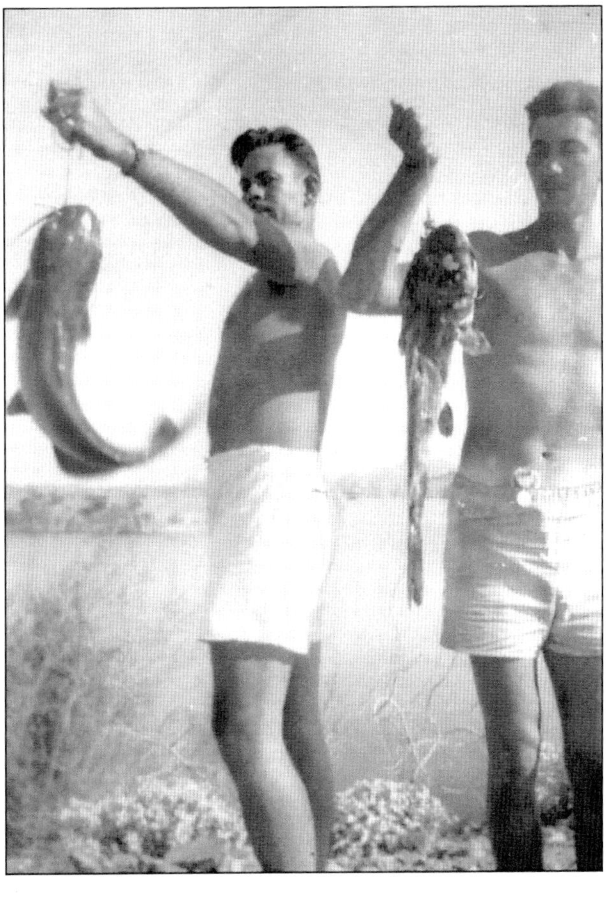

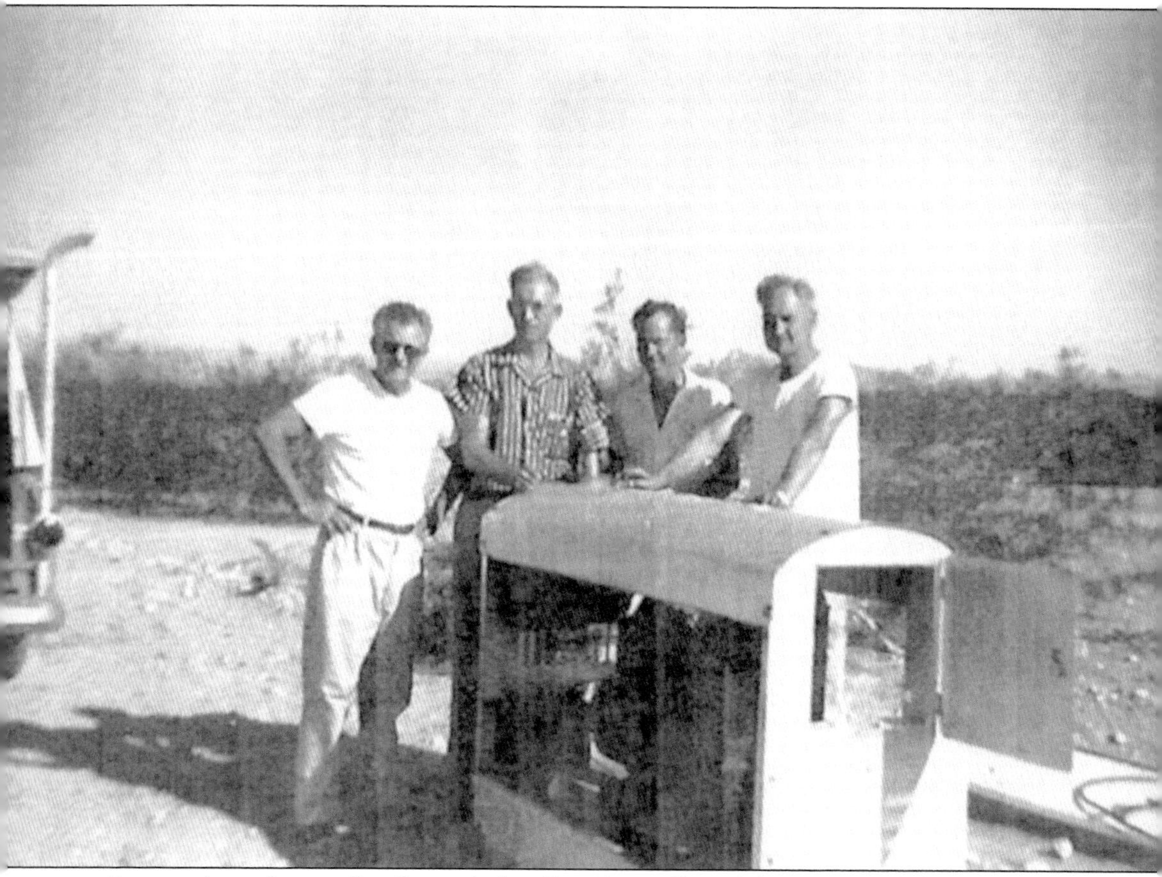

Some early residents at Site Six, including Doc Young (far right), pose around the generator Doc Young repaired. Doc remembered when he and his wife first came here in 1957 they were kept awake by this generator making a racket all night. The next morning, Doc fixed it, figuring it had a leaky fuel line, and he and his wife were hired on the spot to take over the place. (Courtesy Lake Havasu Museum of History.)

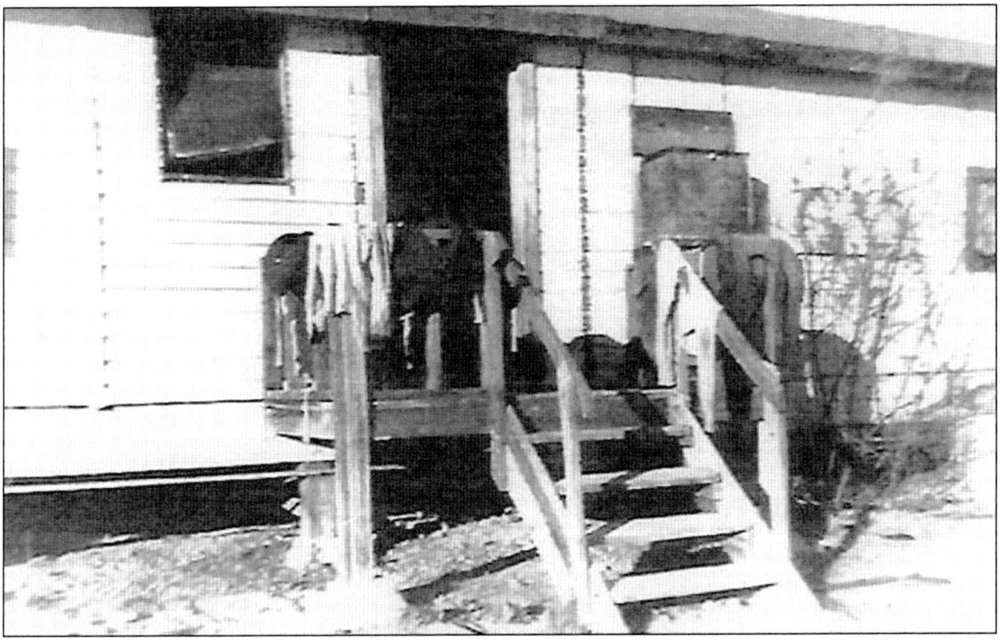

World War II structures were converted into use as dormitories for fishermen at the site. In 1957, there were still some of the old barracks on the site, the restaurant and bar, a bait and tackle shop in another one of the old buildings, a small boat dock with a gas pump, five rental boats, and a few new house trailers nearby. (Courtesy Lake Havasu Museum of History.)

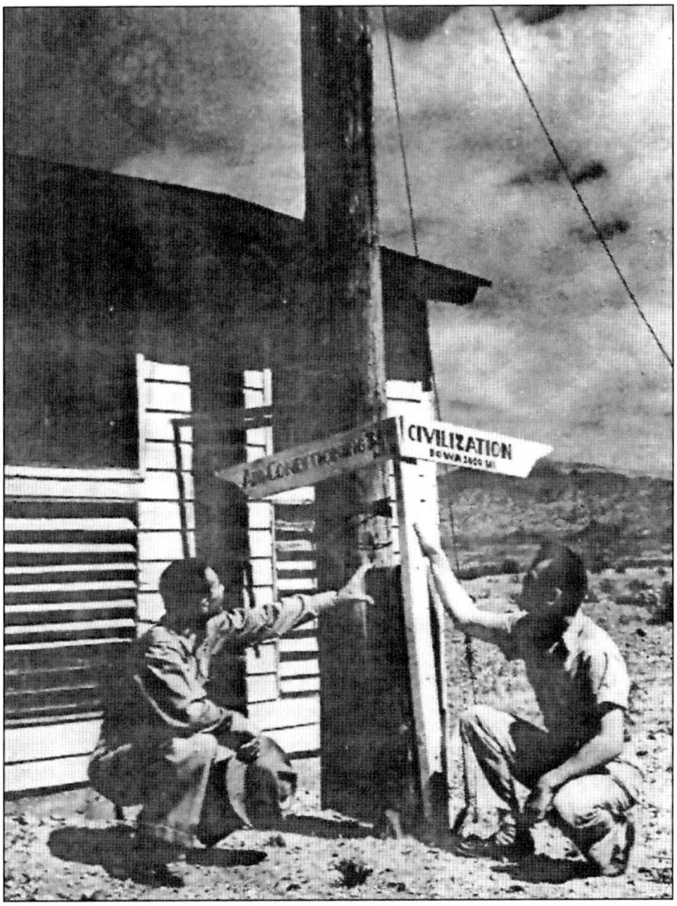

Fishermen rented beds in the barracks for $2 a night. Doc Young's wife ran the bed rentals and took over the restaurant in the mess hall. According to the *Lake Havasu City Herald* ,one Sunday morning, 16 people showed up for breakfast. "Luckily," Mrs. Young said, "one of the wives asked me if she could help." (Courtesy Lake Havasu Museum of History.)

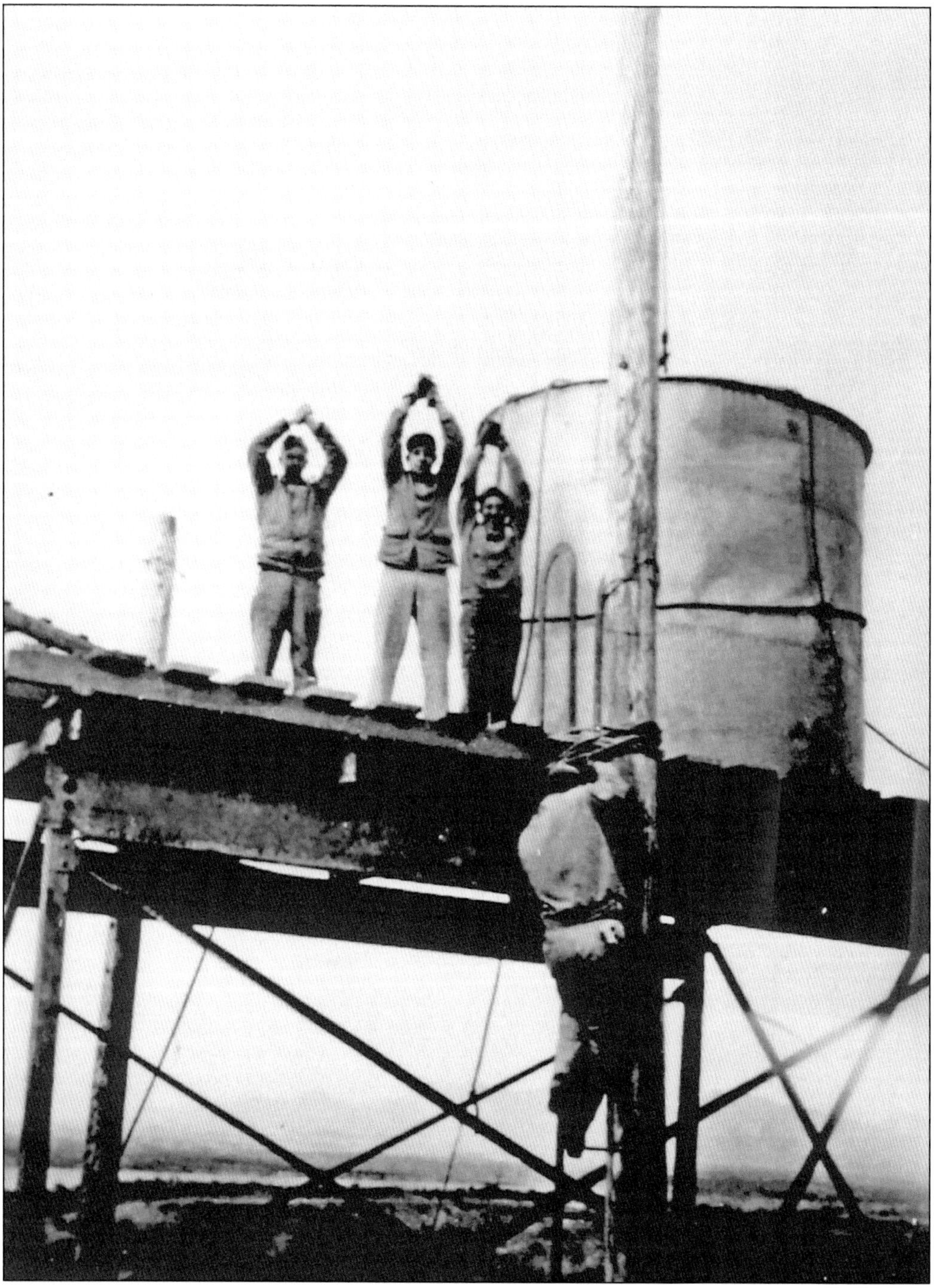

Locals celebrate the installation of the water system at Site Six. Water came from a 2,100-gallon tank filled from a well leftover from the Army Air Corps days. The bathroom facilities were two rickety outhouses marked "His" and "Hers." "When you went in there," said Mrs. Young (*Lake Havasu City Herald*), "you never knew if the house would fall over." "Our cook would feed the wild burros; we even found them in the privy," added Doc . (Courtesy Mohave Museum of History and Art, No. 8380.)

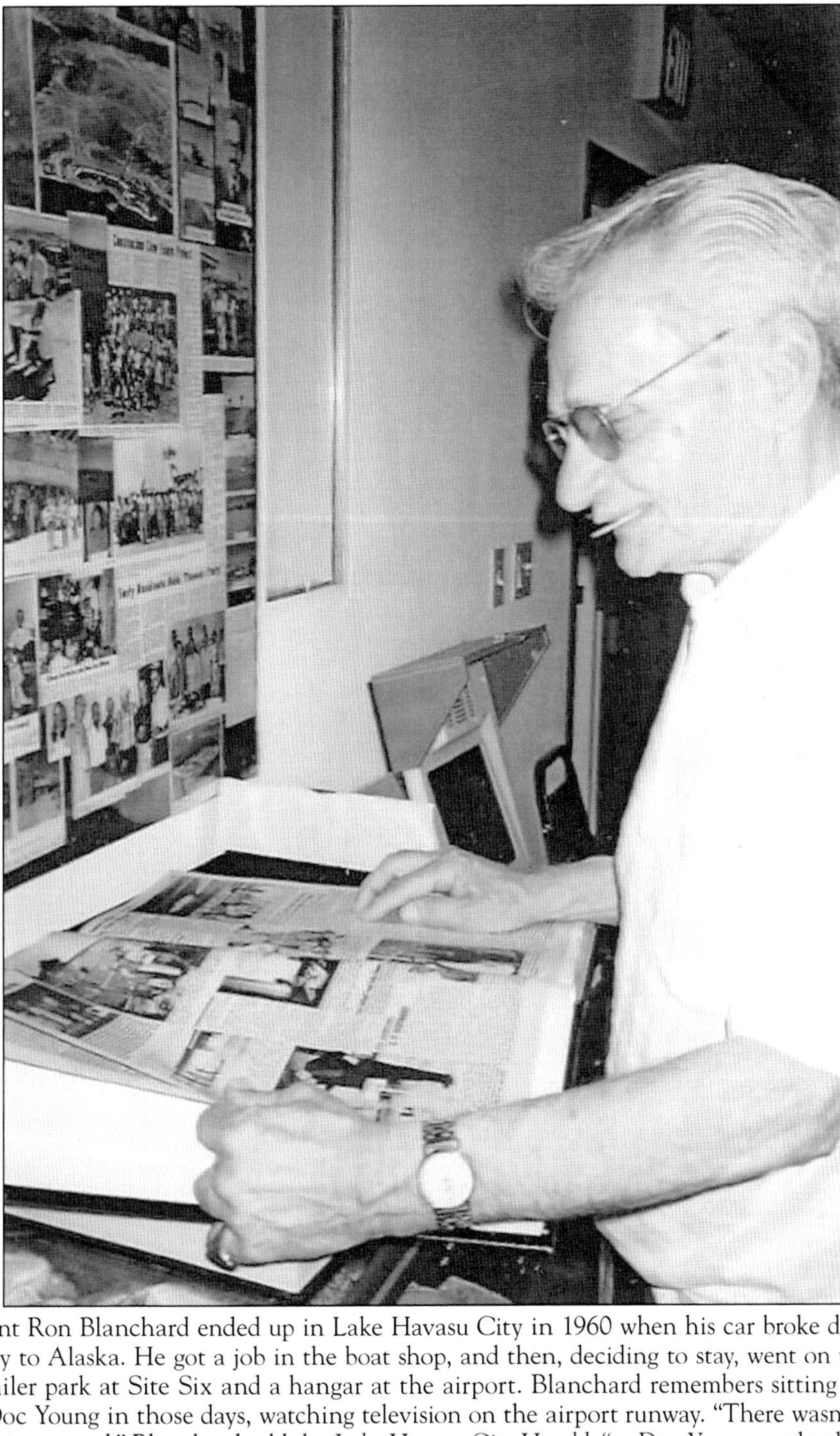

Resident Ron Blanchard ended up in Lake Havasu City in 1960 when his car broke down on the way to Alaska. He got a job in the boat shop, and then, deciding to stay, went on to build the trailer park at Site Six and a hangar at the airport. Blanchard remembers sitting around with Doc Young in those days, watching television on the airport runway. "There wasn't much electricity around," Blanchard told the *Lake Havasu City Herald*, "so Doc Young used to hook up all the televisions to one of the landing lights . . . We all brought stools and sat and watched." "Television reception then, at its best was poor," he added. "As soon as a cloud passed over, the program ended." (Courtesy Lake Havasu Museum of History.)

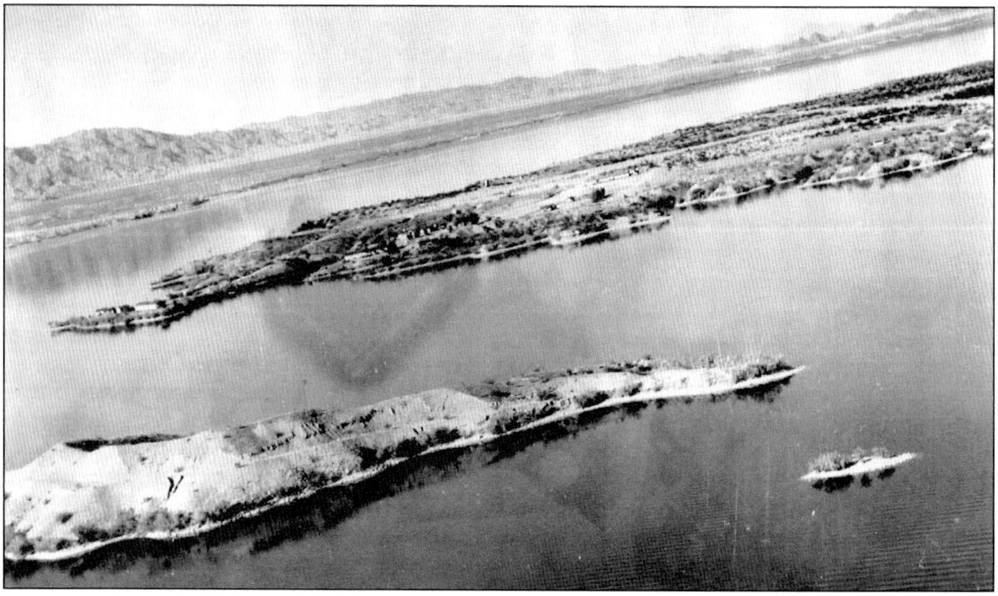

In 1958, when McCulloch flew into Site Six, it must have looked something like this. Note the barrack buildings out on the point (left) and other barely discernible buildings just inland (center). (Courtesy Lake Havasu Museum of History.)

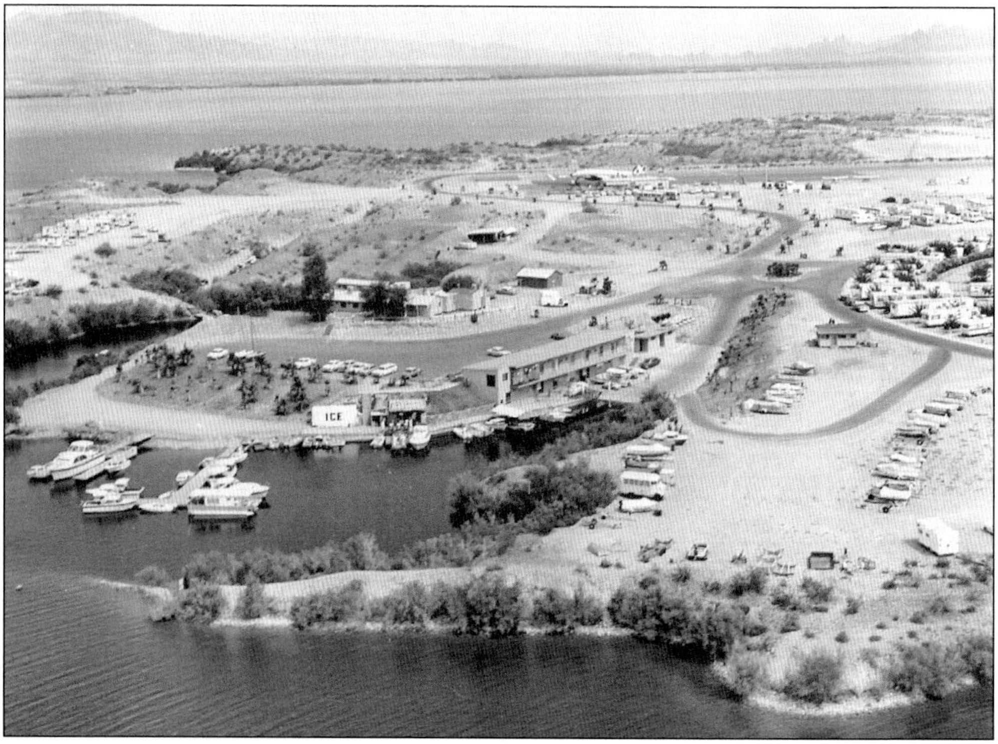

This 1965 photograph shows Site Six after the addition of the marina (foreground, left) and McCulloch's outboard motor testing site, with boat ramp, boat shop, and McCulloch's small motel foreground, right). Note also the trailer park (background, far right) and one of McCulloch's airplanes on the air strip in the background (center). (Courtesy Lake Havasu Museum of History.)

Seven

The Founding of Lake Havasu City

After Robert P. McCulloch Sr. purchased Site Six for the purpose of testing his outboard motors, he began to think about relocating his chain saw business to Lake Havasu as well. He had already moved his small-engine manufacturing operation, renamed McCulloch Motors, to Los Angeles in 1946. But by 1959, the factory land—near the soon-to-be-new international airport—had become too valuable for manufacturing, priced and taxed out of the market for industrial use. Consulting his partner C. V. Wood Jr. for advice, McCulloch then hit upon the idea of creating an entire city at Lake Havasu.

Wood thought the idea was crazy, but agreed to have his research department do a feasibility study "just to prove it's hopeless" (*New City, Old Bridge* by Roger Johnson). In a couple of months the study was finished and to Wood's surprise, if McCulloch moved his employees there to provide an economic base, the project was possible. "If we can make a bunch of pieces go together," exclaimed Wood, "this is a perfect site for a new community."

McCulloch Properties took four years and spent $500,000 to plan the city. Wood, the master-planner, studied topographical maps, scouted every inch of the site, and did the research, consulting the yellow pages of other cities in order to determine how many lawyers, doctors, teachers, grocery stores, electricians, plumbers, etc. the city would need at each stage of growth. Finally he was able to draw up blueprints for a free-standing community with controlled population density, appropriate zoning, and a balanced economy based on tourism, service, retail businesses, and light industry—all initiated by the transplanting of the McCulloch operation from Los Angeles.

McCulloch and Wood then sat down to figure out how to acquire the 16,000 acres adjacent to Site Six, 26 square miles in all, where Lake Havasu City would be built. In addition to the 3,500 acres he had already purchased, McCulloch was able to arrange a long-term lease for another 1,000 acres with the U.S. Bureau of Fish and Wildlife, ultimately providing a 23-mile-long beachfront for the city. In August 1963, after considerable finagling, some 13,000 acres of federal land given to the state of Arizona for schools was bought by McCulloch at a public auction for $73.47 an acre.

In September 1963, Mohave County established Lake Havasu City as an official Irrigation and Drainage District (IDD)—making it a legal entity, "a municipal corporation for all purposes"—and authorized an election for an IDD board of directors to act as "city councilmen." C. V. Wood was elected to the first board. In December 1963, Wood persuaded Charles C. Royall, former assistant attorney general in the state land department, to act as first "city manager."

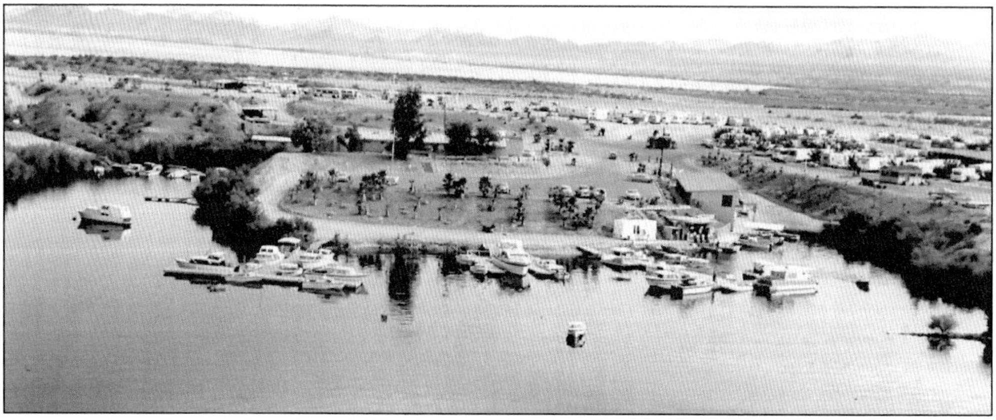

By 1964, Robert P. McCulloch Sr. had set up his outboard motor testing complex at Site Six (shown here), including a small motel at the facility (photograph below). McCulloch had come from a long line of successful businessmen. His father, Richard McCulloch, was president of the United Railway Company in St. Louis. His grandfather, John Irvin Beggs, founded the Milwaukee public utility system. After graduating from high school, Robert P. McCulloch received a substantial inheritance from his grandfather, who had invested wisely in Thomas Alva Edison. (Courtesy Lake Havasu Museum of History.)

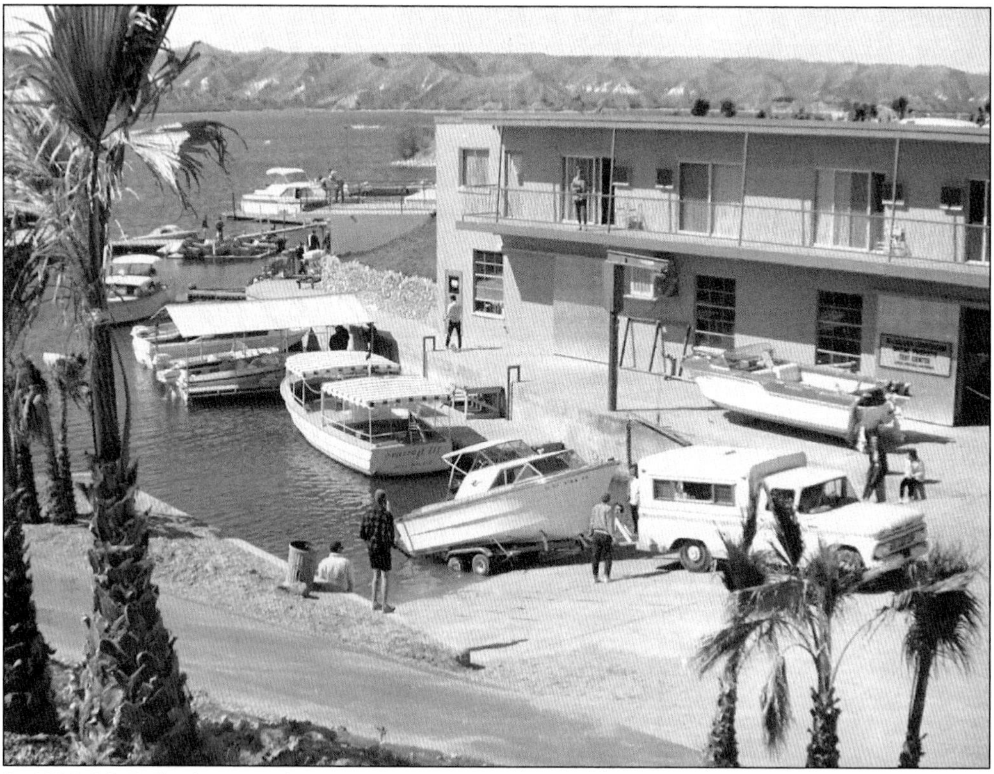

In 1928, McCulloch entered Princeton University. In 1930, he transferred to Stanford, finishing with an engineering degree in 1932. Always an avid fan of boat racing, he won two National Outboard Racing championships while at Stanford. In 1934, McCulloch moved to Milwaukee and married his high school sweetheart, Barbara Ann Briggs, of Briggs and Stratton Motors, a future competitor in his small engine business. (Courtesy Lake Havasu Museum of History.)

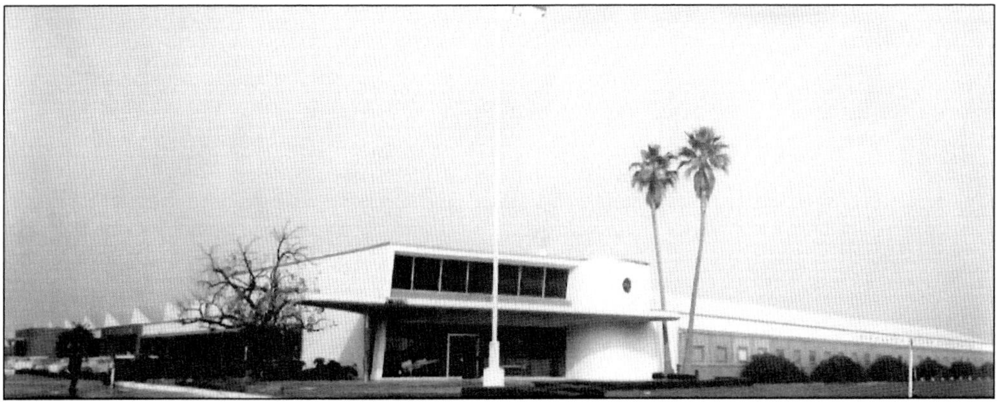

When he was just 20, McCulloch began building small engines and superchargers for midget racing cars. His supercharger business became so successful that when he sold it to Borg Warner for a million dollars in 1943, it was second only to General Motors. During World War II, seeking to further develop lightweight engines, McCulloch founded McCulloch Aviation and began producing engines for military target planes. (Courtesy Lake Havasu Museum of History.)

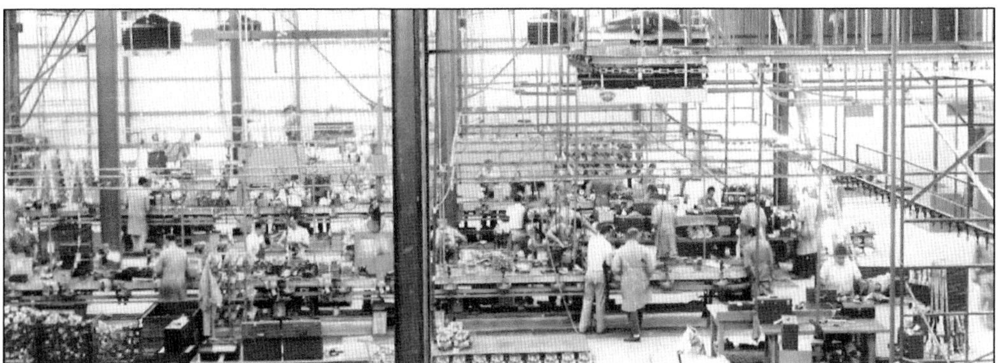

In 1946, McCulloch moved his small-engine plant from Milwaukee to Los Angeles (shown here in these two photographs). In 1948, applying his knowledge of lightweight engines to chain saws, McCulloch produced a five-horsepower chain saw that weighed only 49 pounds. In 1949, McCulloch came out with a one-man chain saw that delivered three horses of power and weighed only 25 pounds. (Courtesy Lake Havasu Museum of History.)

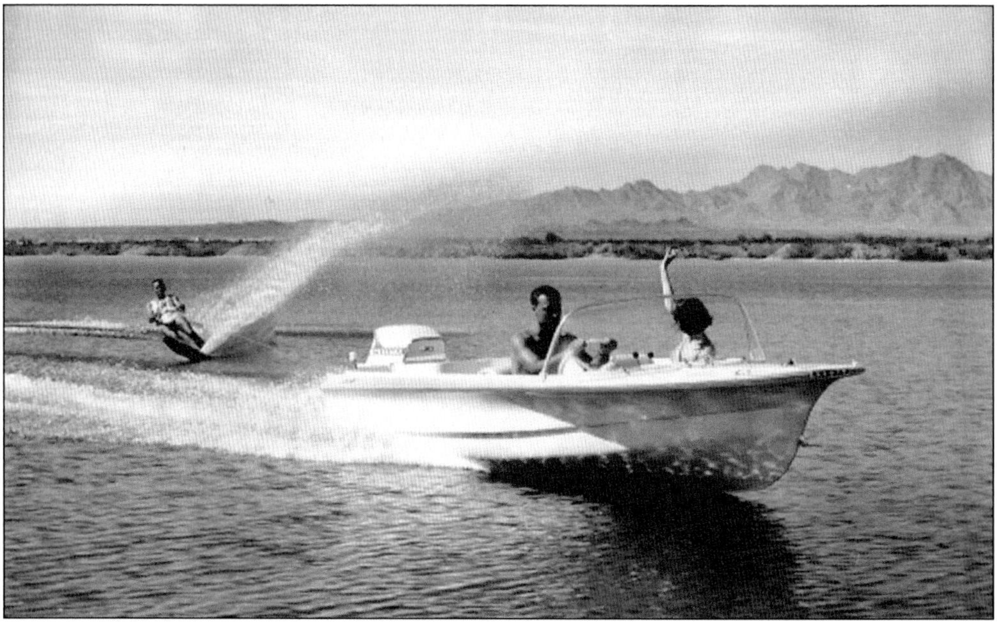

In 1956, McCulloch got back into outboard motors, purchasing the Scott–Atwater Company of Minneapolis. Here is one of his early outboards, c. 1963. (Courtesy Lake Havasu Museum of History.)

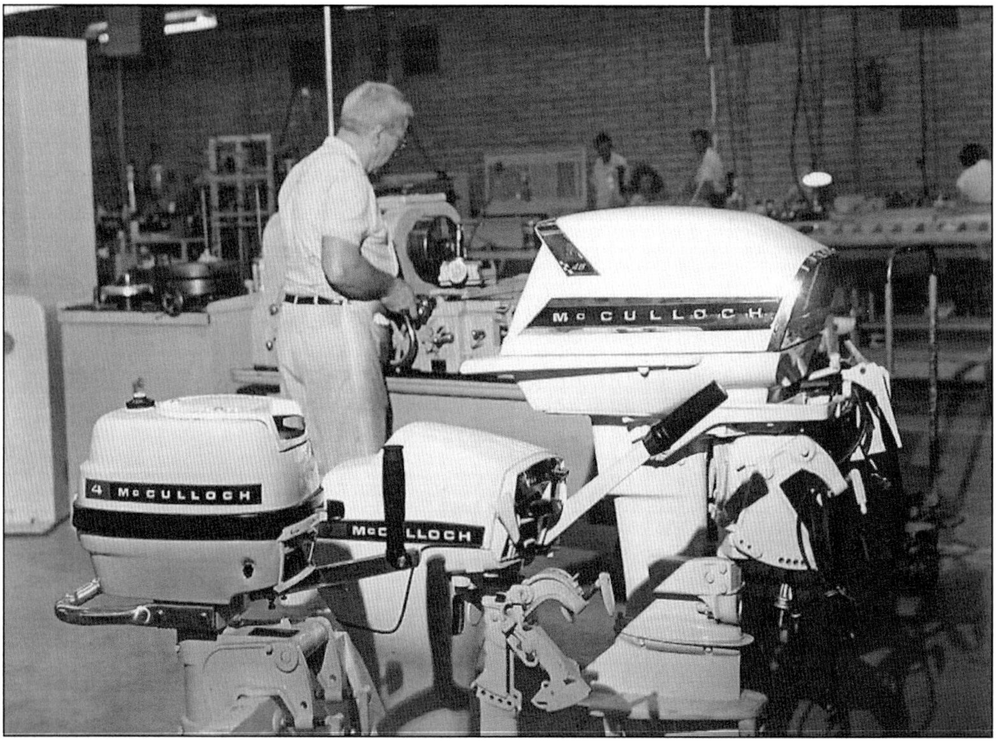

McCulloch eventually became the world's largest manufacturer of chain saws and the world's third largest manufacturer of outboard motors, while at the same time developing his oil and land businesses. (Courtesy Lake Havasu Museum of History.)

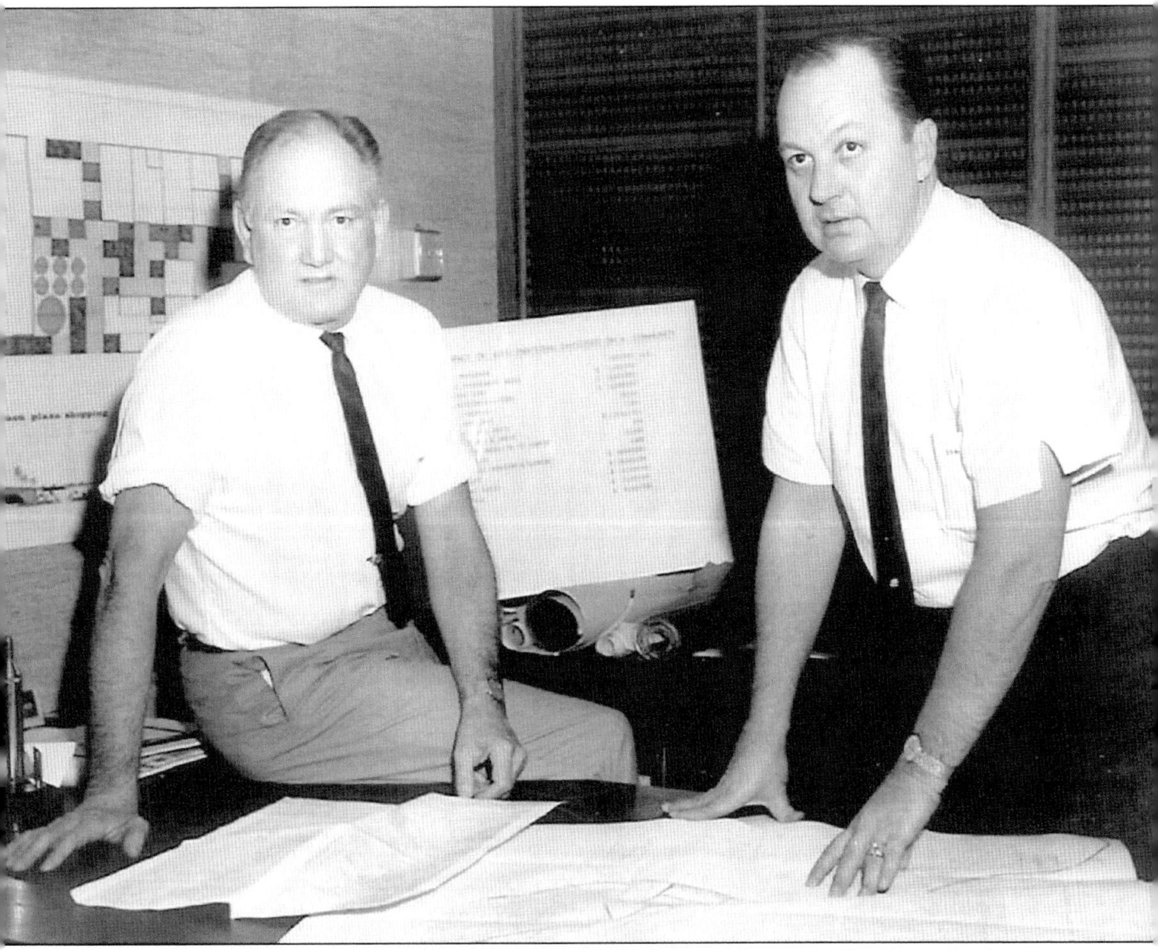

Robert P. McCulloch Sr. (left) first met C. V. Wood Jr. (right) in 1954, when Wood was developing Disneyland. McCulloch was visiting the Disneyland construction site and offered Wood the opportunity to test one of his electric golf carts, as Wood recently had hurt his knee and was on crutches. "Man, there's nothing I'd like more," replied Wood and thus their friendship was born. C. V. Wood came from Amarillo, Texas, by way of Wood County, Oklahoma, where he was born, and Oklahoma University, where he earned a degree in petroleum engineering in 1941. After graduation, Wood got a job with the Convair Corporation, later becoming their chief industrial engineer. In 1950, he became the Southern California director of the Stanford Research Institute. After he left Disneyland in 1956, C. V. Wood formed Marco Engineering, partnering with McCulloch on the development of Lake Mead Marina and Pacific Ocean Park. In 1961, Wood merged with McCulloch Properties and began building master-planned cities. (Courtesy Lake Havasu Museum of History.)

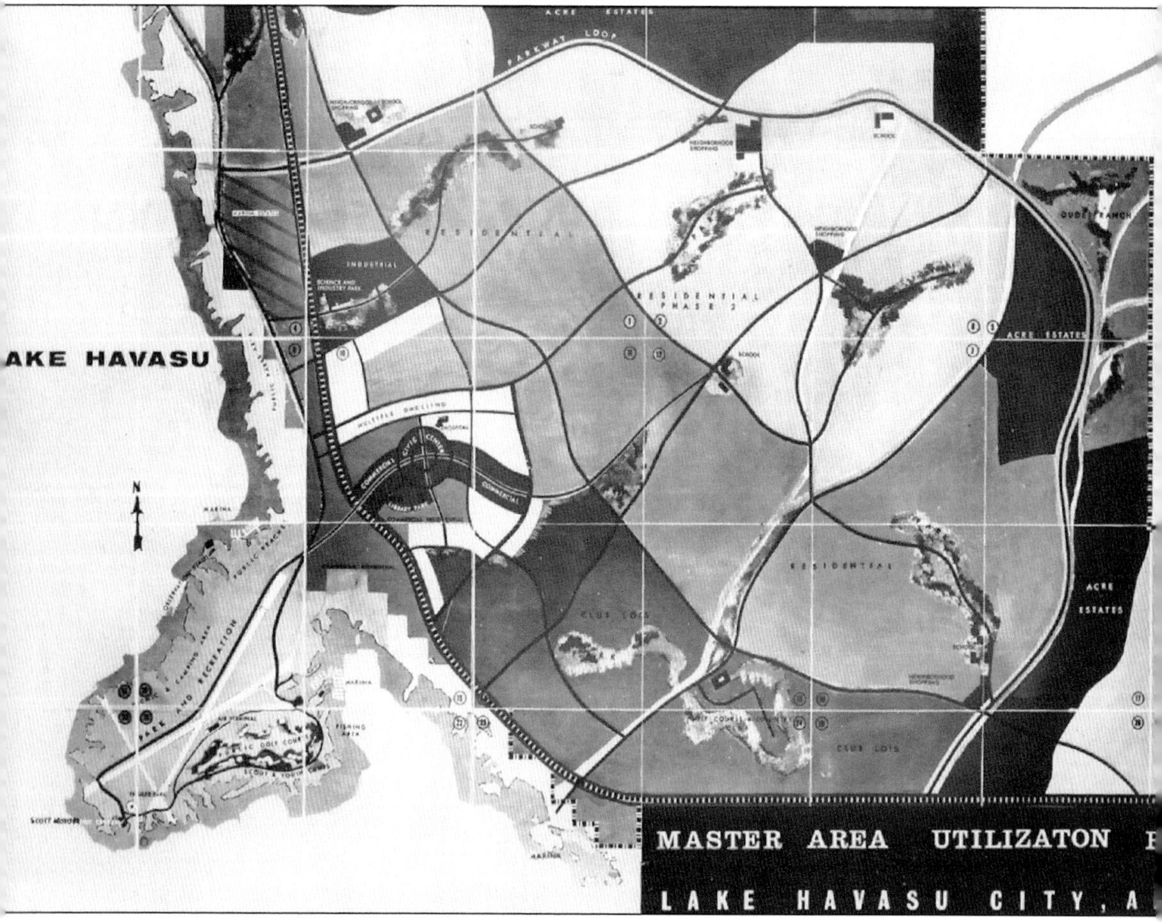

As envisioned by McCulloch and Wood, the economy of Lake Havasu City was to be based on tourism, service, retail businesses, and light industry. On this early planning map, distinctive sectors of the city can be identified that correspond to those concerns: areas reserved for parks and recreation, public beaches, and a golf course (lower left); commercial, a civic center, a library, and a hospital in the center; and industrial, including the science and industrial park, above center. Most of the rest of the map is designated residential. (Courtesy Lake Havasu Museum of History.)

Eight

Early Growth and Sales

Although the construction of Lake Havasu City proper began in 1964, some construction had already occurred at Site Six—McCulloch's test facilities in 1958, a new airplane hangar, and a trailer park in 1962. A significant community had sprung up there. The old Site Six restaurant and bar was the main hangout.

Ron Blanchard, bartender at the bar, remembered being on a jeep ride in the desert with McCulloch and Wood when they told him they were going to build a city there, but he couldn't believe it. "I just died trying not to laugh," said Blanchard in the *Lake Havasu City Herald*. Then Wood "turned around and pointed to a spot and said they were going to build a hotel," continued Blanchard. "And it was hard to believe in those days," he added. "Eight people registered in the trailer park meant a real big weekend."

By 1966, the population of Lake Havasu City had grown to a thousand residents. Also by that time, 50 miles of streets had been paved and utilities had been installed. An official post office had been opened. The Lake Havasu City Volunteer Fire Department came into being. And a new school district had been established, the first elementary school opening its doors in 1964. The first tavern opened in 1964, the first church in 1965. Then came shops, restaurants, gas stations, and the first apartment houses.

In 1964 and 1965, the first doctor and the first dentist opened their offices in the newly-constructed commercial center, Arnold Plaza. Also located in Arnold Plaza were Claypool's Market, the Valley National Bank, the Phoenix Title and Trust Company, and the offices of McCulloch Properties, Incorporated.

Following the construction of the new $2-million factory complex McCulloch built to house his manufacturing business were the construction of various housing developments for his employees.

By 1966, McCulloch's fly-in, "see-before-you-buy" program was in full force. Before it was over, McCulloch's fleet of Lockheed Electras and Constellations brought in 137,000 prospective buyers to Lake Havasu City, in as many as a dozen flights per week, from cities all across America. Buyers were met at the Site Six airport by Holly Development Corporation salespeople and squired in a fleet of 40 white Jeeps to the Nautical Inn or the new Lake Havasu Hotel for a free weekend—rooms, meals, boat cruises, and fishing trips included. Also included, of course, were guided tours around the shore of the lake, up into the hills for the view, by the new golf course, and by potential building sites for new homes. By the time clients had returned to their hotels—in the case of the Lake Havasu Hotel, surrounded by lush landscaping, a waterfall flowing off the roof, a dining room with a floor-to-ceiling fireplace framed by more waterfalls—most were ready to buy.

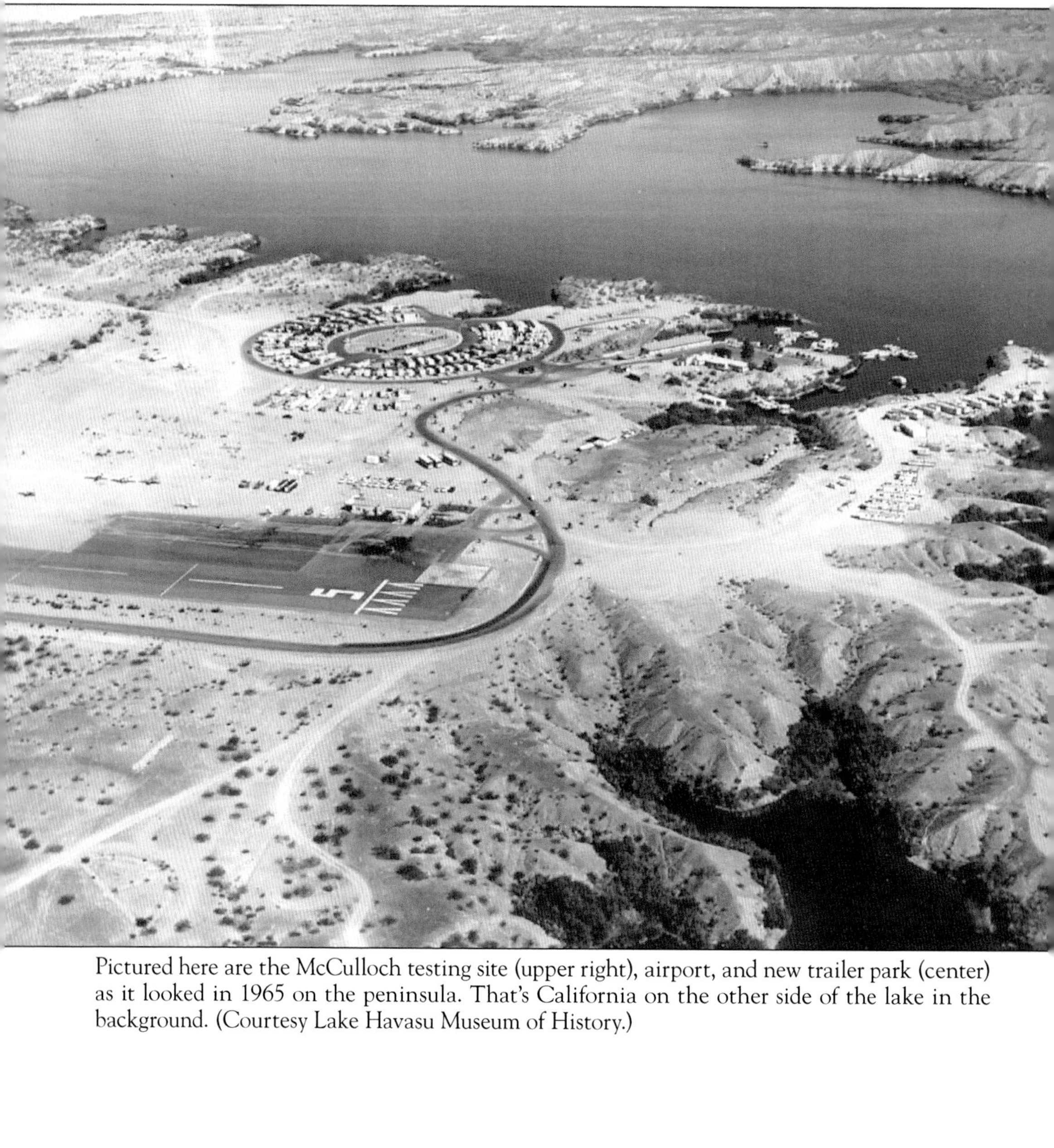

Pictured here are the McCulloch testing site (upper right), airport, and new trailer park (center) as it looked in 1965 on the peninsula. That's California on the other side of the lake in the background. (Courtesy Lake Havasu Museum of History.)

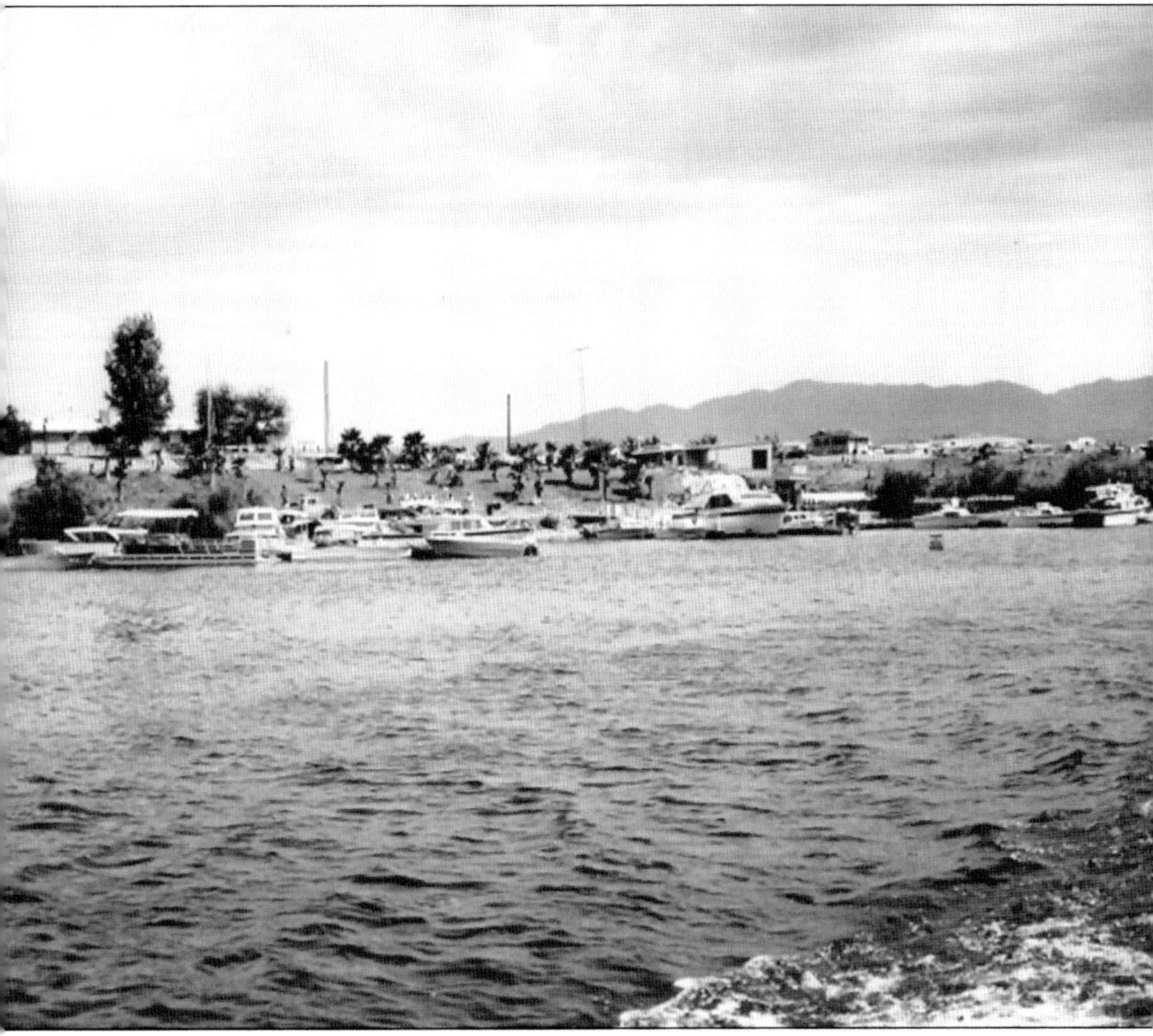

Approaching Site Six by water, one gets a close-up view of the new marina and McCulloch's small motel at the site (right of center). (Courtesy Lake Havasu Museum of History.)

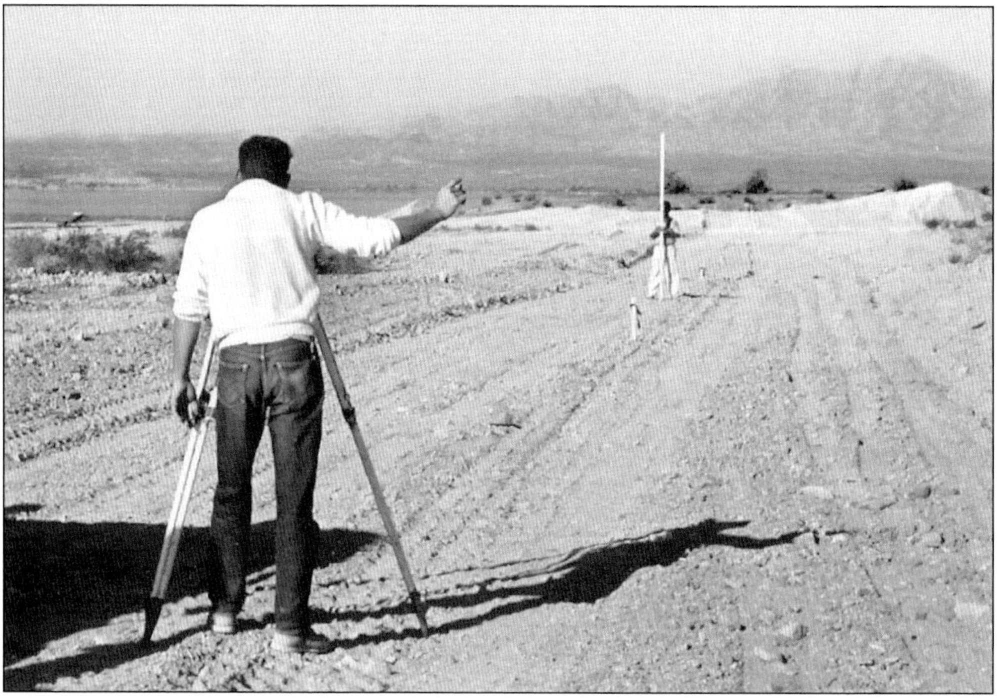

Survey and paving crews work on the first streets in Lake Havasu City. (Courtesy Lake Havasu Museum of History.)

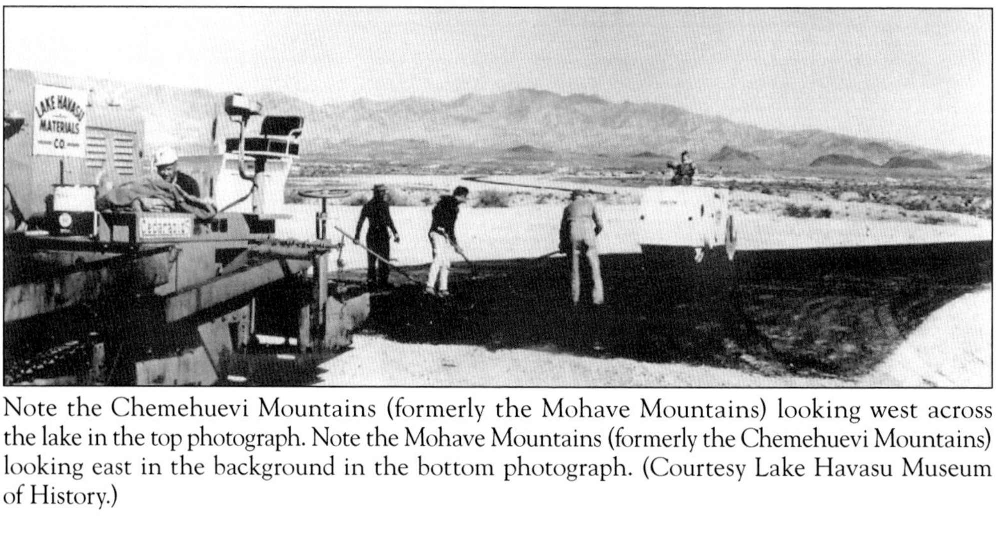

Note the Chemehuevi Mountains (formerly the Mohave Mountains) looking west across the lake in the top photograph. Note the Mohave Mountains (formerly the Chemehuevi Mountains) looking east in the background in the bottom photograph. (Courtesy Lake Havasu Museum of History.)

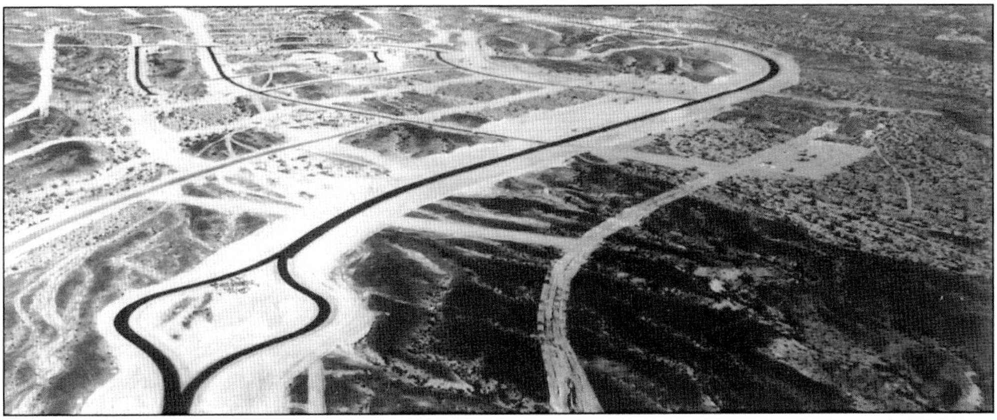

By 1965, paving of McCulloch Boulevard had gone as far up as Wheeler Park (lower left). Note the construction beginning on the Havasu Hotel (upper right) even further up. (Courtesy Lake Havasu Museum of History.)

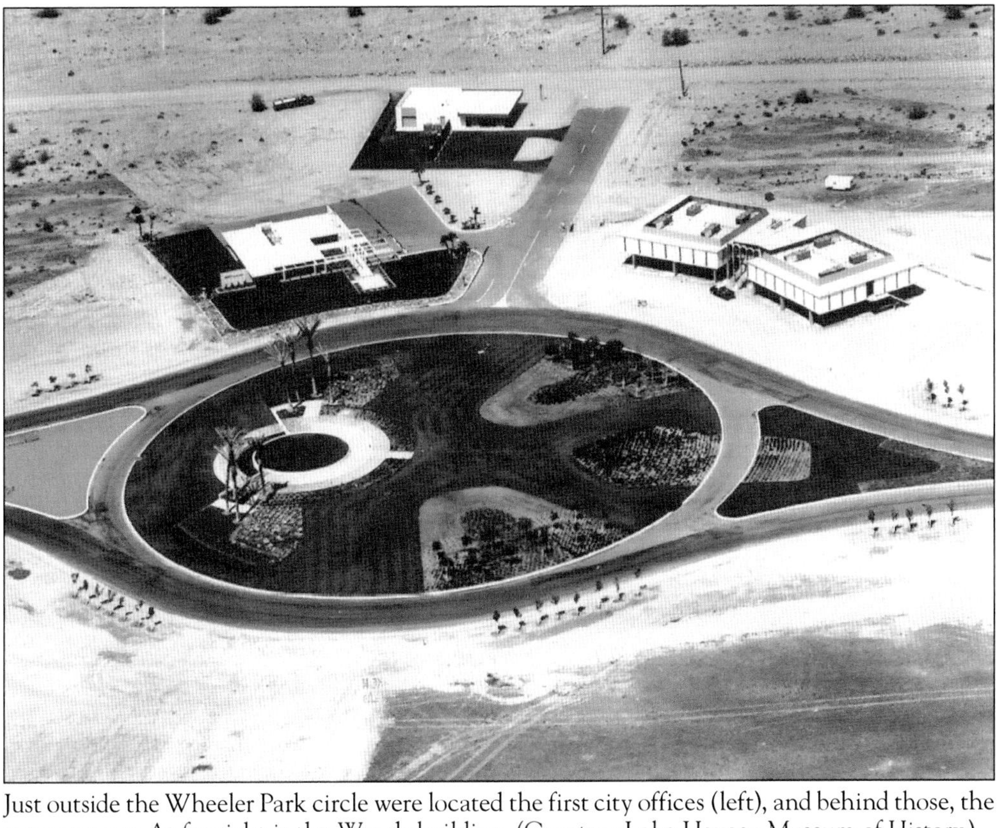

Just outside the Wheeler Park circle were located the first city offices (left), and behind those, the gas company. At far right is the Woods building. (Courtesy Lake Havasu Museum of History.)

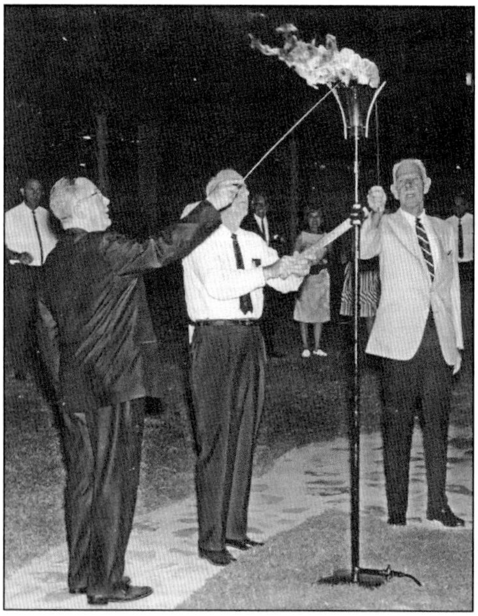

Natural gas comes to Lake Havasu City. The first bond of the newly formed Lake Havasu Irrigation and Drainage District was passed in 1964, in the amount of $7,140,000, in order to provide utilities for the fledgling city. (Courtesy Lake Havasu Museum of History.)

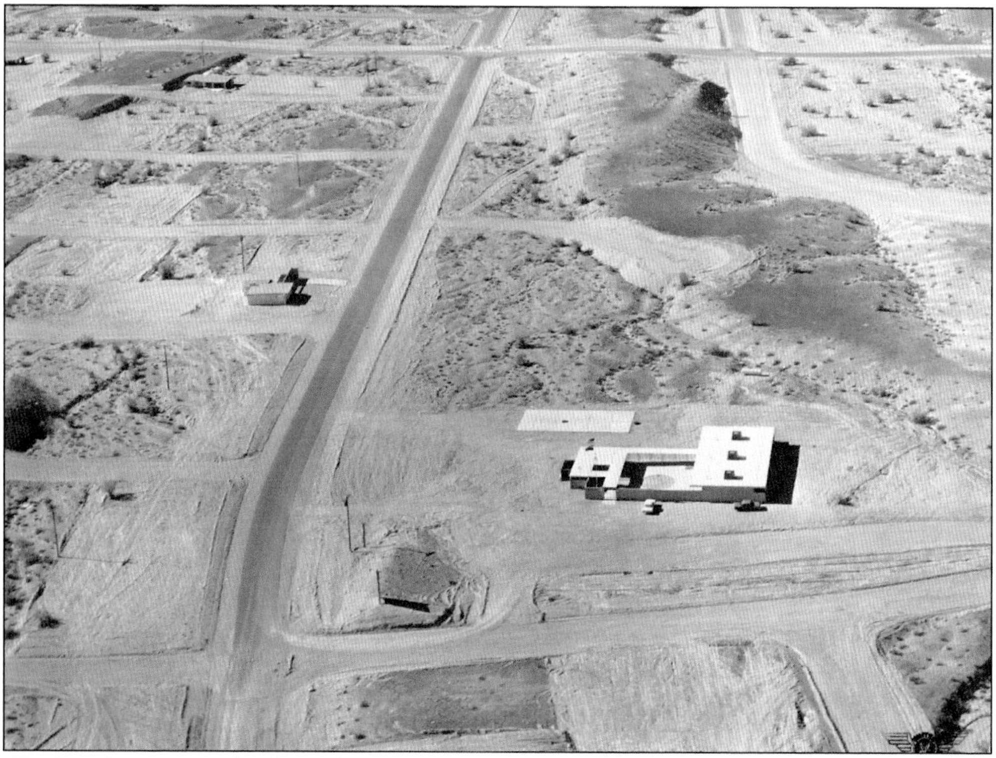

The first elementary school in Lake Havasu City, built on land donated by McCulloch Properties, opened in 1964. It had five classrooms, a cafeteria, offices, and a small auditorium. But "it wasn't ready in time for classes," recalled Mary Fraze DeWees, who was in eighth grade at the time (*Lake Havasu City Herald*). And the cafeteria wasn't quite finished, so "the McCulloch catering truck would stop at noon at the school, bringing hot lunches." (Courtesy Lake Havasu Museum of History.)

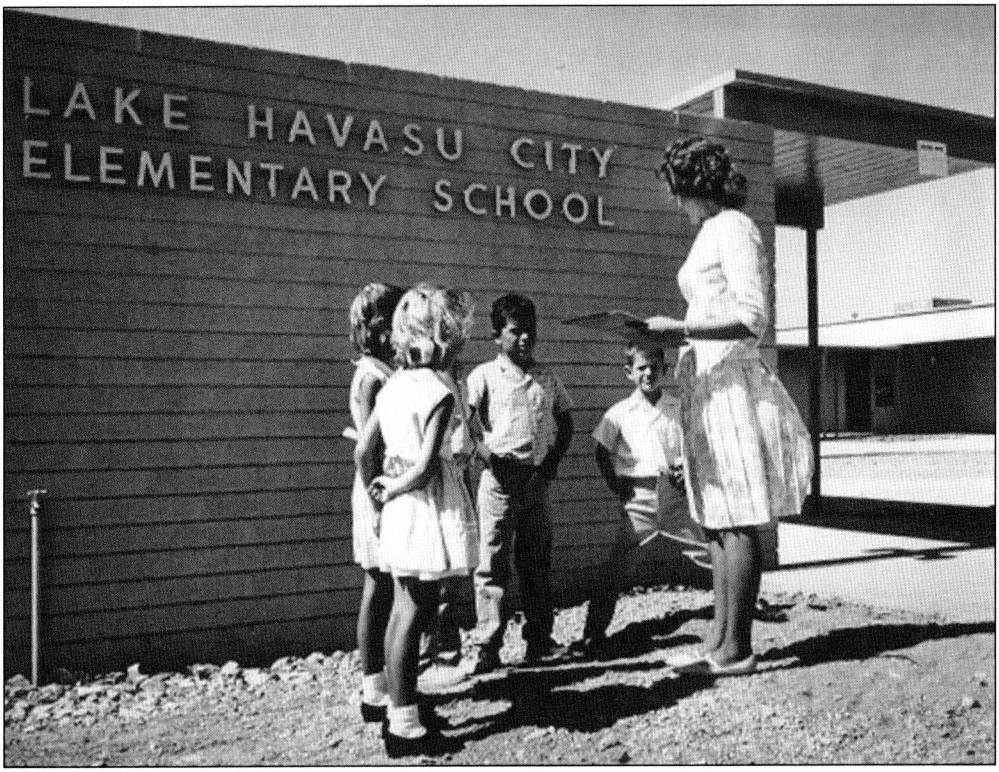

Three teachers and the principal taught first grade through eighth grade that first year. Of the 14 students, 10 graduated. "We walked into the graduation hall with candles and received our diplomas in style," said Mary (*Lake Havasu City Herald*). "A small party followed in our classroom." (Courtesy Lake Havasu Museum of History.)

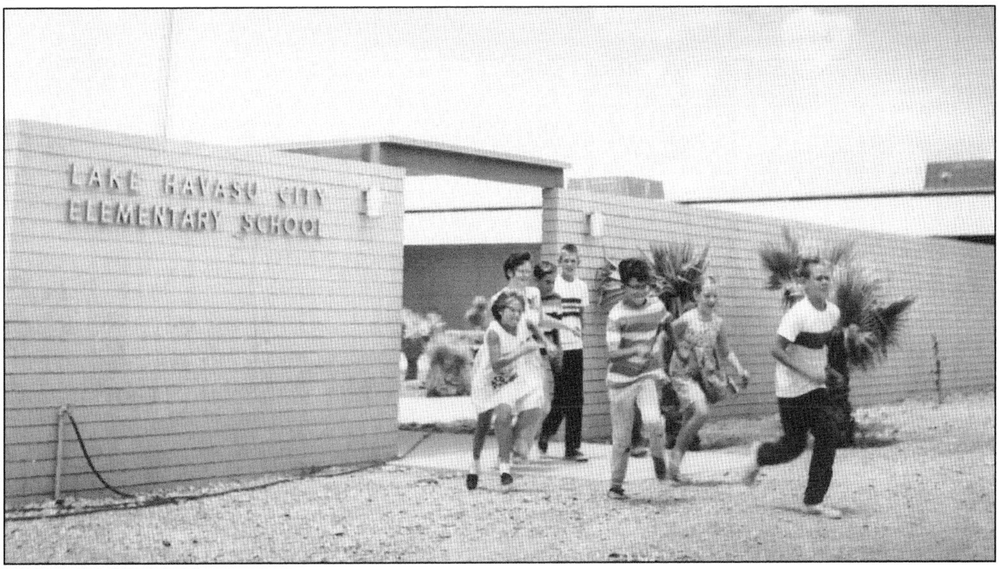

After finishing grade school, students had to catch the county bus on Route 66 to go to high school in Kingman, 40 miles away. A high school wasn't built in Lake Havasu City until 1969. (Courtesy Lake Havasu Museum of History.)

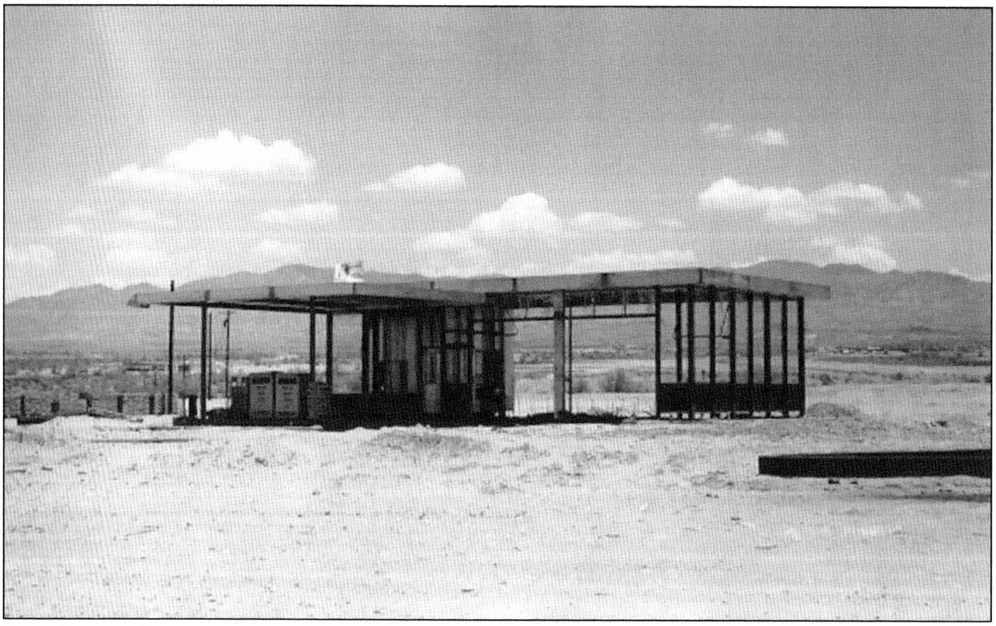

Seen here under construction in 1964 is the first service station in Lake Havasu City, the Standard station on McCulloch Boulevard. (Courtesy Lake Havasu Museum of History.)

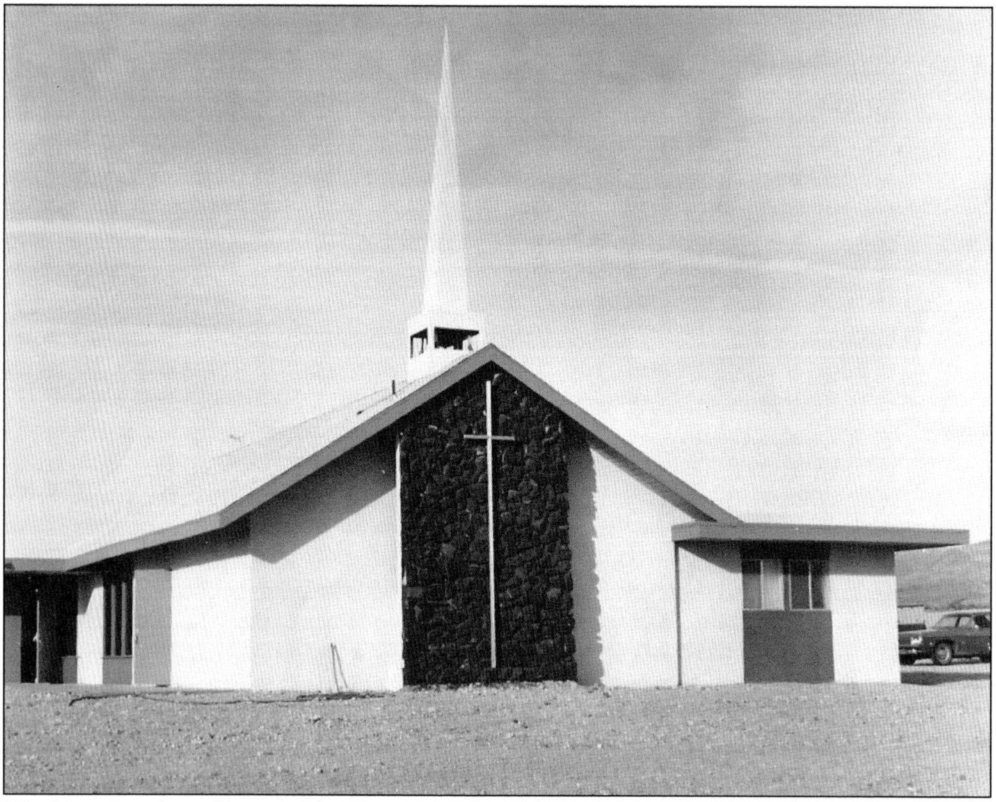

The First Southern Baptist Church on North Palo Verde Drive was the first church in Lake Havasu City. It was dedicated in 1965. (Courtesy Lake Havasu Museum of History.)

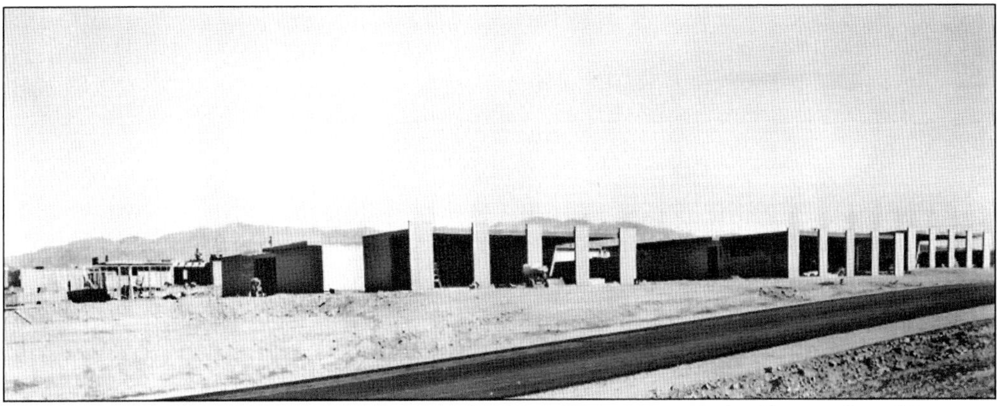

Built in 1964, the Andrus Apartments were the first apartments in Lake Havasu City. (Courtesy Lake Havasu Museum of History.)

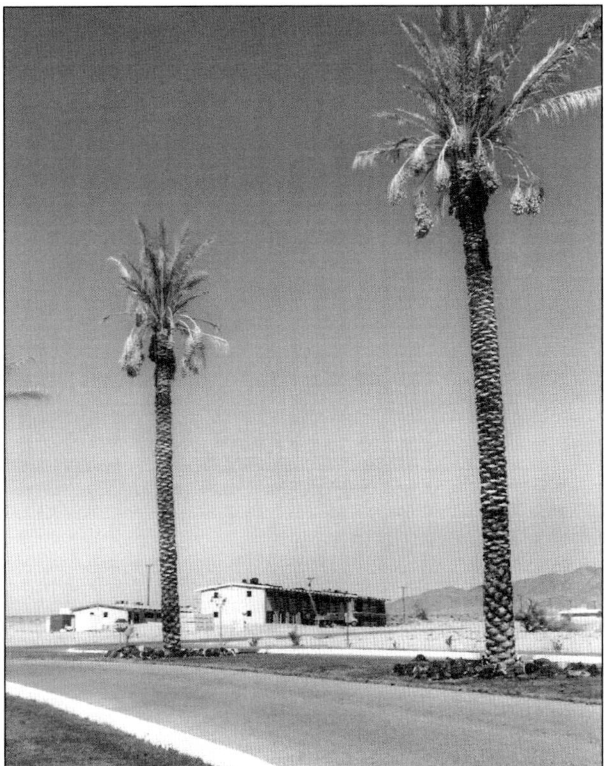

The Briggs Apartments on McCulloch Boulevard across from the new Havasu Hotel were also built in 1964. (Courtesy Lake Havasu Museum of History.)

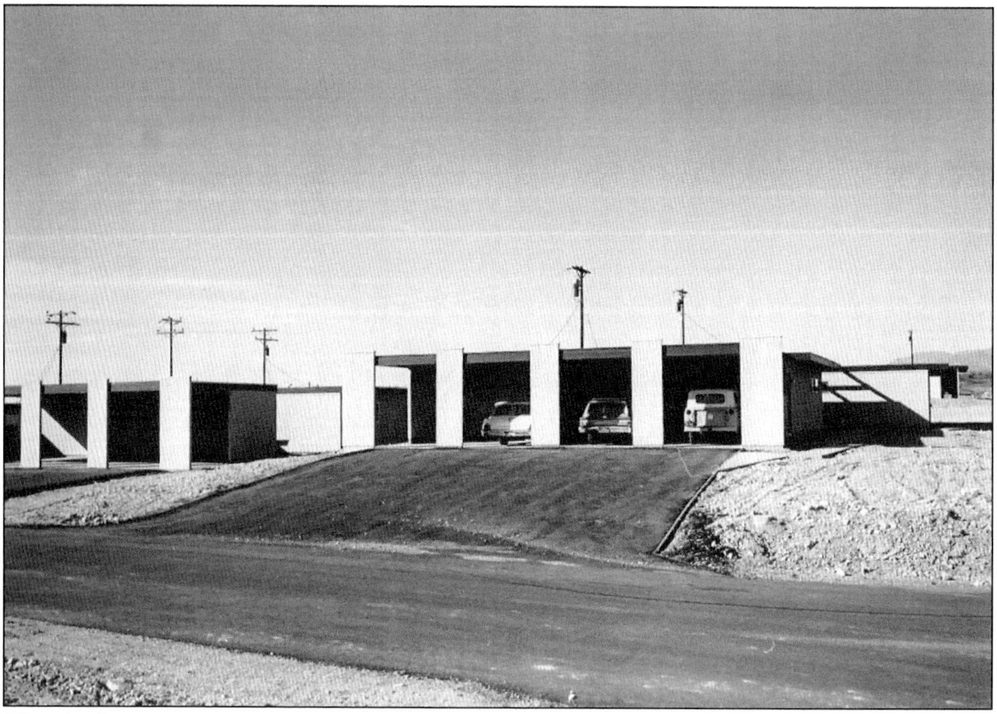

The Anderson Apartments, 10 units, were built in 1965. (Courtesy Lake Havasu Museum of History.)

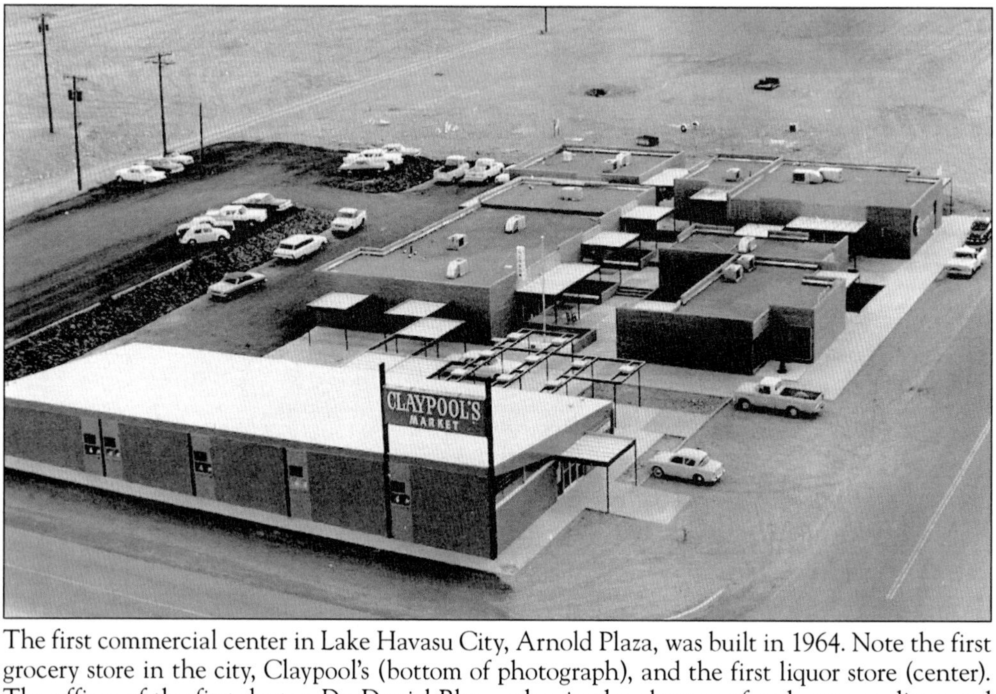

The first commercial center in Lake Havasu City, Arnold Plaza, was built in 1964. Note the first grocery store in the city, Claypool's (bottom of photograph), and the first liquor store (center). The offices of the first doctor, Dr. Daniel Blez—who, in the absence of a pharmacy, dispensed drugs out his office—and the first dentist, Dr. Hal Torgersen, were located in Arnold Plaza. Later the post office was moved there. (Courtesy Lake Havasu Museum of History.)

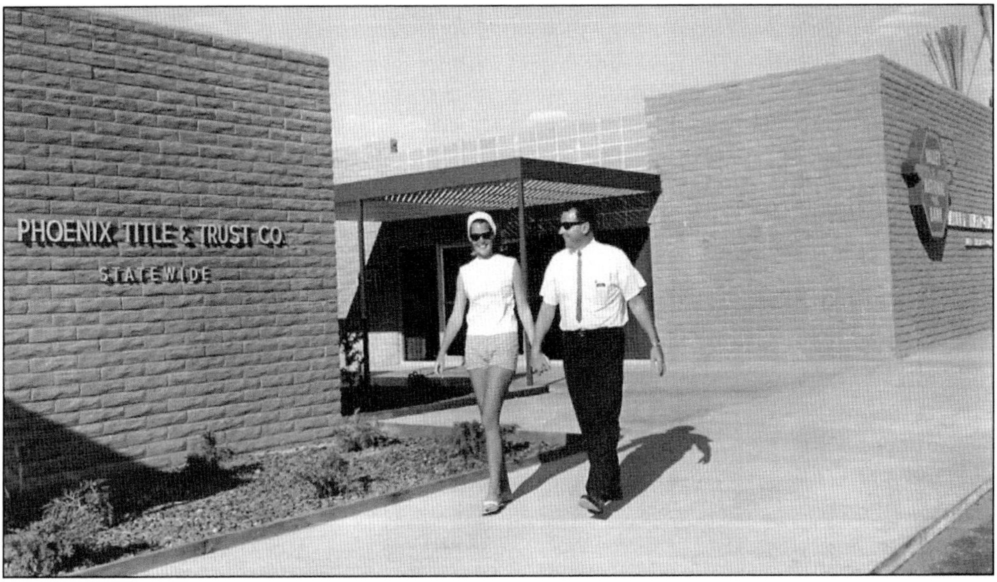

Several other businesses also set up office in the plaza, including The Phoenix Title and Trust Company. (Courtesy Lake Havasu Museum of History.)

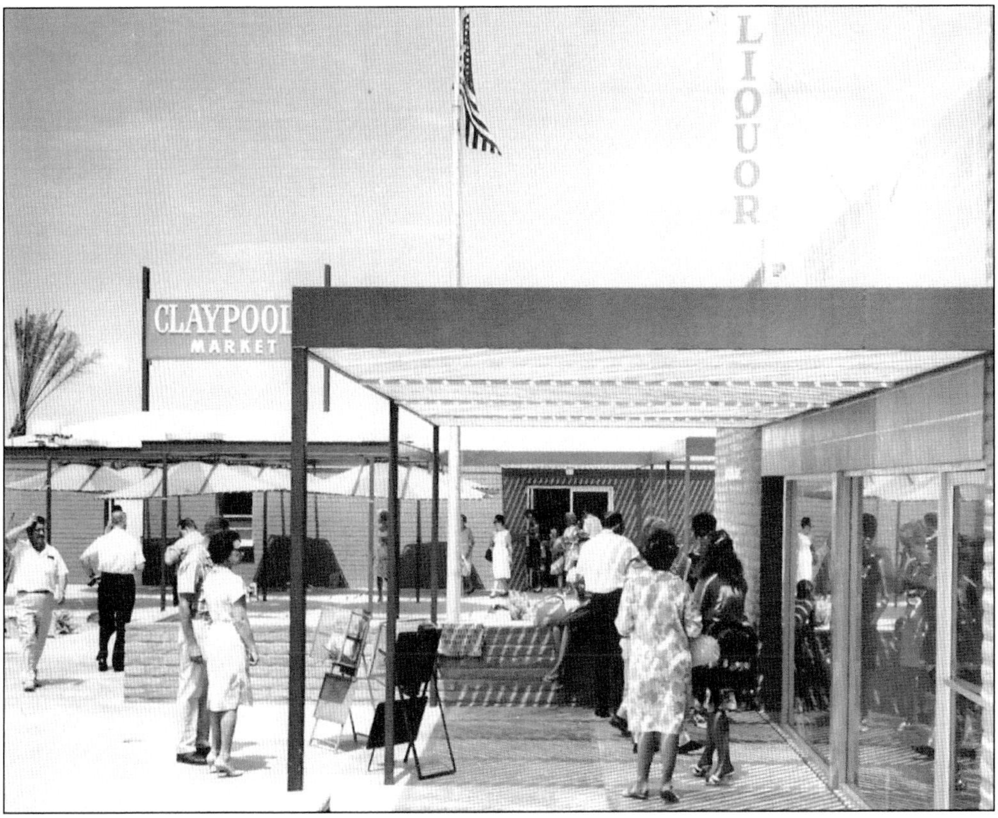

One of the first buildings on Arnold Plaza was also the first grocery store in Lake Havasu City—Claypool's Market, the top retail chain in western Arizona at that time. (Courtesy Lake Havasu Museum of History.)

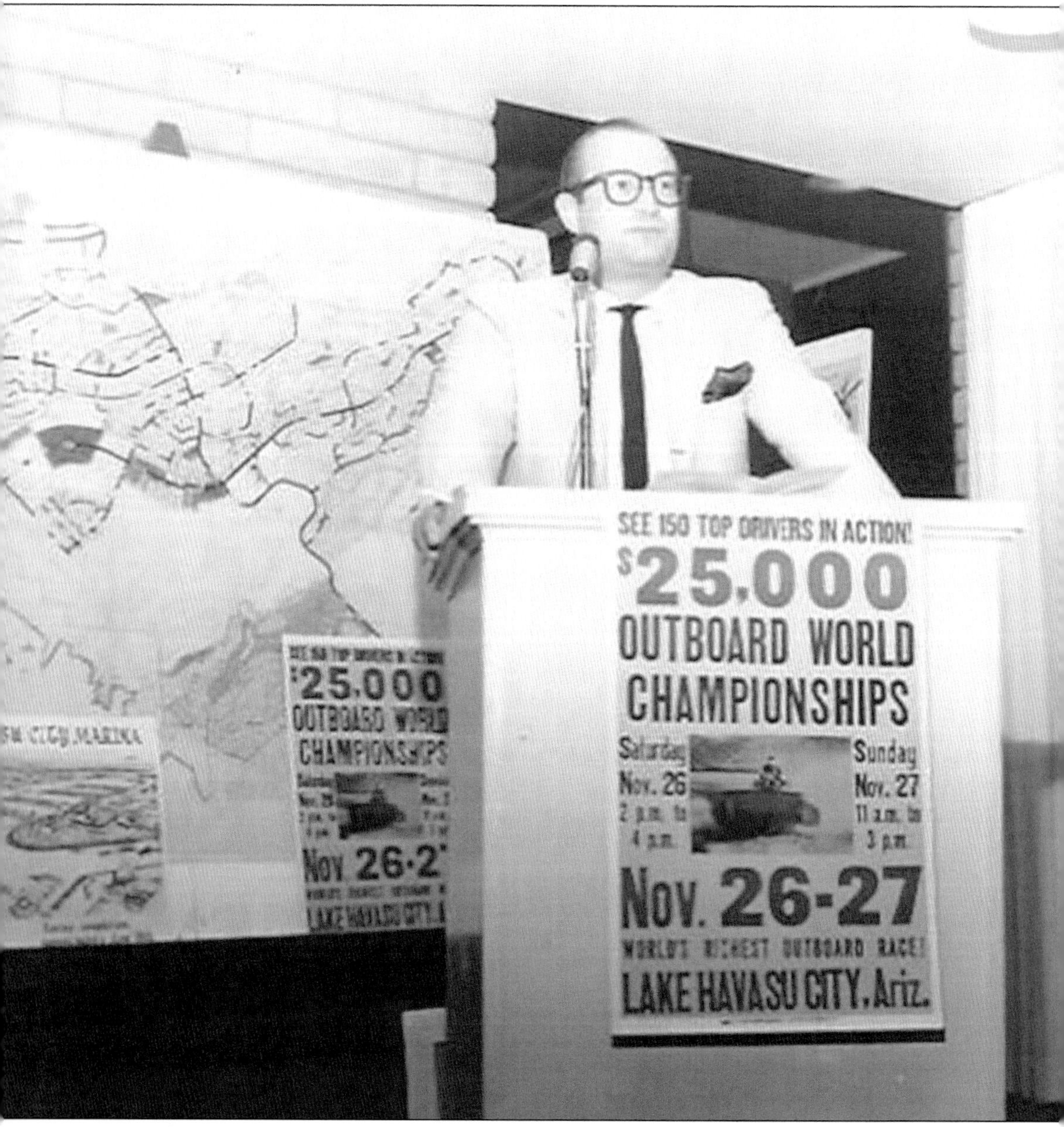

Located in the Arnold Plaza commercial center was the office of McCulloch Properties, Inc., the company that developed Lake Havasu City. Robert P. McCulloch Jr., the son of Robert P. McCulloch Sr., was the president of McCulloch Properties and served as the guiding force in the development of the city during its first eight years. Lorne B. Pratt was the executive vice president and supervised planning, engineering, design, and construction in the city. (Courtesy Lake Havasu Museum of History.)

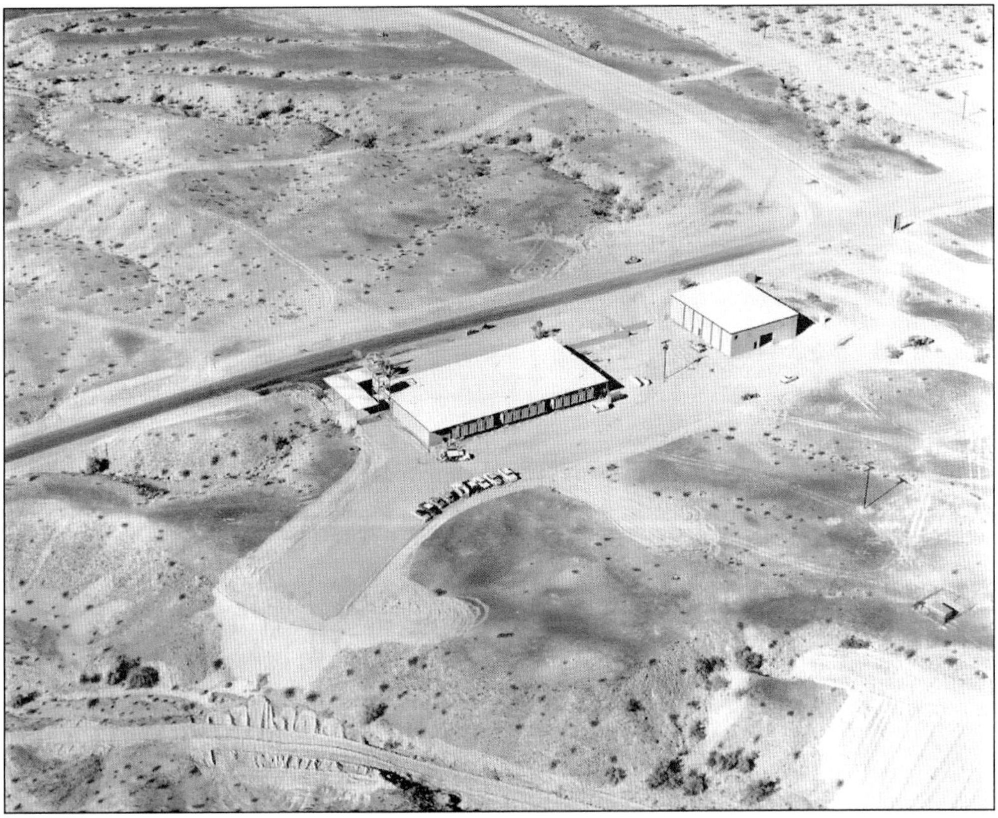

In 1964, under the auspices of the McCulloch Corporation, the parent company and manufacturing arm of the McCulloch family conglomerate—one of the largest in the United States, grossing $75 million annually—Robert P. McCulloch Sr. moved his chain saw manufacturing operation from Los Angeles to Lake Havasu City. (Courtesy Lake Havasu Museum of History.)

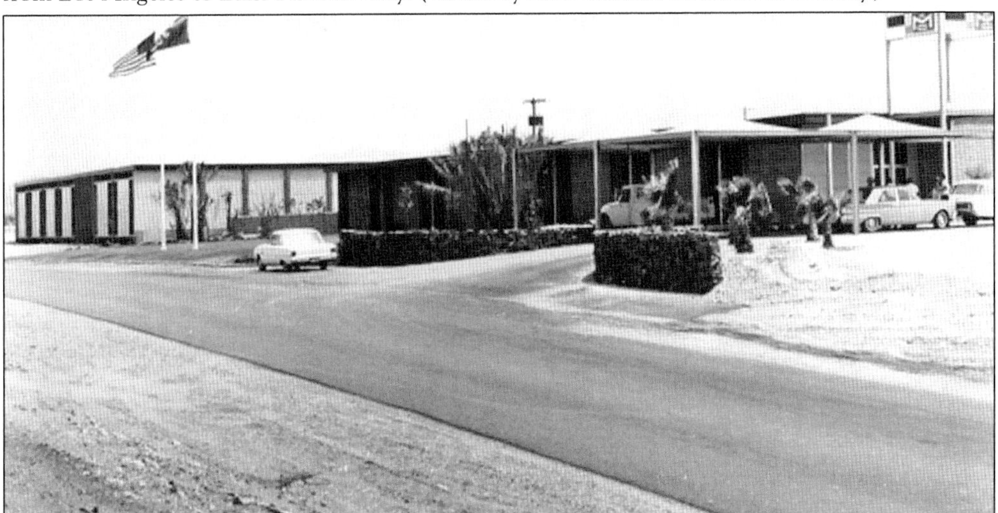

McCulloch invested $2,000,000 in his new chain saw plant (shown here), and invited other manufacturers to join him in the development of an entire industrial complex in Lake Havasu City. (Courtesy Lake Havasu Museum of History.)

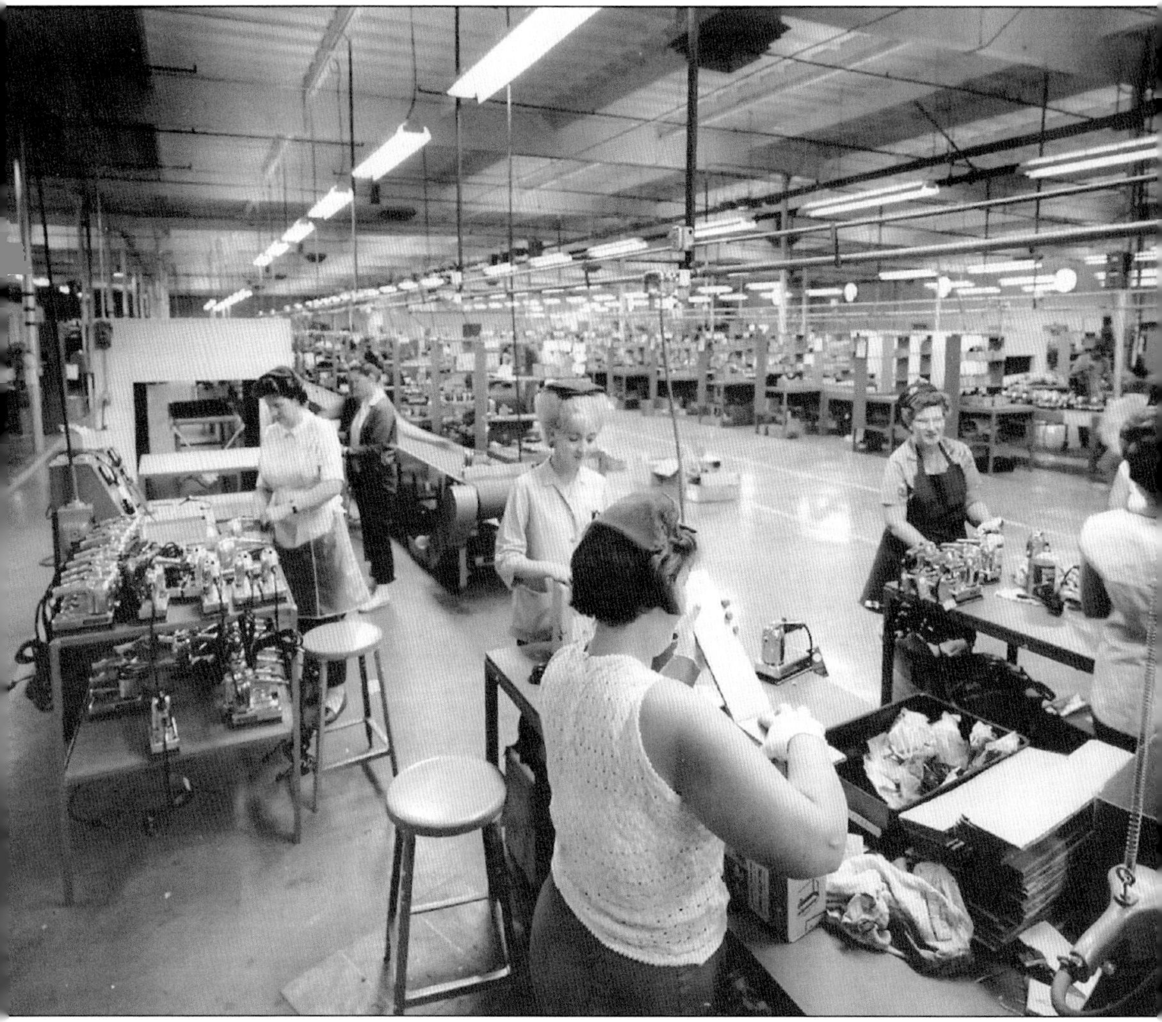

After building its first plant for the manufacture of chain saws, the McCulloch Corporation eventually increased its number of employees to 500 people. Ultimately, McCulloch added two other plants. Next to join the complex was Walters Publications Incorporated, a commercial printing company, investing over $800,000 in their facilities and employing 75 workers. Then came the Campbell Boat Company, starting a $250,000 plant with 20 or so employees, not counting 30 subcontractors. Milne Truck Lines, an international freight company, developed a four-acre site at the cost of $100,000. And, finally, The Mode of Arizona, a furniture-making company, brought their business to the complex, employing some 100 workers in their plant and 20 more in their lumber yard. (Courtesy Lake Havasu Museum of History.)

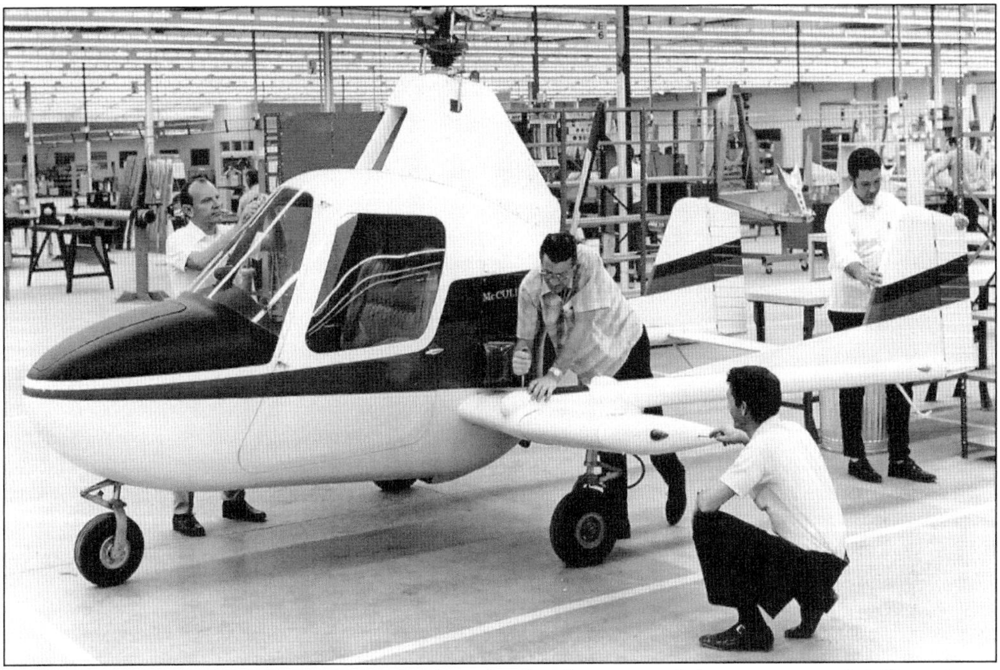

At one time McCulloch became involved in the development of the innovative J-2 Gyroplane. Designed as a two-passenger hybrid combination of airplane and helicopter, the J-2 was marketed as personal aircraft intended to become as common as the automobile. It was easy to fly and could be stored in a backyard or garage. Unfortunately, however, the J-2 never caught on with the public. (Courtesy Lake Havasu Museum of History.)

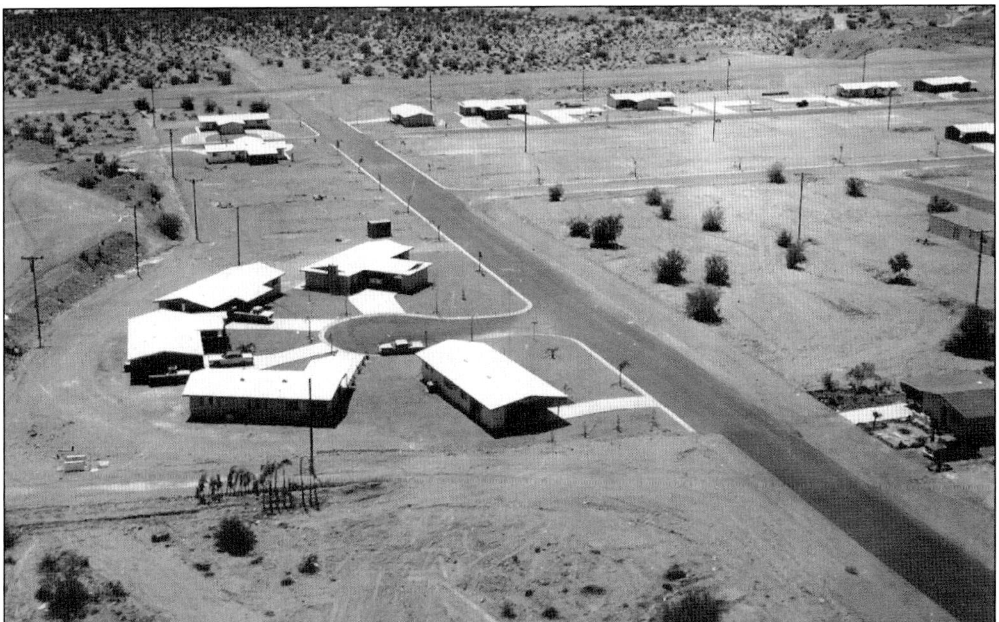

The first suburbs in the city were the tract homes provided for McCulloch employees on Smoketree Avenue. Everyone else had to either commute back and forth to Needles or Kingman or live in tents on Thompson Bay. (Courtesy Lake Havasu Museum of History.)

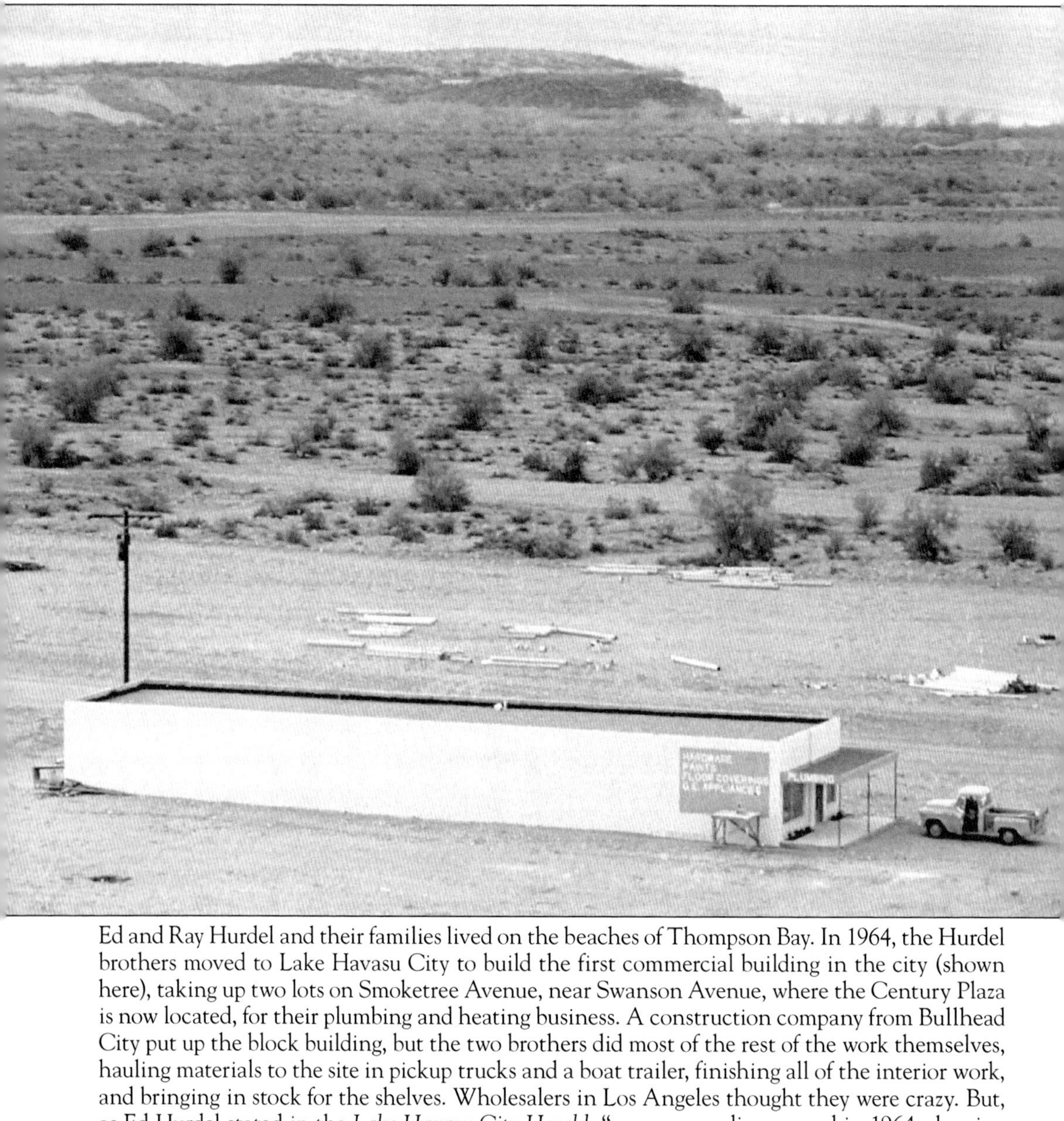

Ed and Ray Hurdel and their families lived on the beaches of Thompson Bay. In 1964, the Hurdel brothers moved to Lake Havasu City to build the first commercial building in the city (shown here), taking up two lots on Smoketree Avenue, near Swanson Avenue, where the Century Plaza is now located, for their plumbing and heating business. A construction company from Bullhead City put up the block building, but the two brothers did most of the rest of the work themselves, hauling materials to the site in pickup trucks and a boat trailer, finishing all of the interior work, and bringing in stock for the shelves. Wholesalers in Los Angeles thought they were crazy. But, as Ed Hurdel stated in the *Lake Havasu City Herald*, "no one was discouraged in 1964, sleeping on the beach, traveling long distances for food, fighting the heat with no air conditioning . . . That's why most of who have been here . . . since . . . feel like pioneers." (Courtesy Lake Havasu Museum of History.)

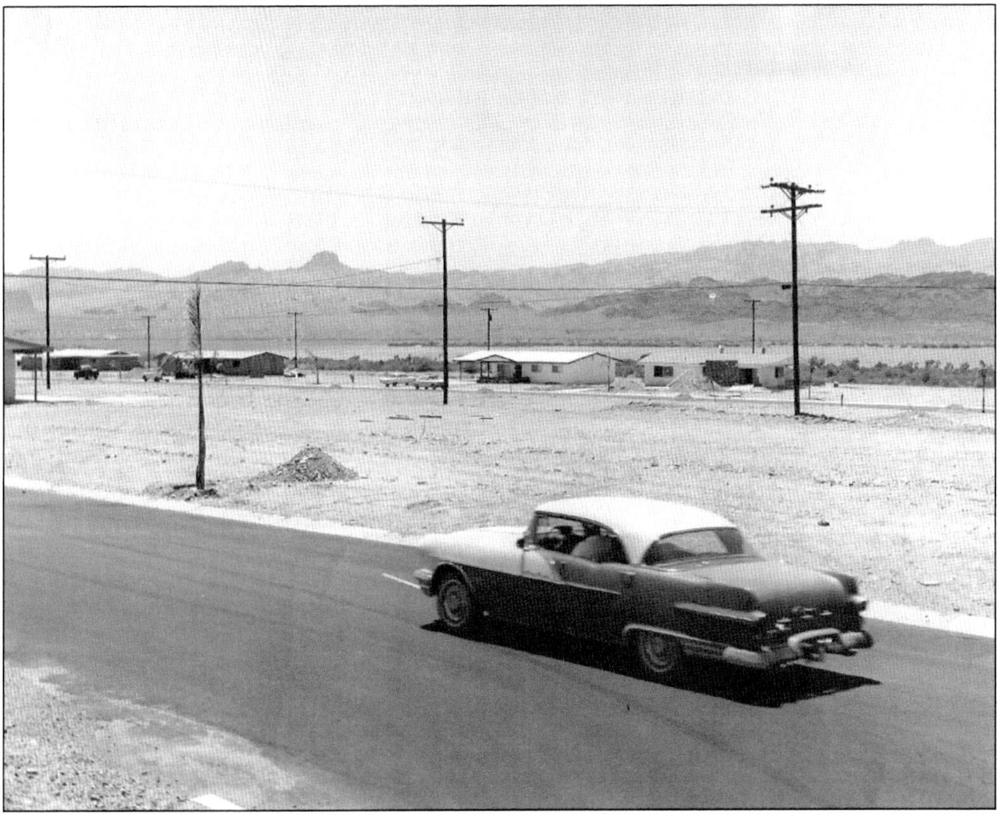

Other FHA–VA tract homes were developed on Sunflower Drive in 1964 (above) and Columbine Drive in 1965 (below). (Courtesy Lake Havasu Museum of History.)

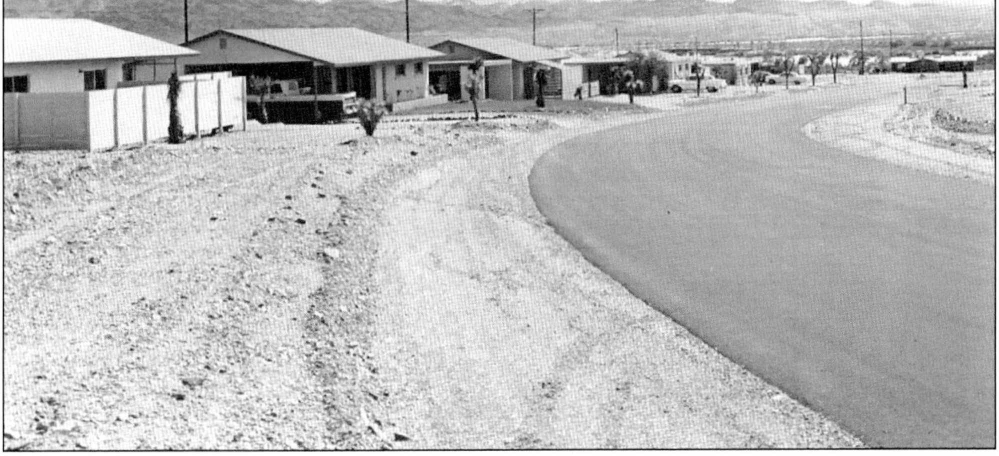

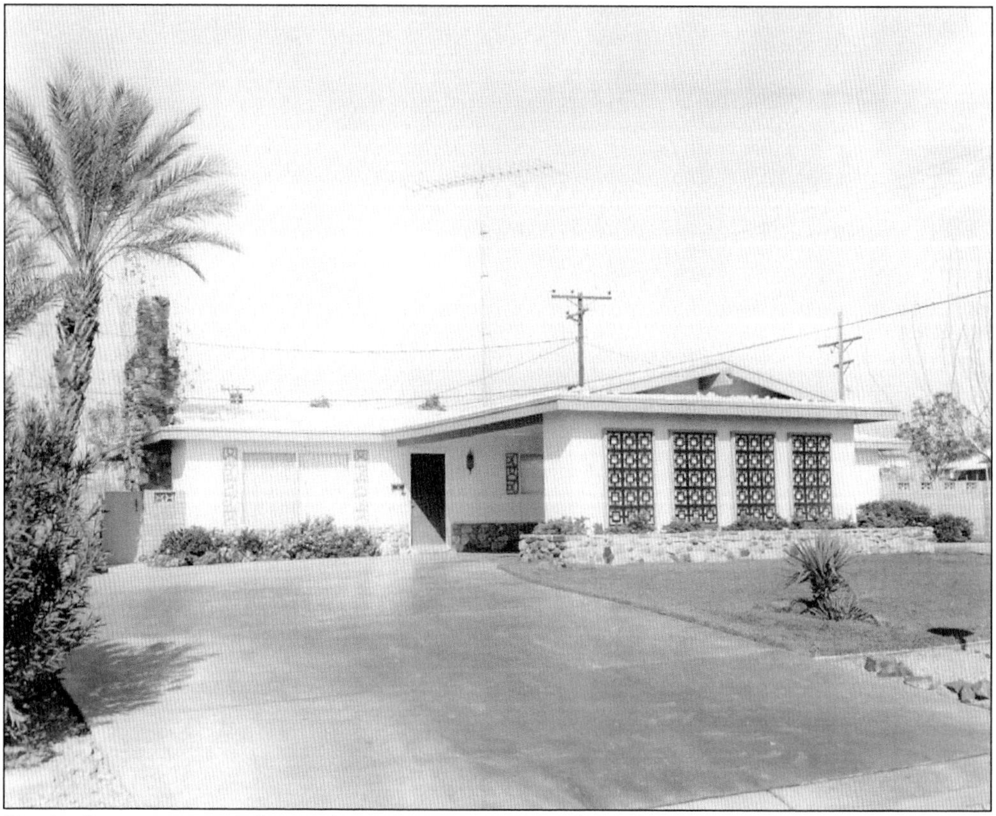

Gradually, more upscale homes began to spring up, such as these early models. (Courtesy Lake Havasu Museum of History.)

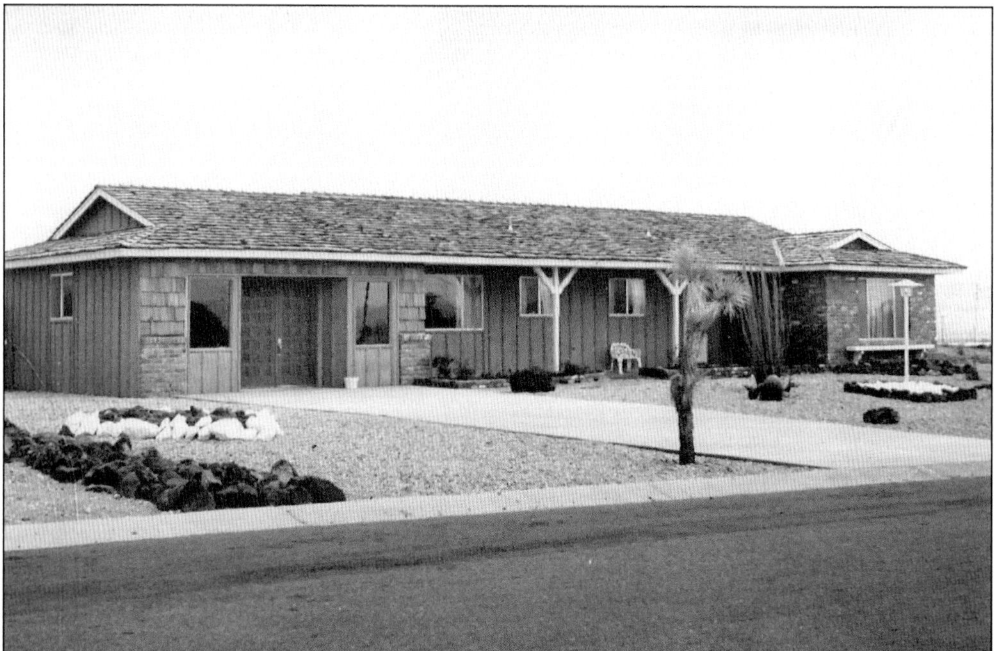

Adding the leisure industry to the tourism, service, retail, and manufacturing sectors of the economy, a new million-dollar marina was built in 1966. Here the owner George Foster (left) and C. V. Wood discuss plans for the marina, which included a restaurant, snack bar, general store, boat repair facilities, boat sales and rentals, a paved launching ramp, and acres of parking. Note the Nautical Inn across the inlet in the background. (Courtesy Lake Havasu Museum of History.)

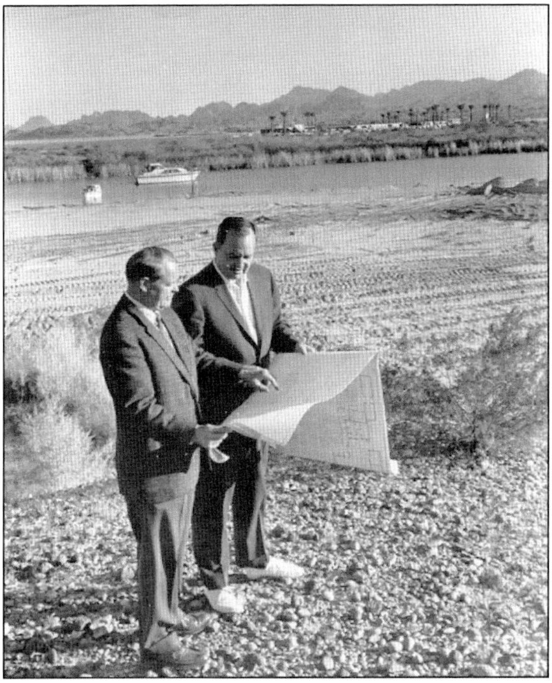

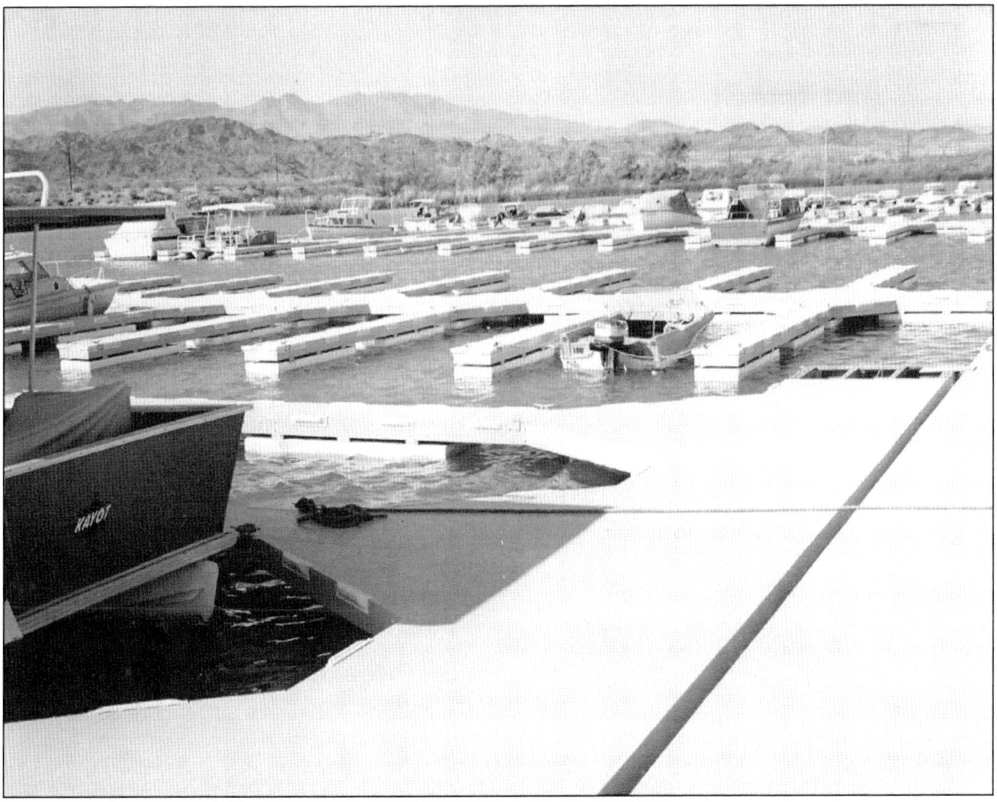

The marina is shown here after completion in June 1966. (Courtesy Lake Havasu Museum of History.)

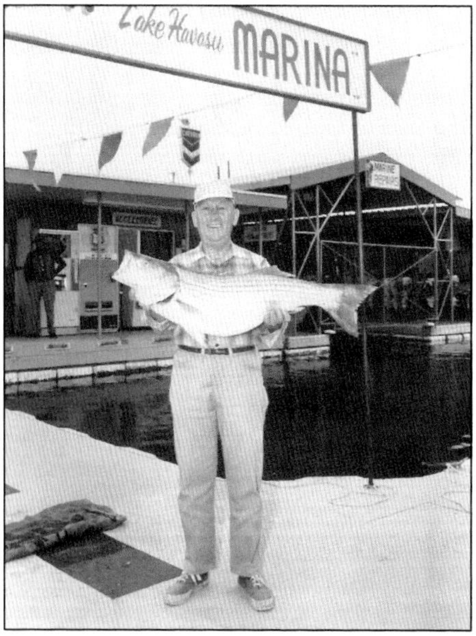

There was also a bait shop with fishing supplies at the marina. Lake Havasu is still famous for its striped and large-mouth bass. (Courtesy Lake Havasu Museum of History.)

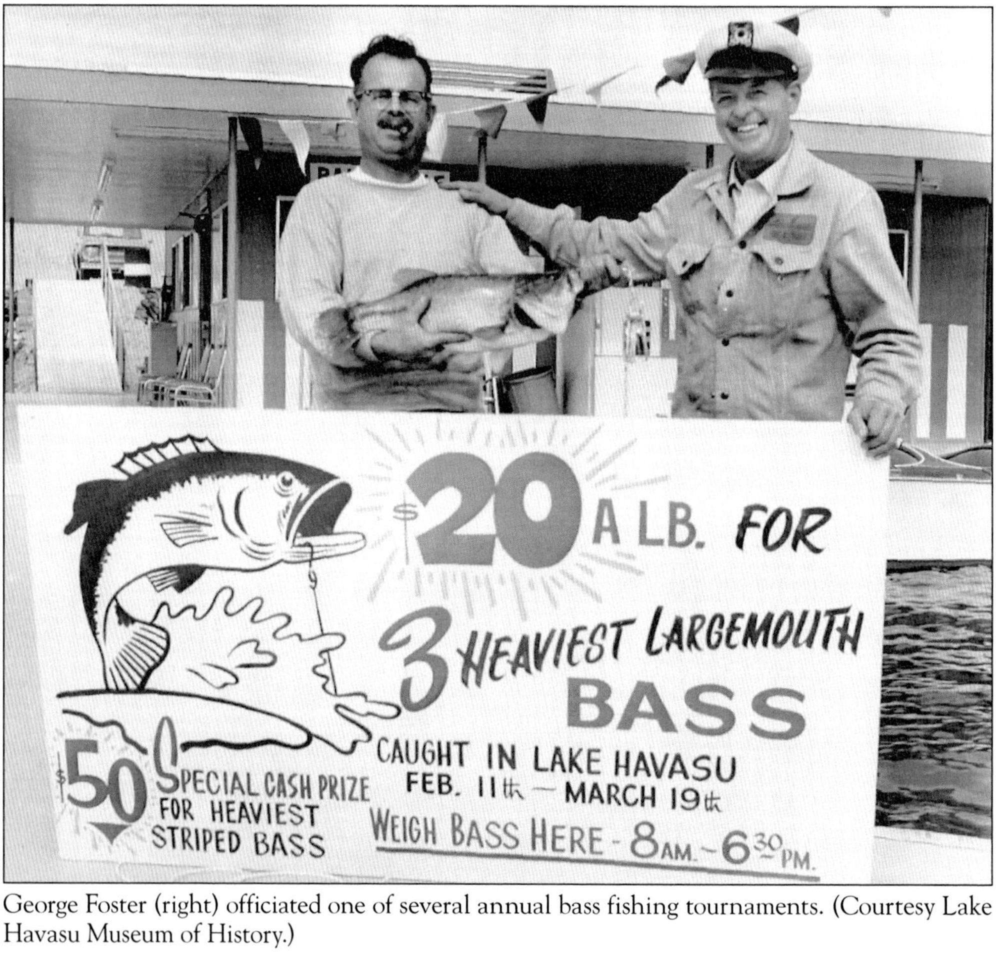

George Foster (right) officiated one of several annual bass fishing tournaments. (Courtesy Lake Havasu Museum of History.)

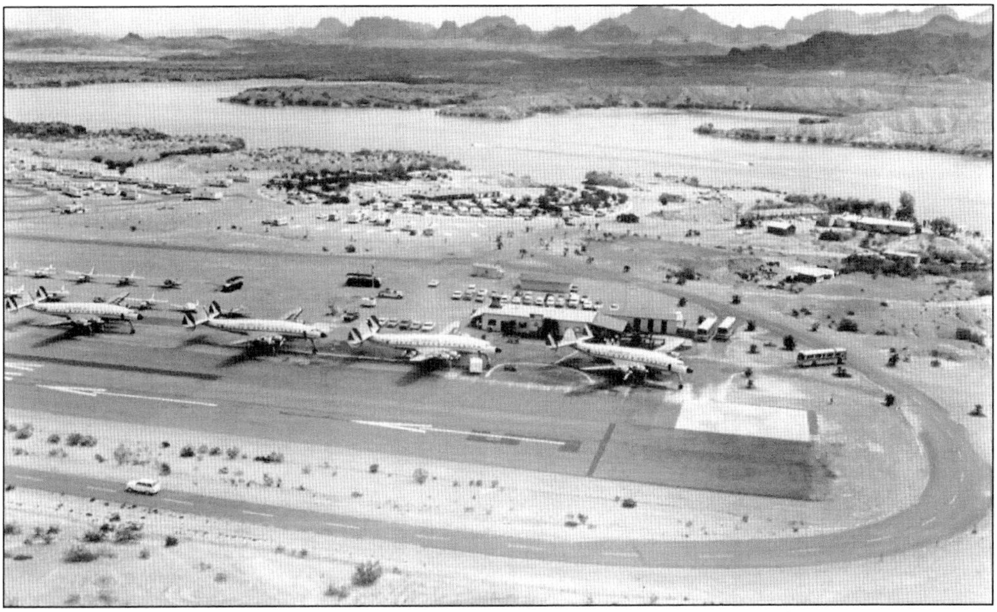

Making use of the two 6,500-foot runways at Site Six, McCulloch began flying in prospective buyers for homes in early January 1964. (Courtesy Lake Havasu Museum of History.)

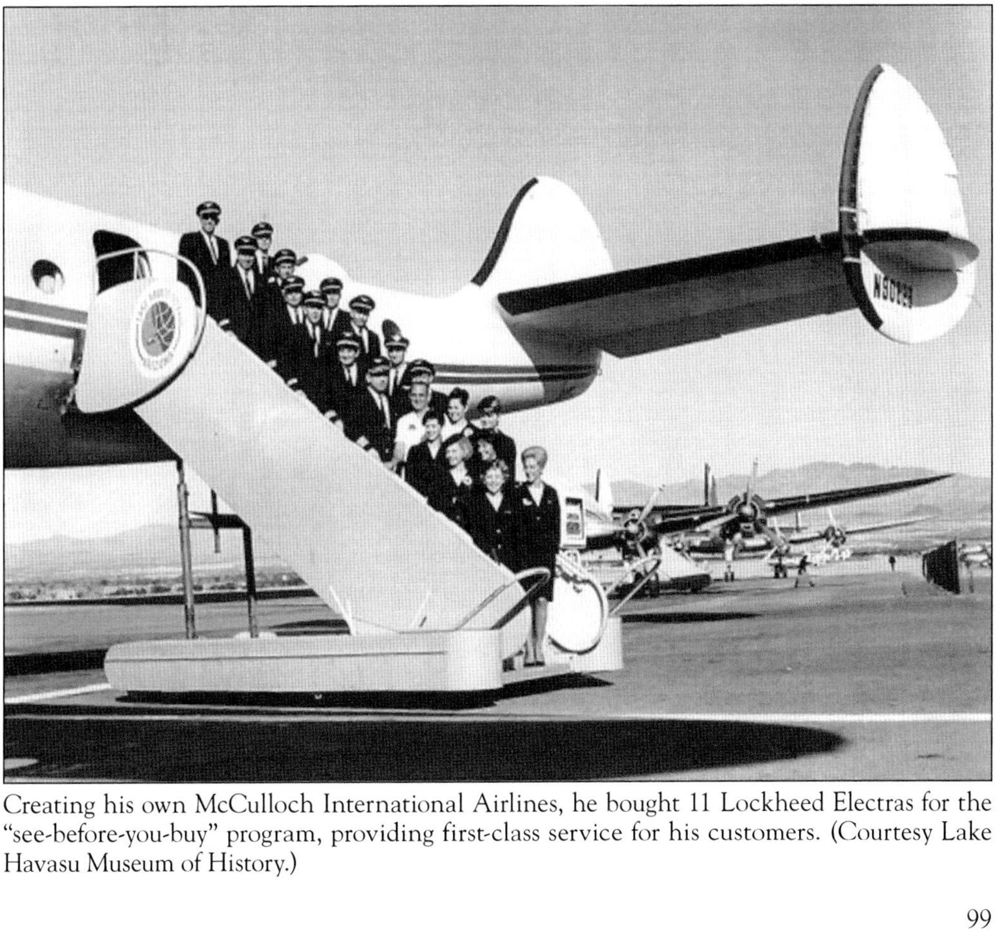

Creating his own McCulloch International Airlines, he bought 11 Lockheed Electras for the "see-before-you-buy" program, providing first-class service for his customers. (Courtesy Lake Havasu Museum of History.)

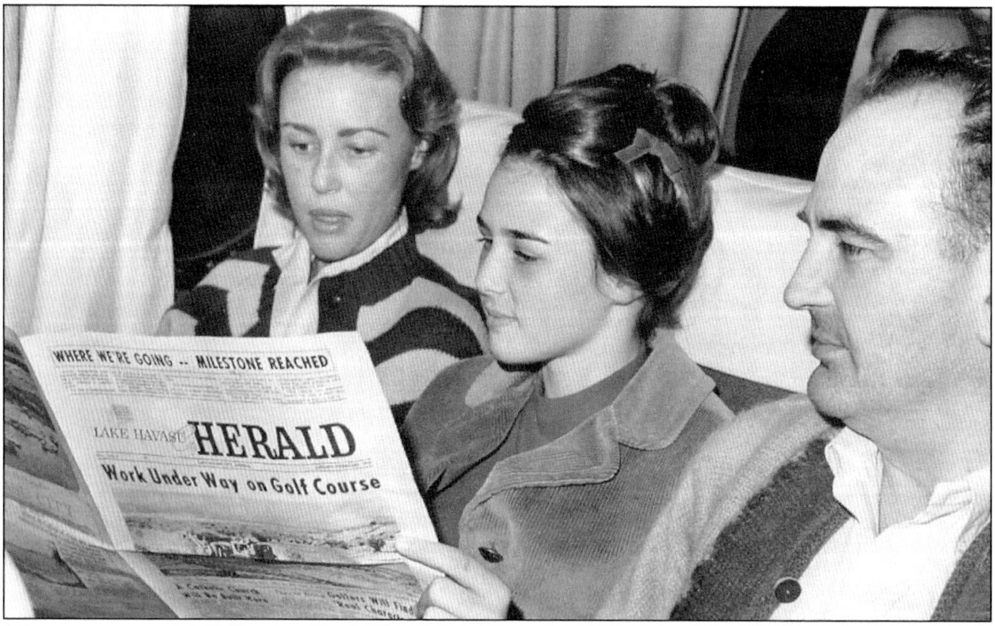

Clients were prepped for the trip with advertisements and brochures in their hometowns, then flown in free—circling around a few times to appreciate the magnificent view. "I first learned of the Lake Havasu City project," recalled local businessman, Carlton R. Fraze in the *Lake Havasu City Herald*, "when the full advertisement came out in the Tucson paper." (Courtesy Lake Havasu Museum of History.)

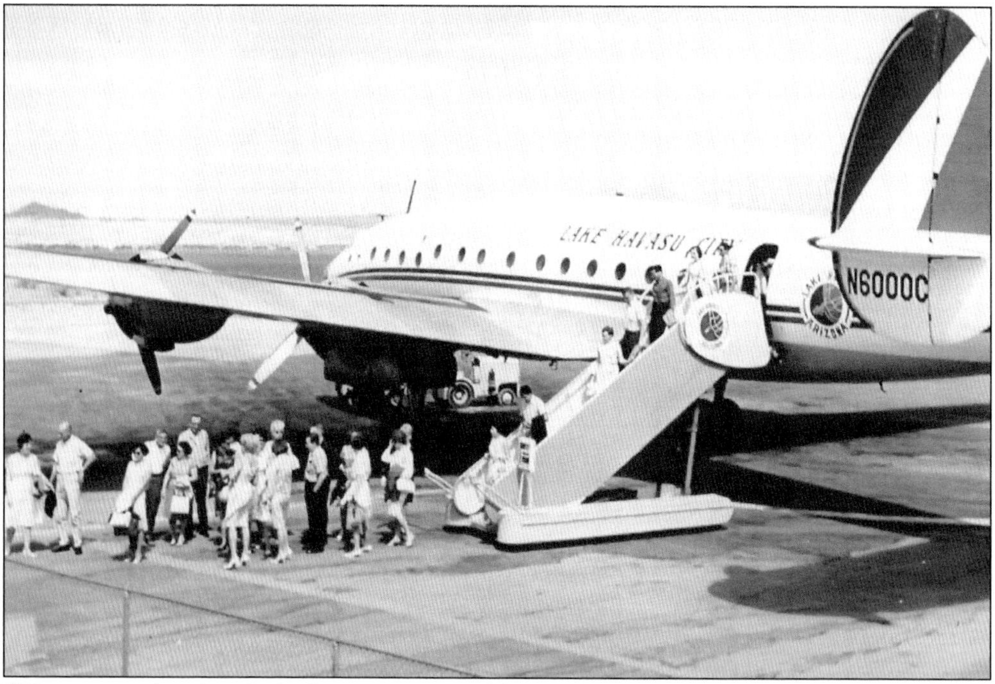

"We were on that first flight from Tucson, and before the plane touched down, I said, 'This is the place,' " recalls Fraze. By 1978, when the fly-in program was discontinued, 2,702 flights had taken place. (Courtesy Lake Havasu Museum of History.)

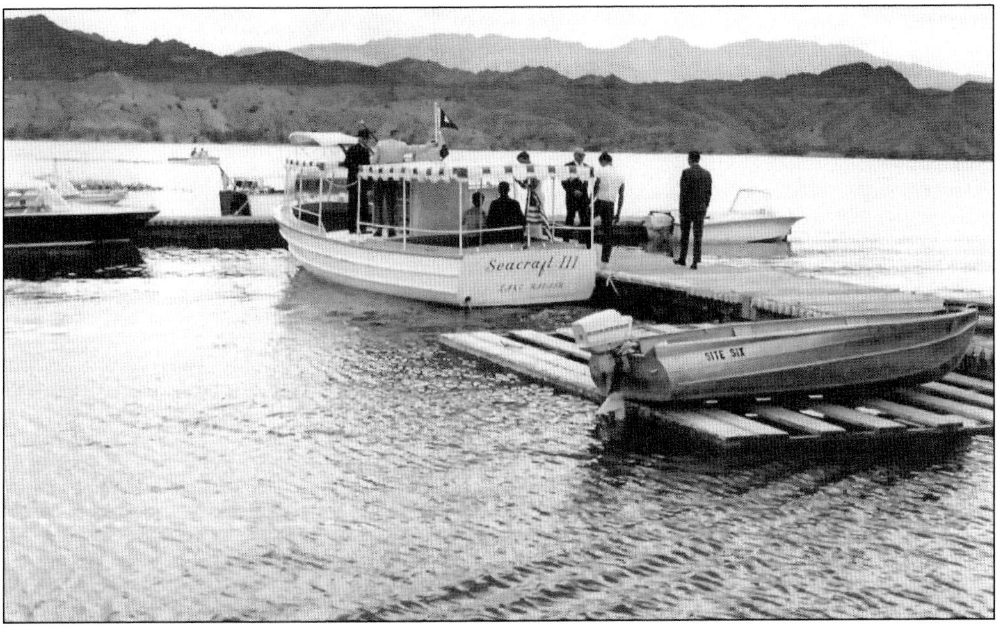

Once settled in their hotels, prospective buyers were given a comprehensive sales pitch by representatives of the Holly Development Company, purchased by McCulloch for its expertise in selling large-scale projects. Buyers were then squired around the 16,000 acres reserved for home sites in the company's fleet of 40 white jeeps or given a cruise around the bay for a lakeside view of the project on the *Captain Kirk*. In the photograph above, clients board the *Captain Kirk* at Site Six, with the California shore of Lake Havasu in the background. Below, clients disembark from the *Captain Kirk* at the Nautical Inn, with the Arizona shore in the background. (Both photographs courtesy Lake Havasu Museum of History.)

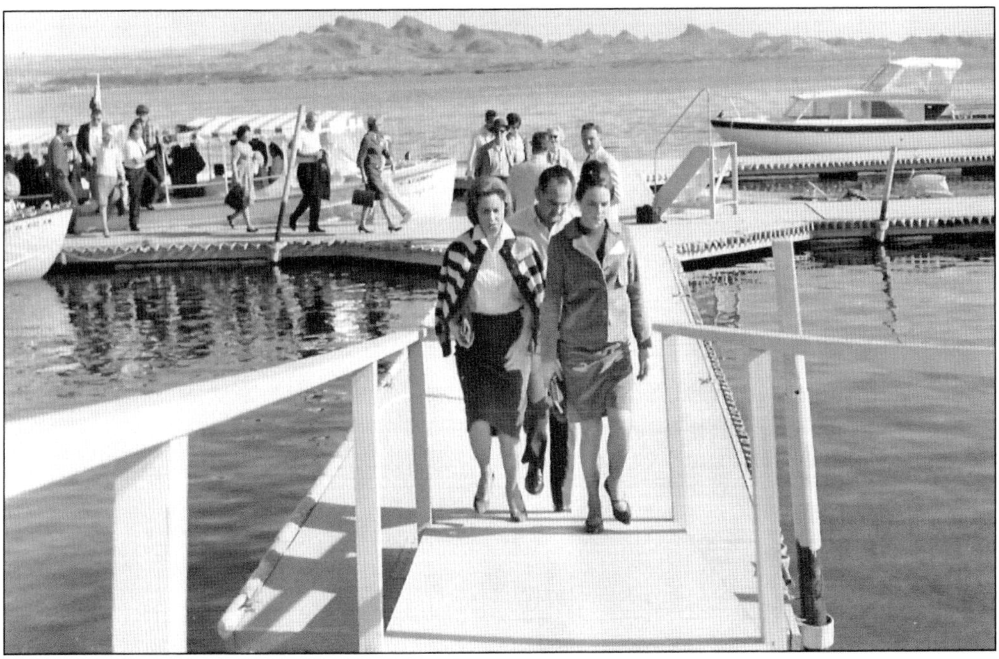

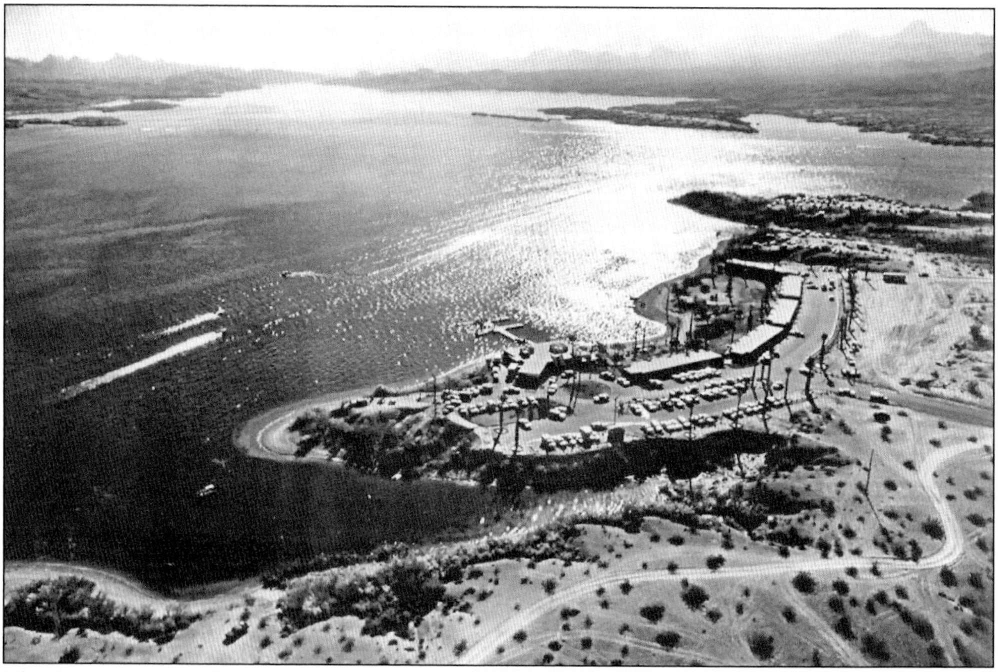

The first prospective buyers were put up at the Nautical Inn, shown here in these two photographs. (Courtesy Lake Havasu Museum of History.)

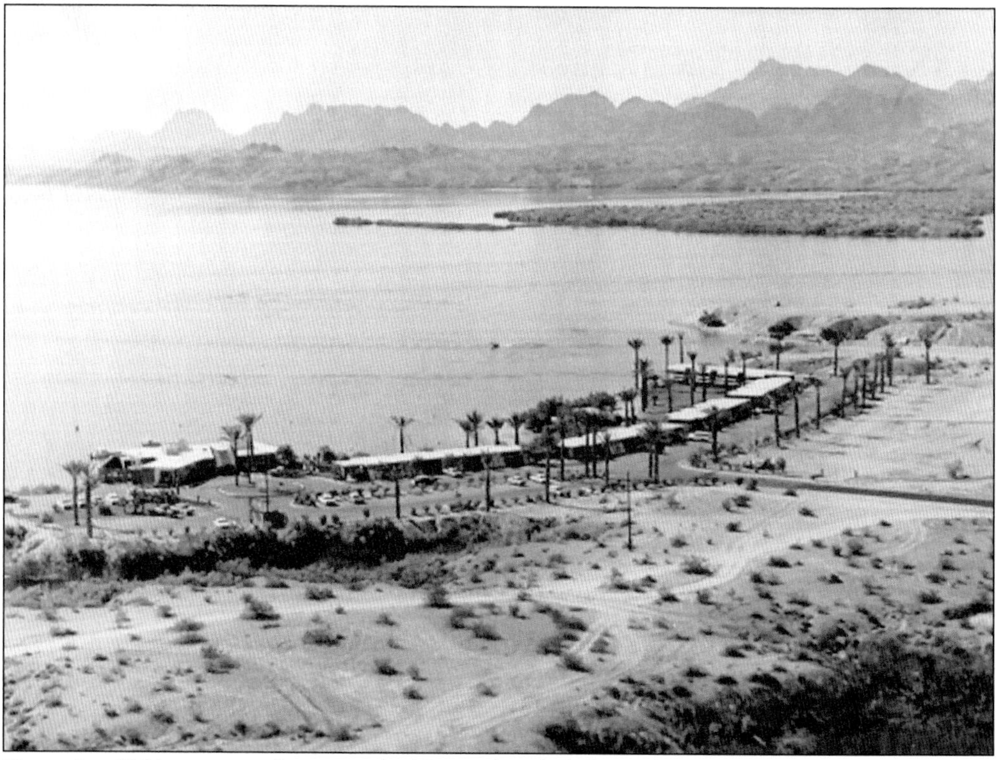

Opened in 1964, accommodations at the Nautical included a cocktail lounge and a 180-seat dining room with a view of Thompson Bay. (Courtesy Lake Havasu Museum of History.)

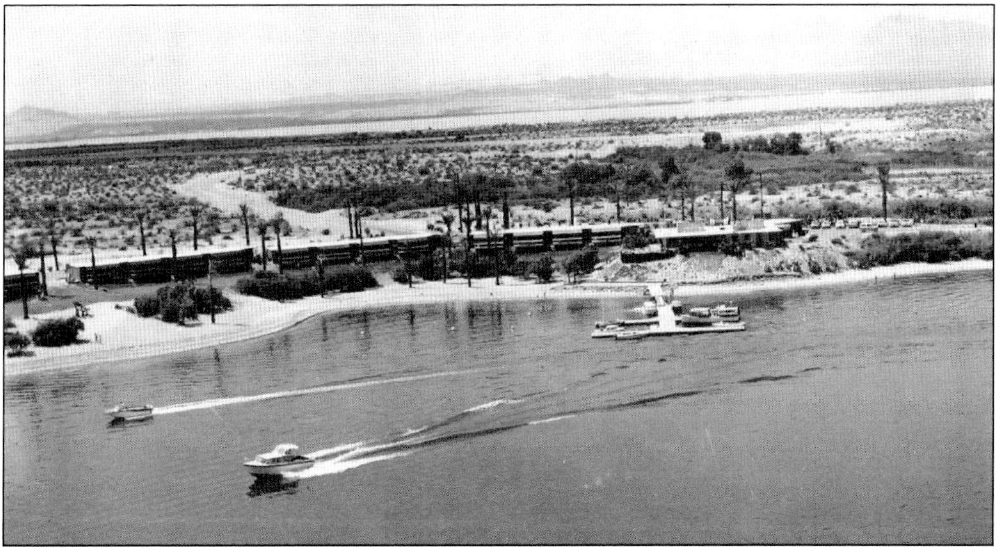

Not only was the Nautical Inn available for prospective buyers, it was also one of the nicest places for locals to gather. (Courtesy Lake Havasu Museum of History.)

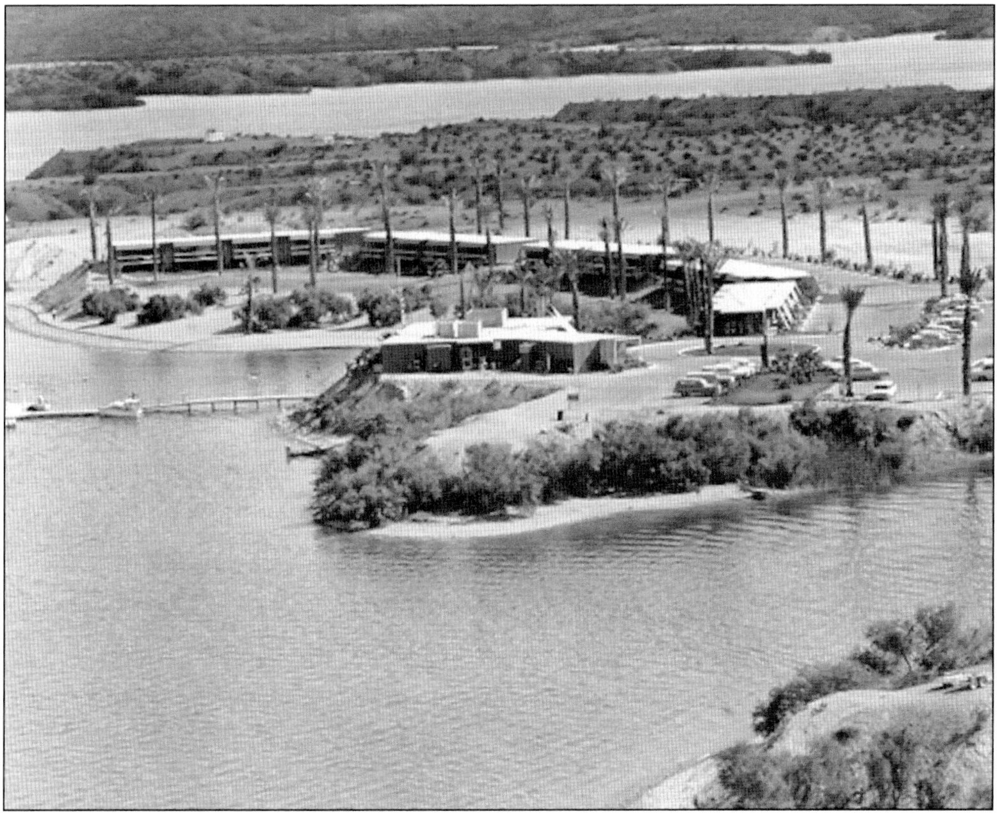

Carlton Fraze, one of the first residents of Lake Havasu City, remembered "how we used to hurry people through dinner at the Nautical Inn, so we could push back the tables and dance to Smokey Rogers and his musical group" (*Lake Havasu City Herald*). (Courtesy Lake Havasu Museum of History.)

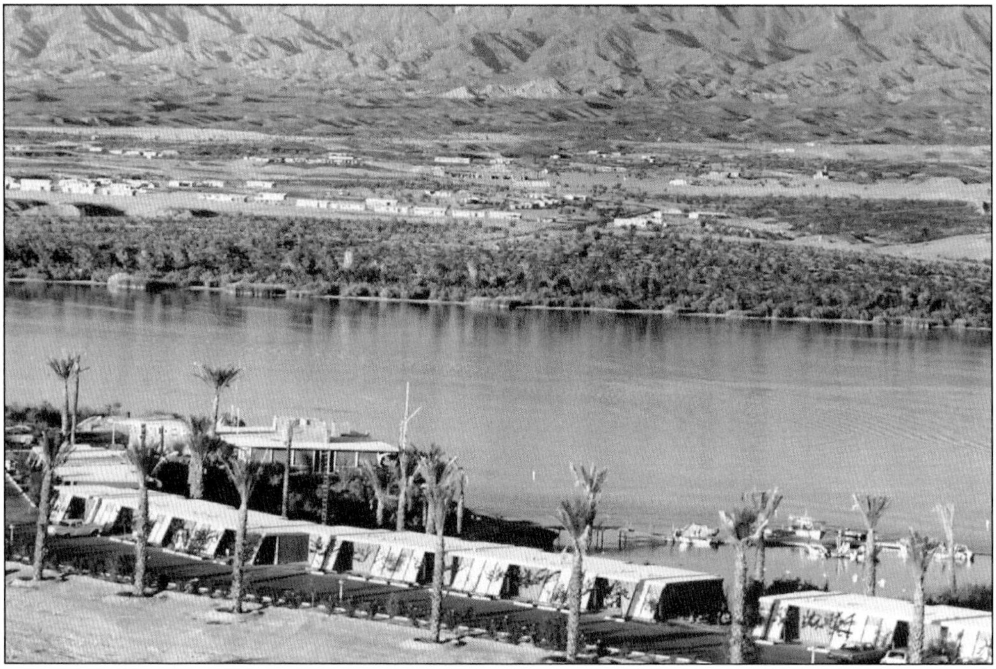

Note the first houses going up on Smoketree Avenue in the city proper across the bay from the Nautical. Houses were selling at the rate of two houses a week, starting at $12,500, and lots were going for $2,390. (Courtesy Lake Havasu Museum of History.)

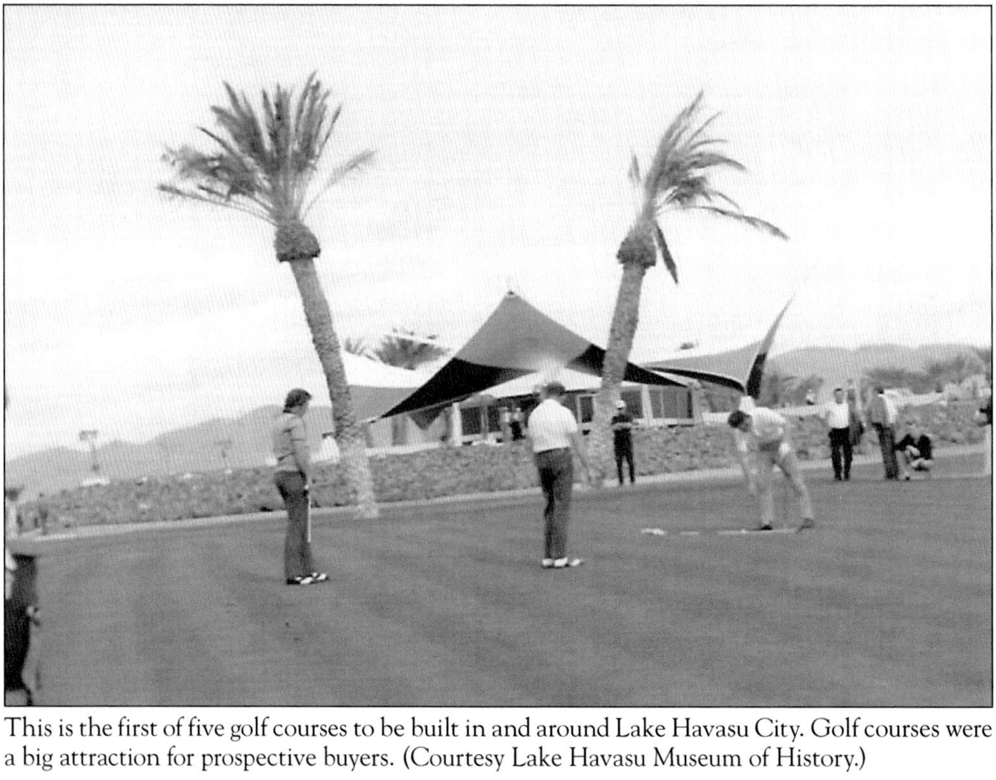

This is the first of five golf courses to be built in and around Lake Havasu City. Golf courses were a big attraction for prospective buyers. (Courtesy Lake Havasu Museum of History.)

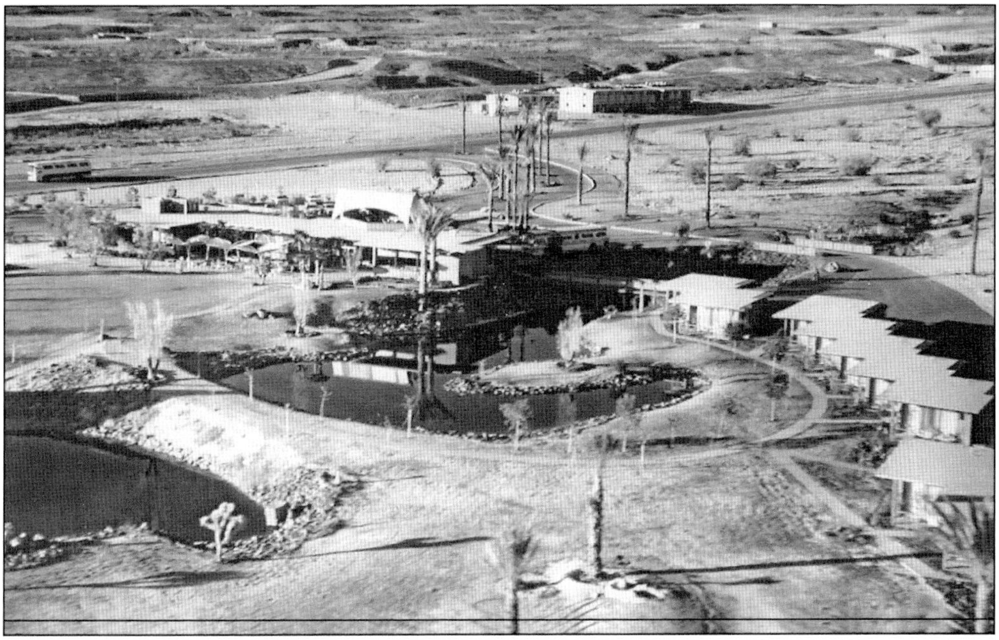

In 1970, the exotic Lake Havasu Hotel opened up for business. Located in the blow sand and sagebrush at the top of McCulloch Boulevard, where the new city hall now stands, the hotel was an oasis in the desert. The 200 bungalows, cocktail lounge, and dining room, featuring waterfalls and rain gardens, provided a welcome retreat for prospective buyers. (Courtesy Lake Havasu Museum of History.)

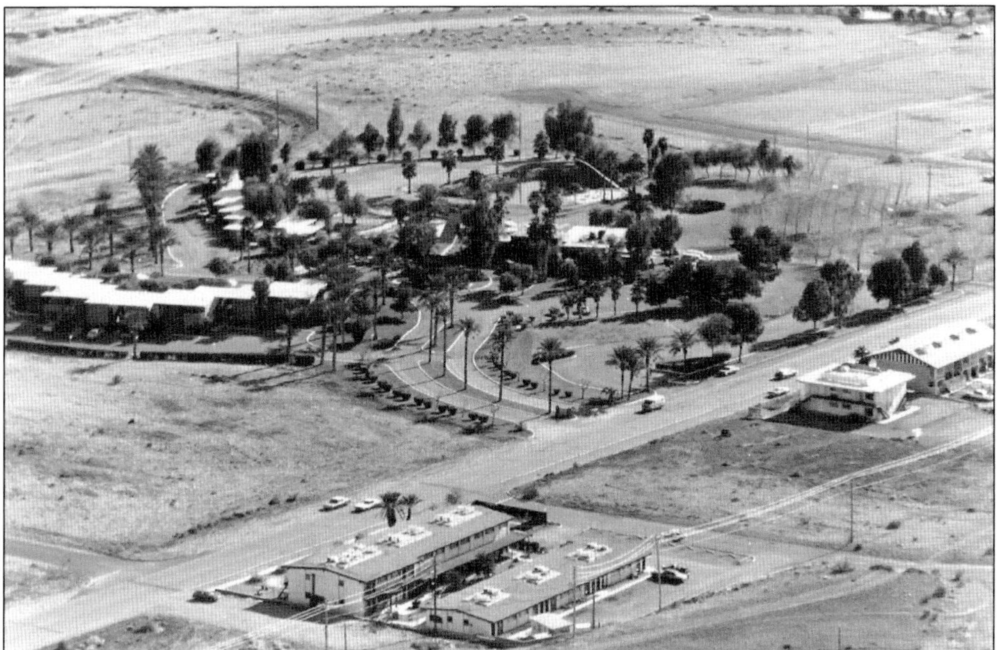

There was still little else in the city in the way of buildings at the time, however. Only the 32-unit Briggs apartment building can be seen across the way. In 1990, the Havasu Hotel was demolished to make room for the new city hall complex. (Courtesy Lake Havasu Museum of History.)

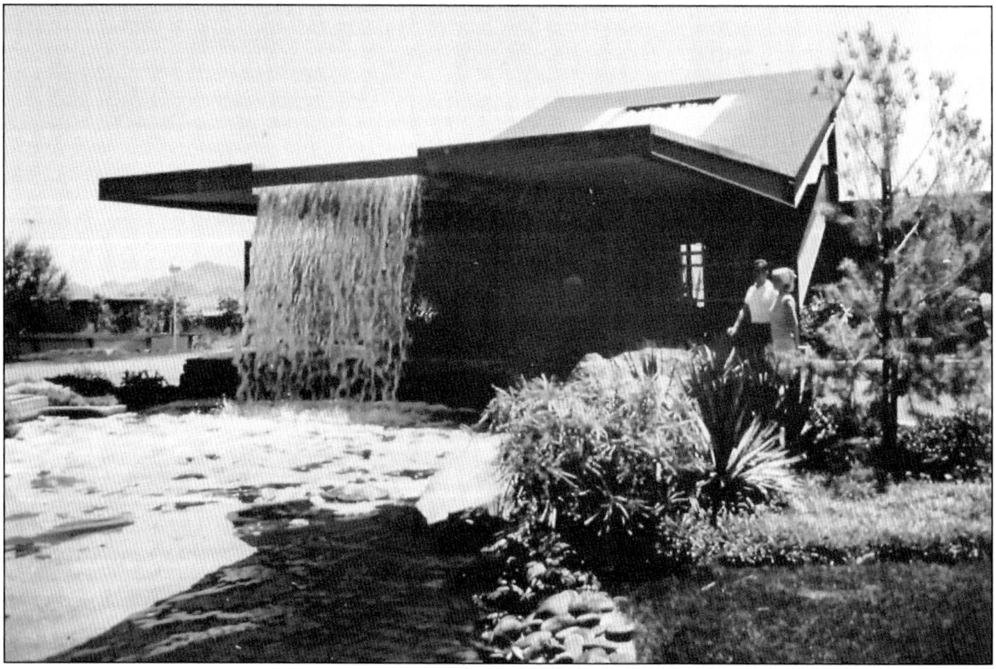

Visiting prospective buyers were enthralled by the exotic waterfall flowing over the entrance to the Havasu Hotel. (Courtesy Lake Havasu Museum of History.)

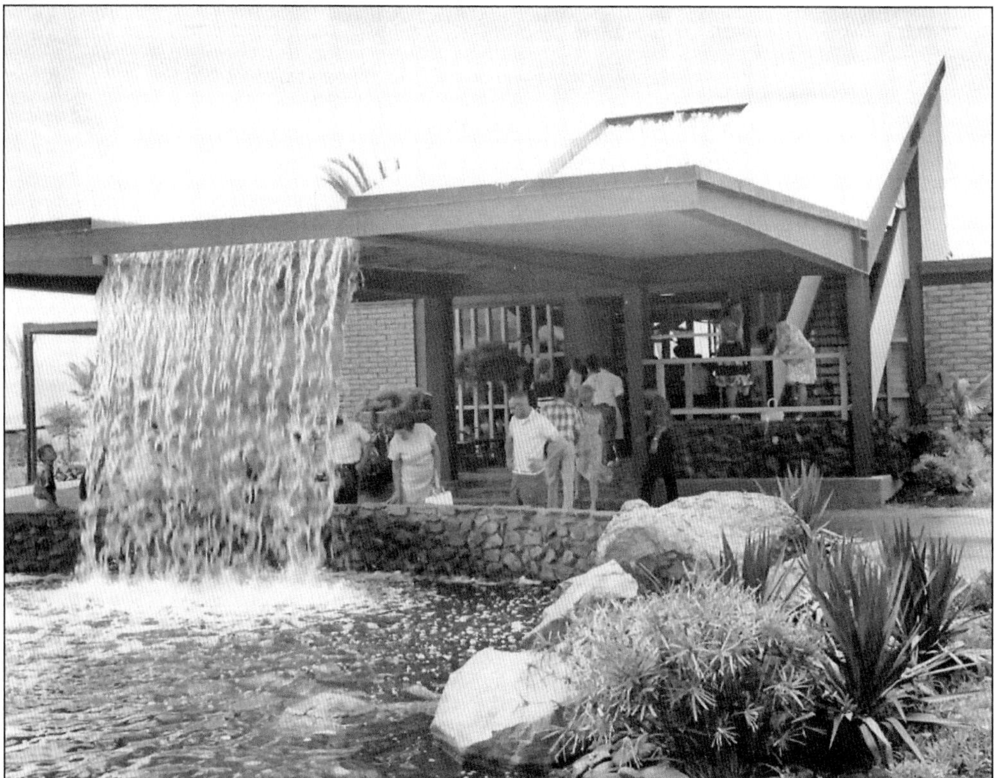

Nine

The London Bridge

In 1968, in order to create a centerpiece for his new city, and perhaps to boost sales, Robert P. McCulloch Sr. decided to bring the London Bridge to Lake Havasu City. C. V. Wood suggested it when he was in New York and heard the bridge was for sale. The bridge was no longer able to handle the heavy traffic and was sinking into the Thames. "I thought Wood was drunk," said McCulloch (*New City, Old Bridge* by Roger Johnson), "and I'd better get out there so I could bail him out." But Wood told him the bridge would be a great tourist attraction and would pay for itself.

The next question was how much to offer. After turning down three bids, the salesman hinted that since the cost of dismantling the bridge would be $1,200,000, McCulloch should offer twice as much. McCulloch did, adding another $60,000—$1,000 for each year of his life—to make sure the deal got done.

On March 23, 1968, McCulloch bought the London Bridge, listed in the Guinness Book of Records as "the largest antique ever sold," for $2,460,000. By the time the bridge was shipped to Havasu and reconstructed, the cost grew to over $5,000,000.

Before dismantling, the bridge had five arches, was 1005 feet long, and was built with 10,276 granite blocks, quarried in Devon, Cornwall, and Aberdeen, Scotland. Designed by John Rennie in 1824 and completed in 1831, it was the last stone bridge to span the Thames. Symbolizing 2,000 years of English history, it is best known for its association with the popular nursery rhyme.

Reconstructing the bridge in Lake Havasu was a difficult process. Shipped across the ocean to Long Beach, California, and then trucked to Lake Havasu, the three-ton granite blocks were laid out in pre-arranged patterns next to the site of the bridge, at the base of the Pittsburg peninsula. Each stone was marked by four numbers, indicating the span, the row number, and the position of the stone in that row. Under the supervision of the engineer, Robert Beresford, each stone was to be reassembled in exactly the same order as the original Rennie design.

On September 23, 1968, Sir Gilbert Ingelfield, lord mayor of London, and Honorable Jack Williams, governor of Arizona, laid the corner stone for the bridge.

In 1969, foundation work was begun and the piers were poured. Earth was mounded up between the piers. Following the exact curves of the arches, wooden forms were built and concrete was poured, arch by arch, until the span was complete. After that, the dirt was removed. Next, the corbels were connected to the underside of the bridge to support a roadway. Finally, the granite blocks were attached to the concrete core of the bridge in their exact specified positions. In 1971, a channel was dug, making the Pittsburg peninsula an island and allowing the waters of Lake Havasu to flow under the bridge.

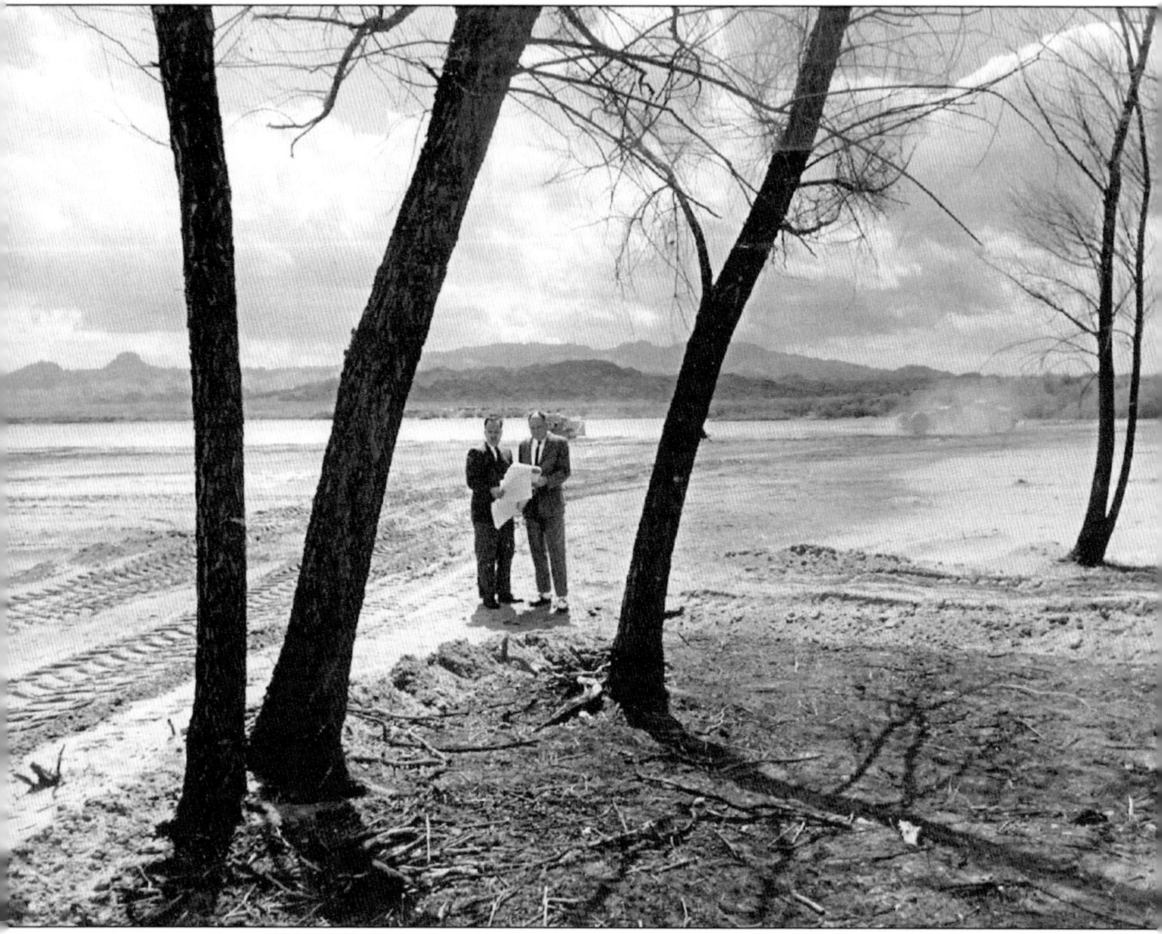

Here are C. V. Wood (left) and Robert P. McCulloch Sr. standing in front of Thompson Bay, the Nautical Inn in the background, looking over plans for the city. One of the concerns that prompted McCulloch to buy the London Bridge in the first place was the stagnating waters of Thompson Bay due to the fact that the downstream flow of water from the main body of Lake Havasu was blocked by the Pittsburg peninsula. Early on, it was thought that a channel might have to be dug across the narrow isthmus connecting the peninsula to the mainland in order to remedy the problem, thus creating the need for a bridge. (Courtesy Lake Havasu Museum of History.)

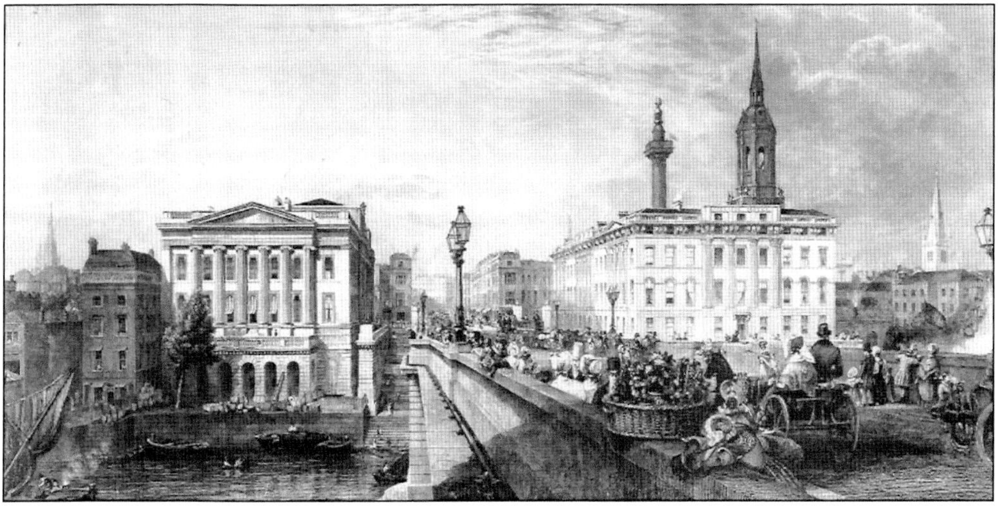

The London Bridge, purchased by McCulloch in 1968, had a history of over 140 years, but was slowly sinking into the soft river bottom of the Thames and had to be replaced. The weight of the 130,000-ton bridge and 50,000 pedestrians daily was causing the bridge to sink an eighth of an inch each year. The decision to sell the bridge was made by the City of London at the suggestion of Ivan F. Lucklin, former member of the Court of Common Council for London. (Courtesy Lake Havasu Museum of History.)

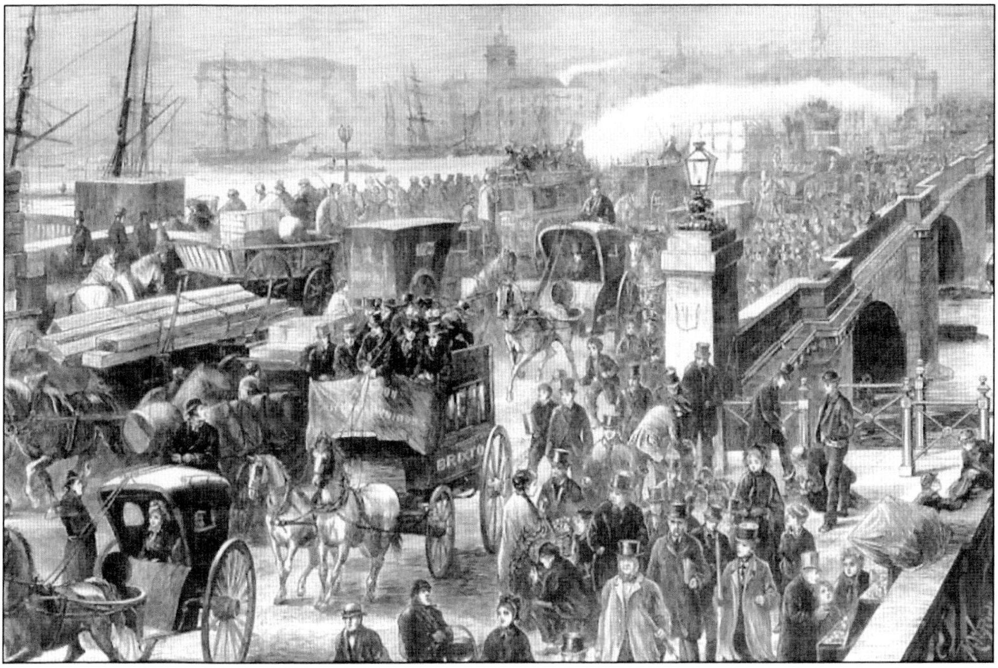

Lucklin had spent three years trying to talk his Guildhall colleagues into the idea. "I based my story on the bridge being the heir to nearly 2,000 years of history," said Lucklin (*New City, Old Bridge* by Roger Johnson), "going back to the time of Roman Londonium, touching upon the years of the Danes, Saxons, and Normans, and referring to the Colechurch Bridge, as one of the wonders of the Medieval World." (Courtesy Lake Havasu Museum of History.)

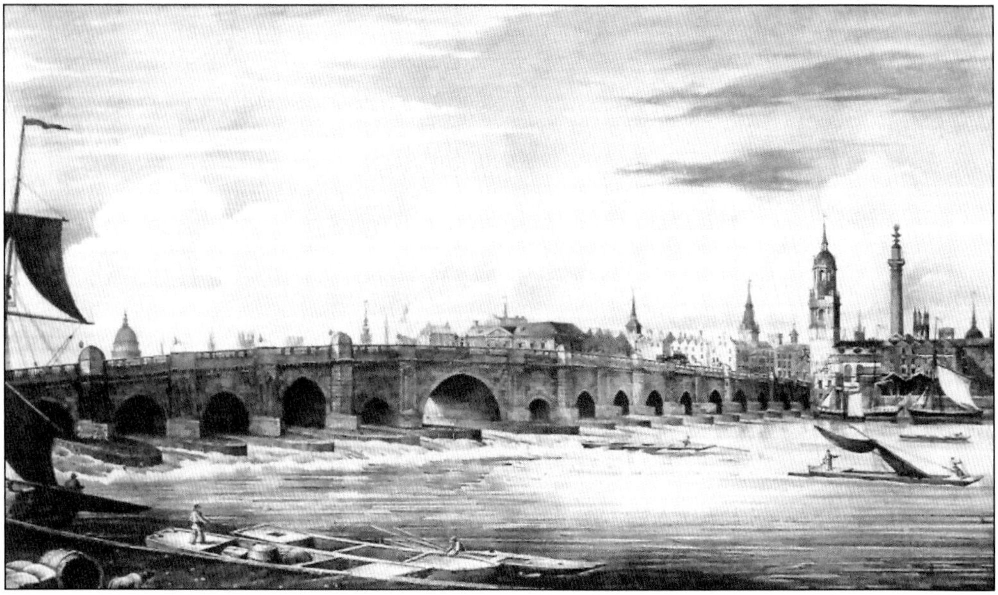

The first stone bridge over the Thames (above), designed by Peter Colechurch, was built in 1209. It was 20 feet wide, 300 yards long, and had 20 arches, with a drawbridge in the center. Houses and shops were built on top of the bridge, and waterwheels below were employed for grinding grain and pumping water into the city. The Stone Gate House on the bridge exhibited the severed heads of traitors. (Courtesy Lake Havasu Museum of History.)

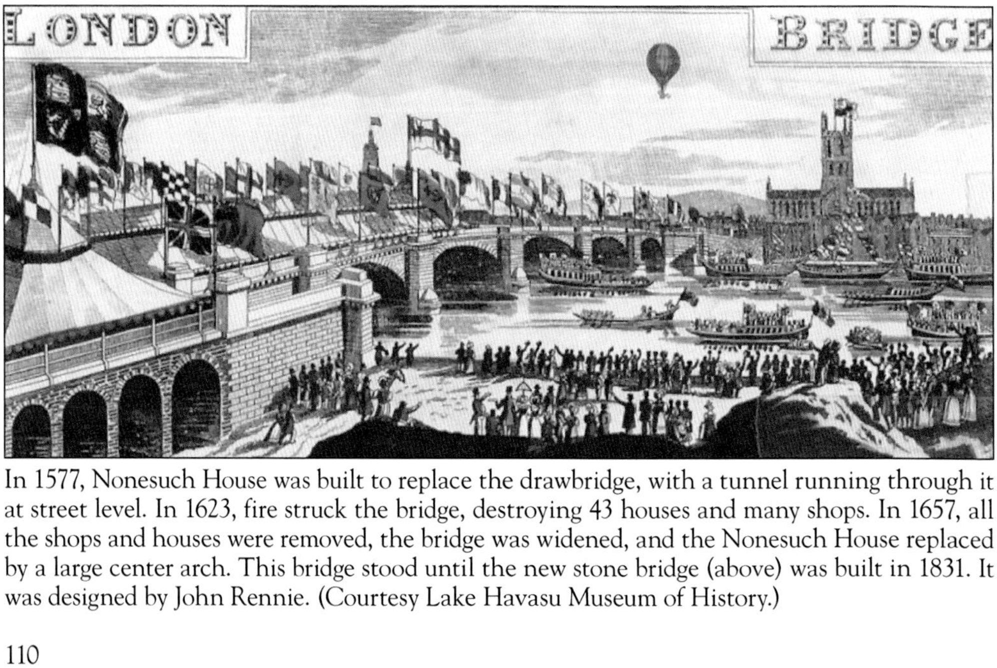

In 1577, Nonesuch House was built to replace the drawbridge, with a tunnel running through it at street level. In 1623, fire struck the bridge, destroying 43 houses and many shops. In 1657, all the shops and houses were removed, the bridge was widened, and the Nonesuch House replaced by a large center arch. This bridge stood until the new stone bridge (above) was built in 1831. It was designed by John Rennie. (Courtesy Lake Havasu Museum of History.)

The Rennie bridge (shown here) was the last stone bridge built over the Thames. The bridge made famous by the nursery rhyme, however, was made of wood. Aside from the pontoon bridges built by the Romans in the first century, the first wooden bridge was built by King Edgar during his reign from 959 to 975. This bridge stood until the Danes took over London. (Courtesy Lake Havasu Museum of History.)

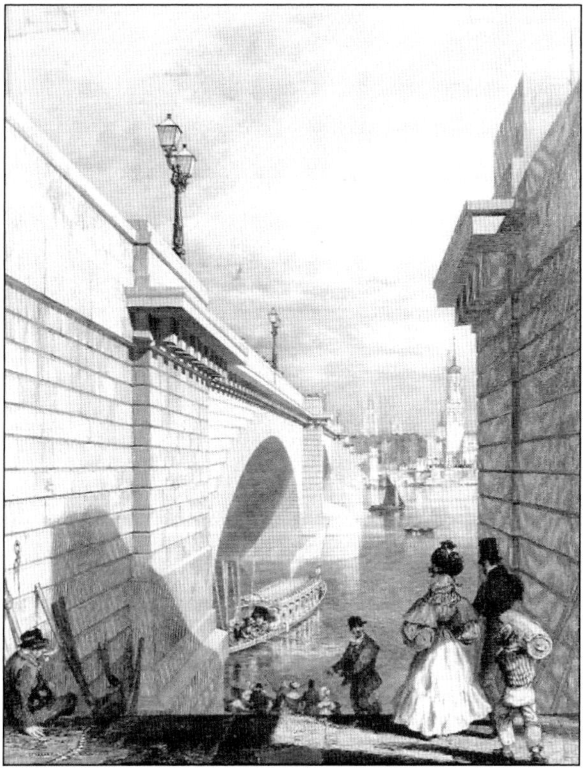

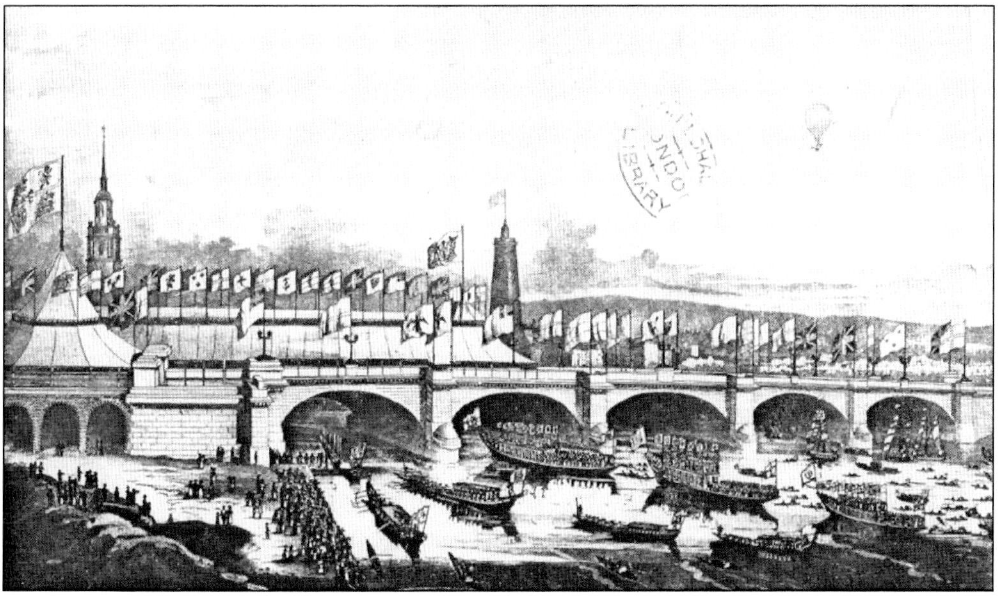

In 1014, the Saxon king, Ethelred, implored a band of Vikings from Norway, under the command of Olaf Haralsen, to help him retake the bridge from the Danes. Olaf and his men sailed up the Thames, their longboats protected from Danish spears by a cover of thatched roofs, attached ropes to the piers that supported the bridge, and pulled the bridge down. The words in Olaf's saga, "*Stradsdjerv Brot Du Londonsbro*" ("London Bridge is broken down"), became the words in the nursery rhyme. (Courtesy Lake Havasu Museum of History.)

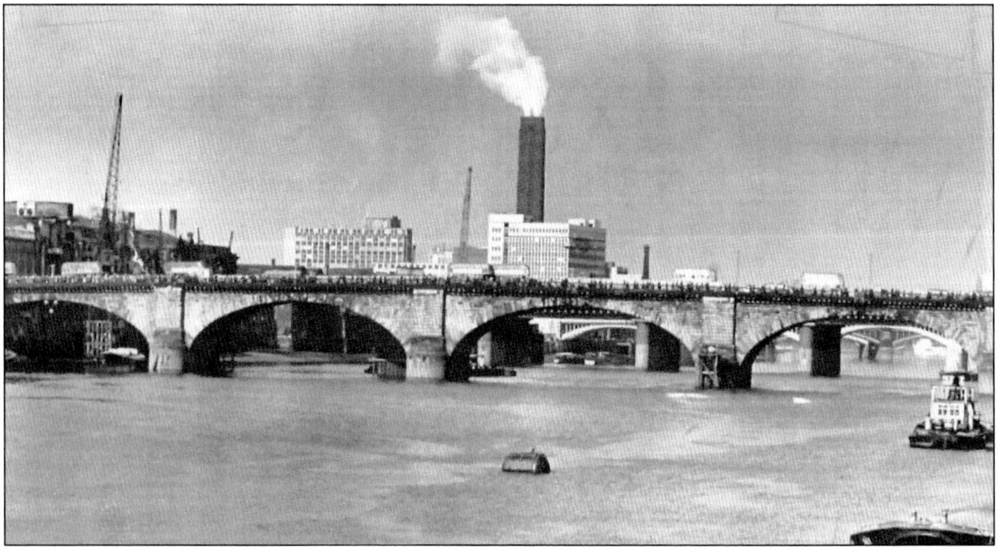

After McCulloch purchased the London Bridge (seen here in London), the three-year-long dismantling process began. In all, 22 million tons of granite blocks were removed, carefully coded, and shipped from the East Indian and Surrey docks in London to Long Beach, California. (Courtesy Lake Havasu Museum of History.)

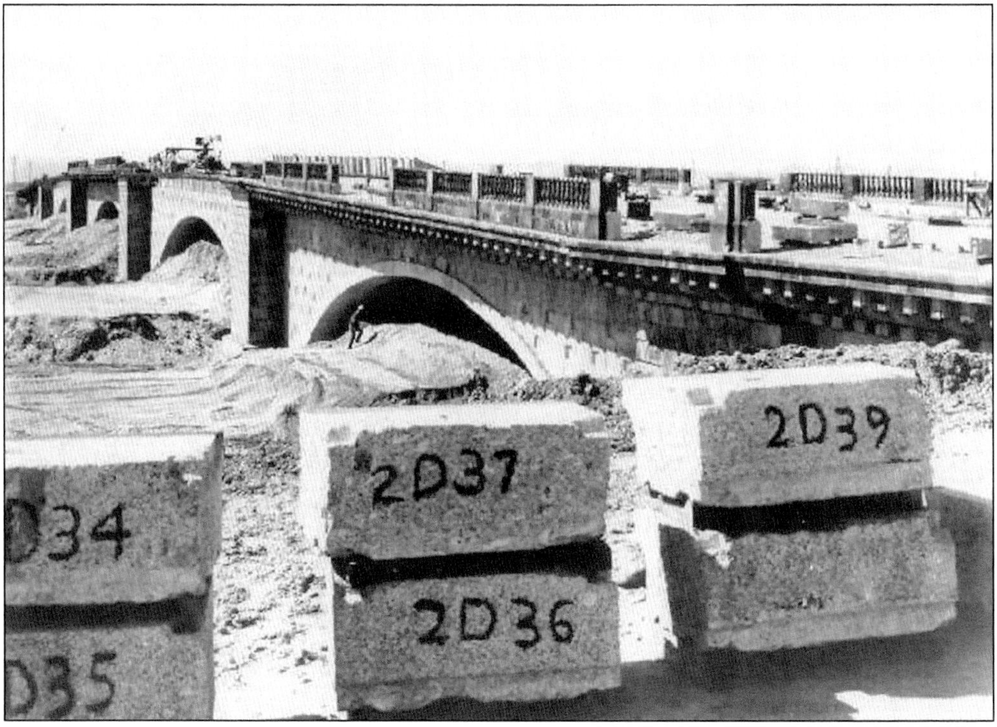

The first shipment of coded blocks arrived in Long Beach aboard the Swedish freighter, the *Agne,* on the Fourth of July, 1968. Some 850 tons of the blocks were shipped aboard the SS *Fossom* of Norway. The rest of the blocks were shipped in container ships on the Johnson Line. The first truckload of blocks from Long Beach arrived in Lake Havasu City on the morning of July 9. (Courtesy Lake Havasu Museum of History.)

During disassembly in London, holes were drilled into the granite blocks and cables attached, by means of a "Lewis" dovetailing device, so that they could be removed from the bridge with winches. Each block was then numbered and lettered to indicate the section, the level, and the sequence in which the blocks would be ordered during reassembly. (Courtesy Lake Havasu Museum of History.)

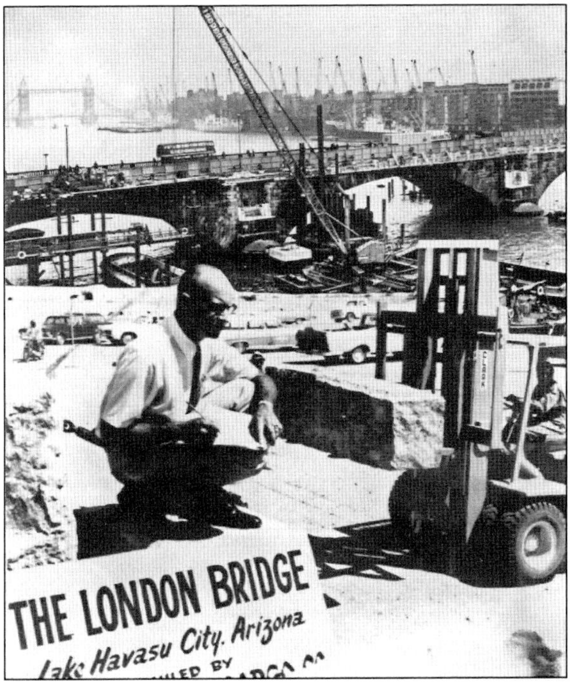

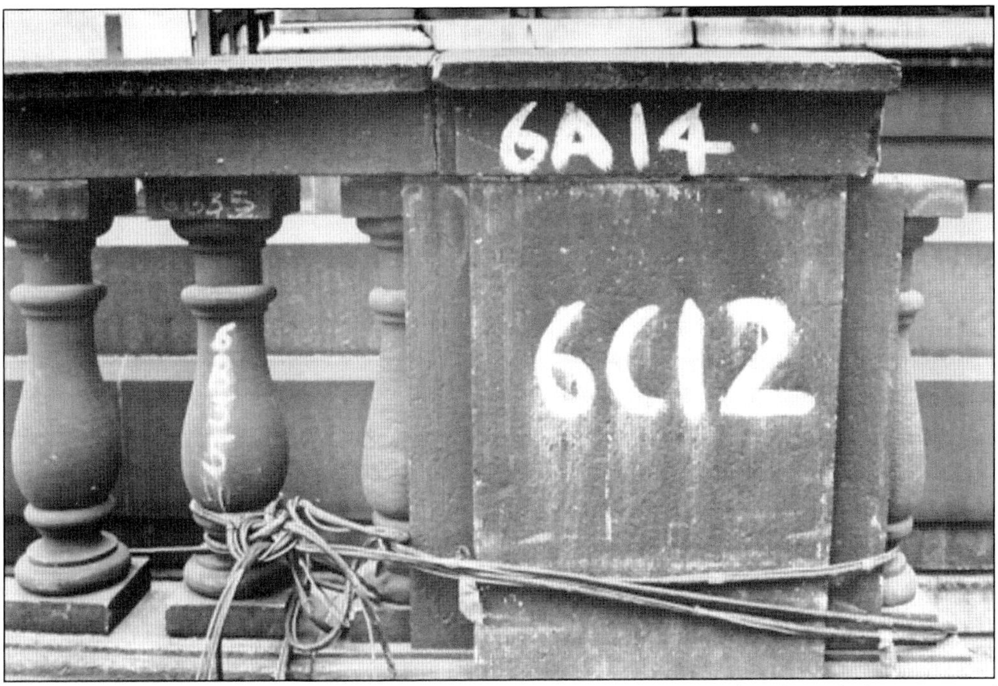

It was discovered during the bridge dismantling that numbers were already coded on many of the blocks. John Rennie most likely used a similar system of organizing the blocks when he built the original bridge. Once the blocks arrived in Lake Havasu City, Robert Beresford, the chief engineer, aided by exact, detailed drawings and photographs (some of them 15 feet long), would make sure the blocks were replaced in their former positions. (Courtesy Lake Havasu Museum of History.)

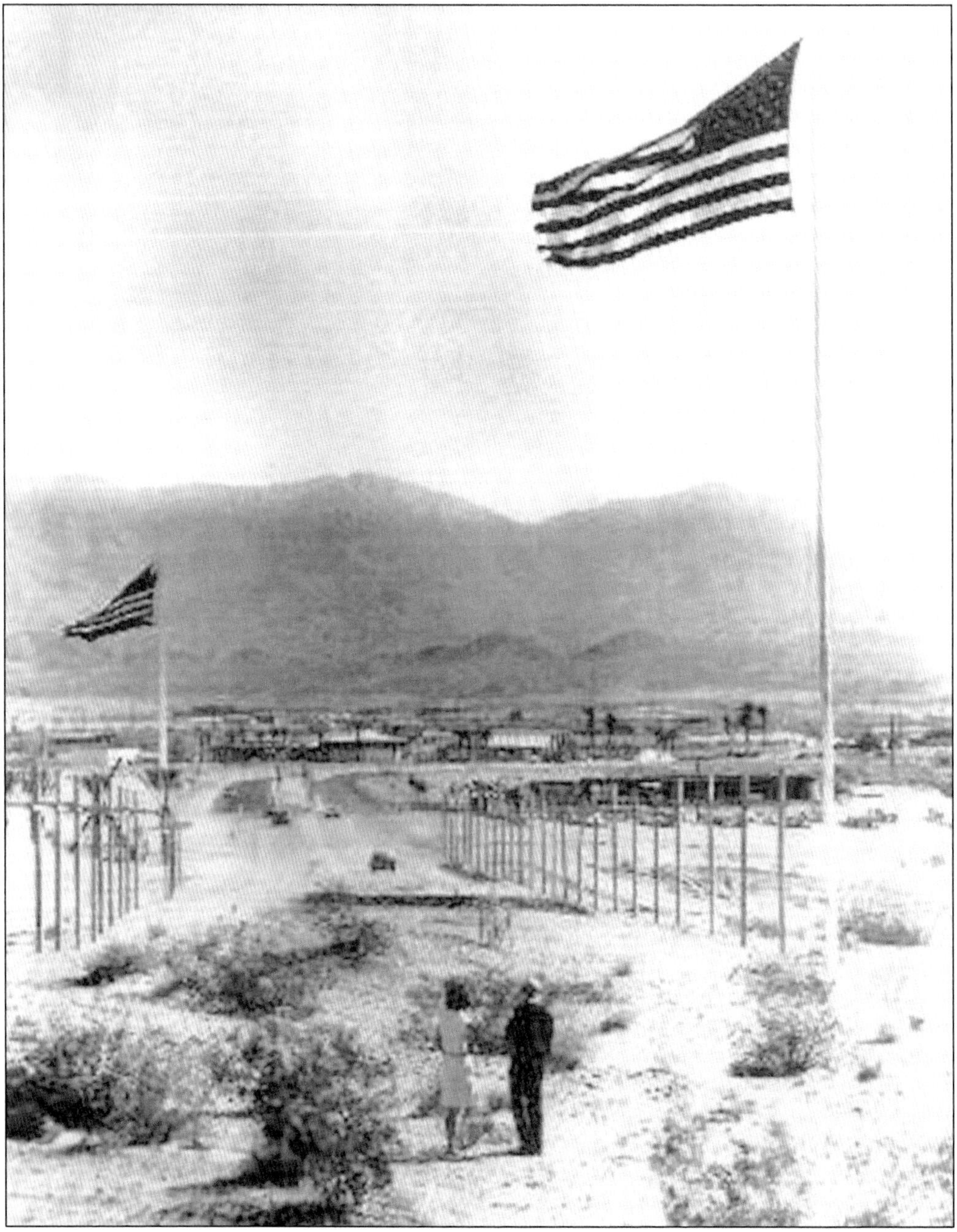

On the isthmus of the Pittsburg peninsula, posts and flags, marked out by Tri-Co Engineering, showed where the London Bridge was to be located—looking toward Lake Havasu City itself, the renamed Mohave Mountains in the background. Tri-Co Engineering, headed by Joe Coombs, was hired by McCulloch and Woods in 1961–1962 to draw maps and do surveys for the proposed city. In 1962, Tri-Co prepared a report for McCulloch that dealt with drainage issues and flood control problems. Later they formulated the first covenants, codes, and restrictions for the city and proposed the formation of the IDD. Tri-Co was ultimately responsible for the management of all the construction in Lake Havasu City, including the London Bridge. (Courtesy Lake Havasu Museum of History.)

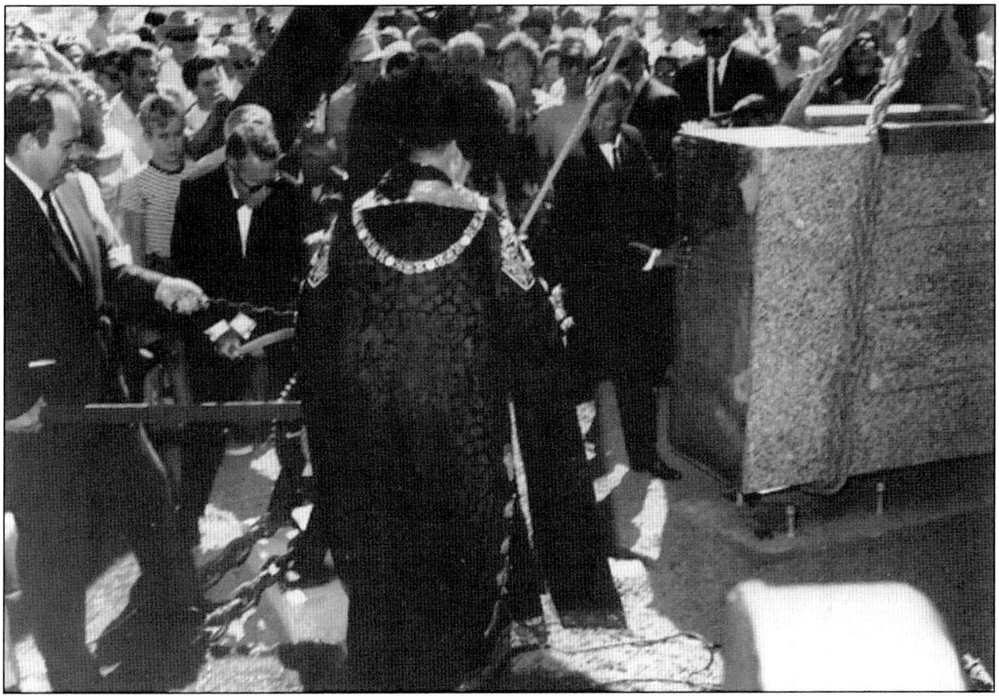

Late in 1968, C. V. Wood Jr. (left), the governor of Arizona; Jack Williams (to the right of Wood), the lord mayor of London; Sir Gilbert Inglefield (facing away); and Robert McCulloch Sr. (not shown) gathered in front of a crowd of onlookers to ceremoniously lay the cornerstone for the London Bridge at its new site in Lake Havasu City. A time capsule was buried beneath the foundation stone. (Courtesy Lake Havasu Museum of History.)

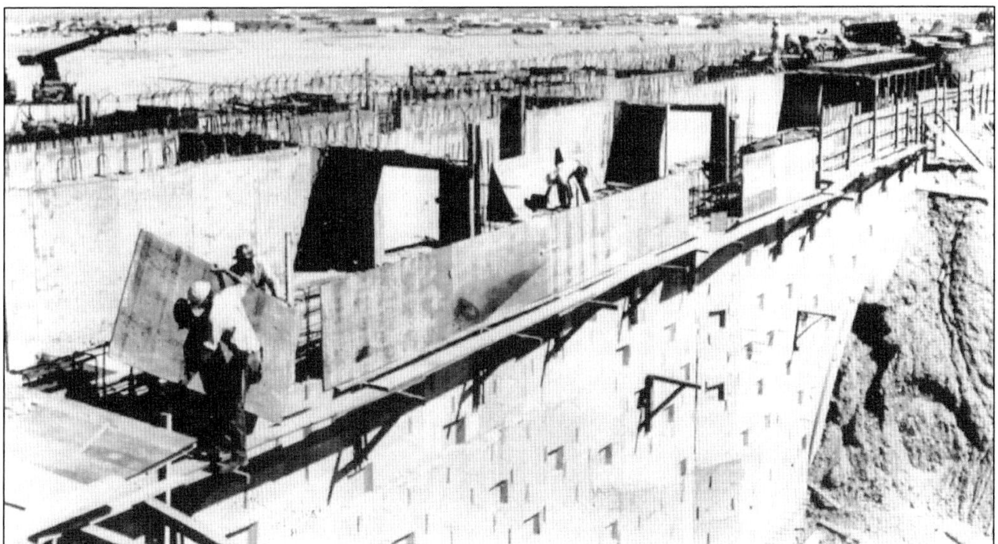

In October 1969, the first contract was awarded to begin the construction of the steel-reinforced concrete core of the bridge. The center of the core was to be left hollow, making the bridge not only stronger, but lighter—weighing 33,000 tons rather than the 130,000 tons it weighed in London—and providing a conduit for utility lines. (Courtesy Lake Havasu Museum of History.)

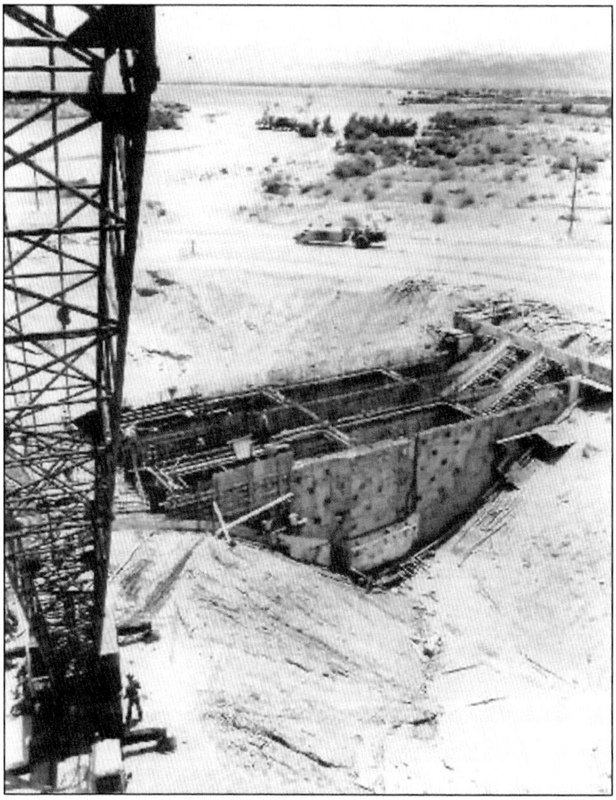

In January 1970, the pouring of the foundation—54-by-18-by-4.5-foot concrete slabs beneath the piers on each end of the bridge with larger footings in the center—was undertaken. Next the piers were poured, and the construction of the arches was begun. (Courtesy Lake Havasu Museum of History.)

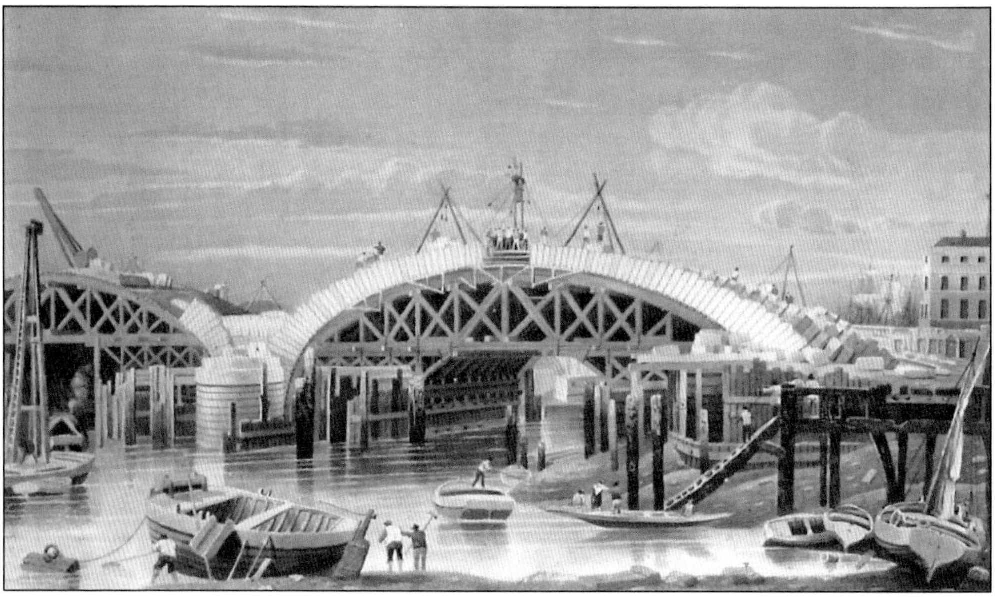

The combined engineering staffs of Mott, Hay, and Anderson of London and McCulloch Properties, Inc. in Lake Havasu City devised the unique dry-land construction technique for building the arches. Excavating mounds of earth up under the arches, rather than erecting scaffolding—as was done when the bridge was first constructed in 1831 (shown here)—made building the arches easy. (Courtesy Lake Havasu Museum of History.)

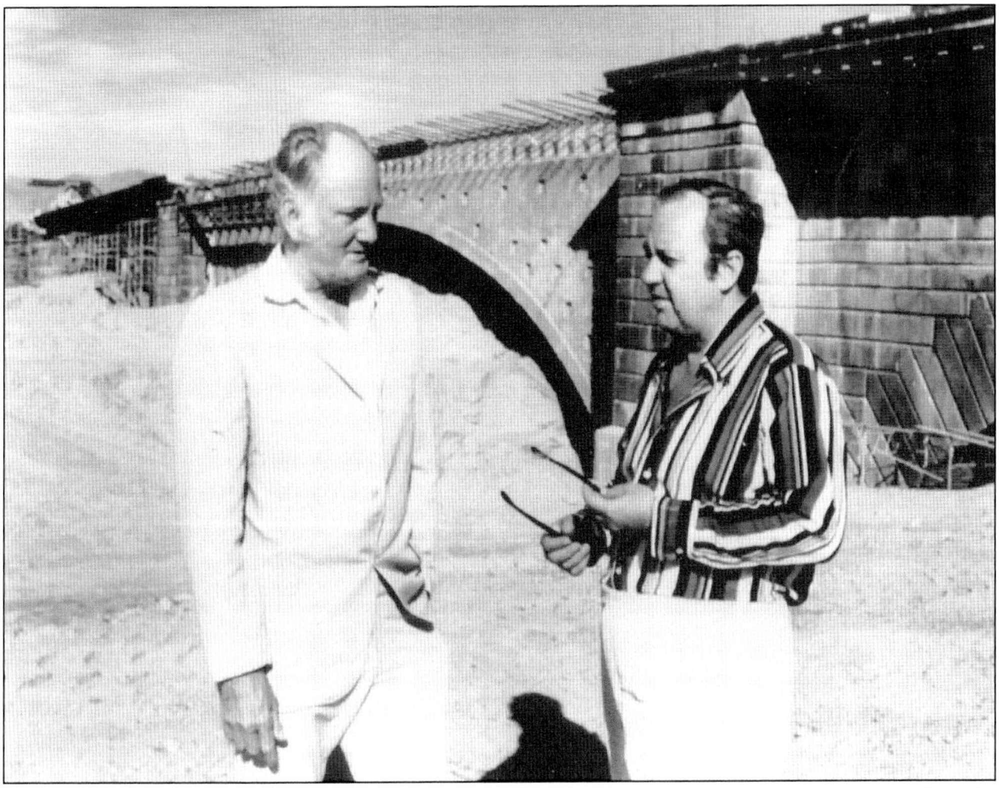

Robert McCulloch Sr. (left) and C. V. Wood discuss the progress being made on the bridge. As the arches were poured, one by one, the bearings of the piers at the ends of the arches were locked tight. Next the corbels were hoisted into position and hooked onto the bridge with 1.5-inch reinforced steel loops. The corbels were the first actual London Bridge stones to be attached to the reconstructed bridge in Lake Havasu City. (Courtesy Lake Havasu Museum of History.)

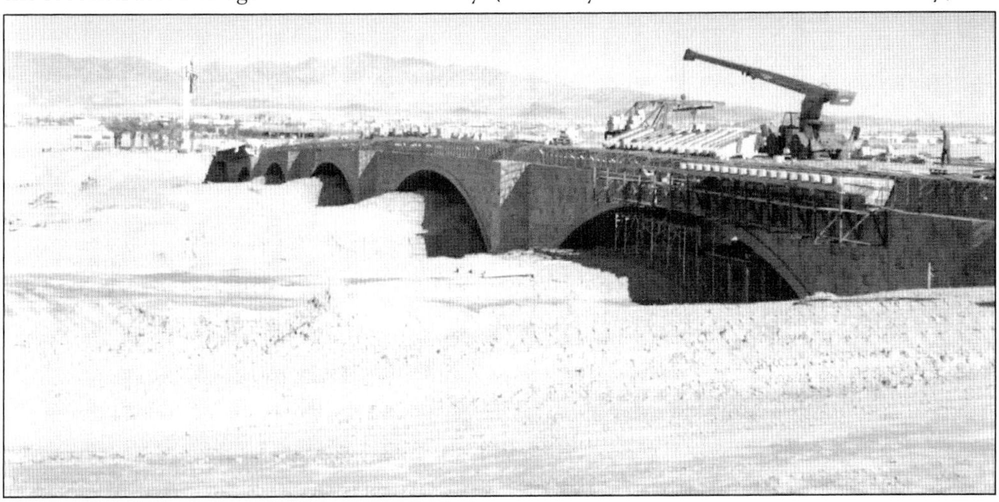

Atop the corbels, a 53-foot-wide and 952-foot-long roadbed was laid. Because the corbels had to support the roadway, as well as all the automobile and pedestrian traffic to follow, those 9.5-foot long, 2.5-ton blocks of Cornish granite would be the most highly stressed stones in the bridge. (Courtesy Lake Havasu Museum of History.)

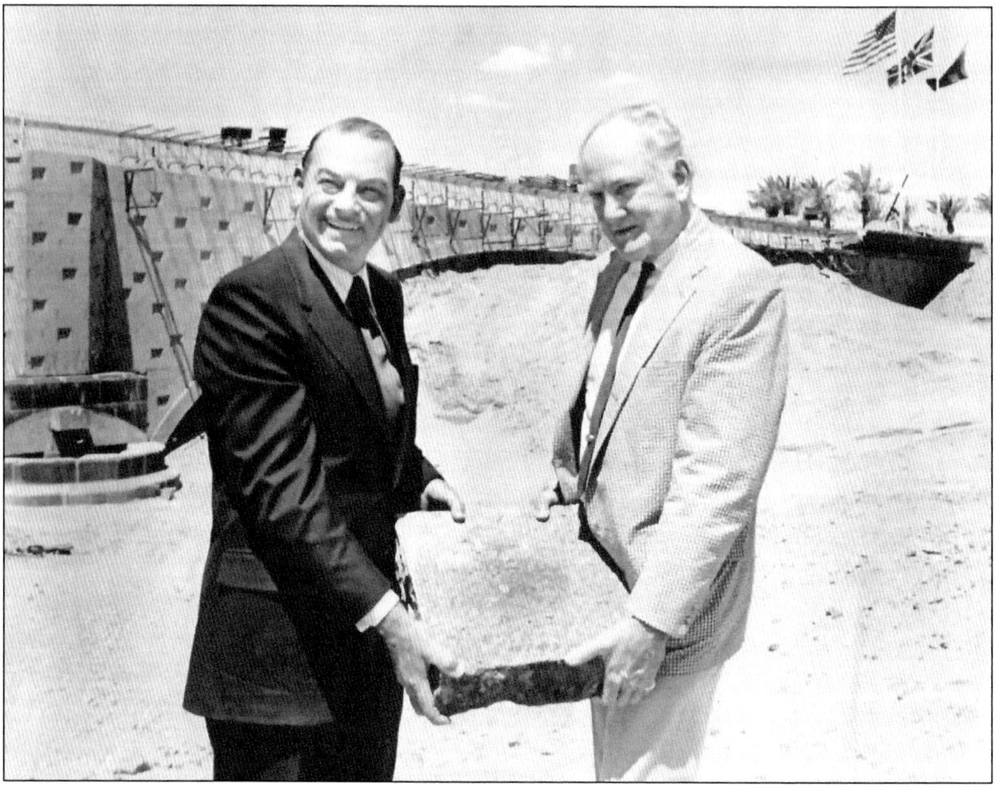

McCulloch (right) helps heft one of the granite facing stones to be attached to the sides of the bridge. Expert stonemasons, some from Mexico and Yugoslavia, attached the stones from the top down, by means of a giant crane. (Courtesy Lake Havasu Museum of History.)

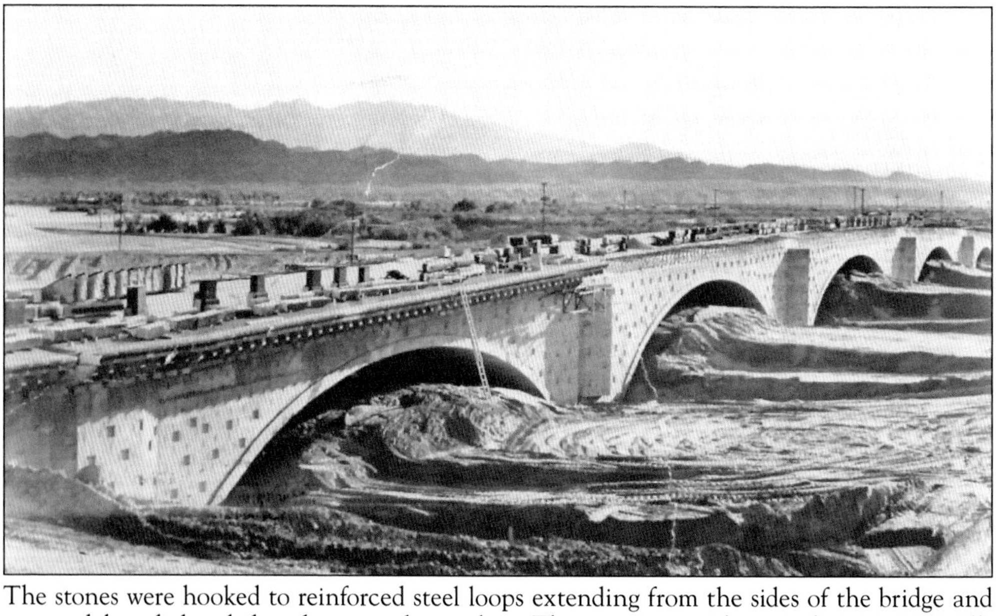

The stones were hooked to reinforced steel loops extending from the sides of the bridge and cramped, keyed, doweled, and mortared into place. The recesses seen here in the concrete walls of the bridge helped to hold the mortar. (Courtesy Lake Havasu Museum of History.)

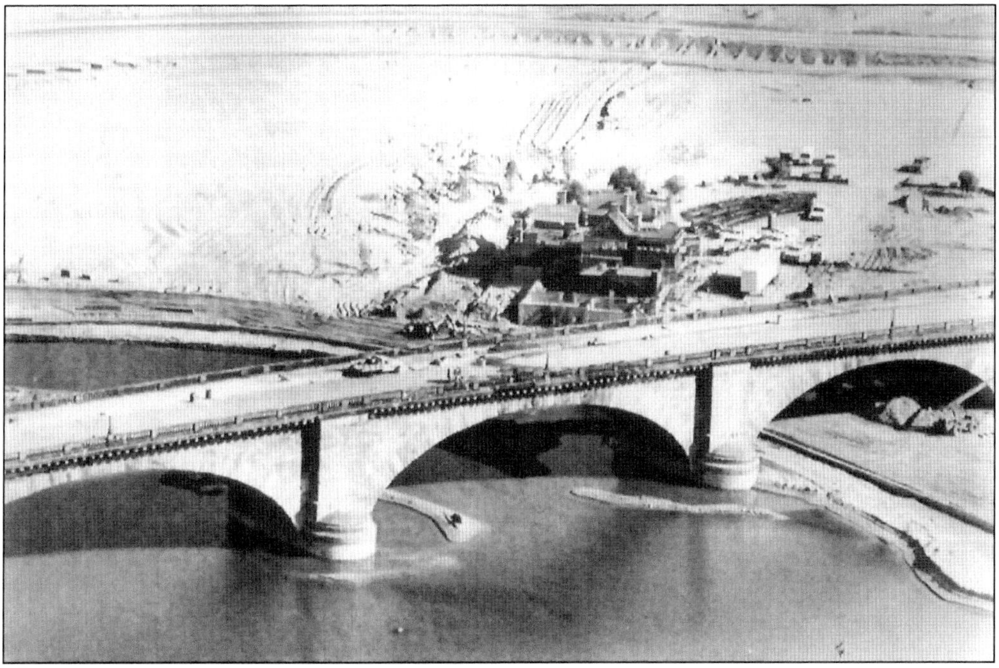

In 1971, after the facing stones were all attached, the job was done. The dirt mounds beneath the arches were removed and the dredging of the channel beneath was begun. (Note the first buildings in the "English Village" going up on the mainland side of the bridge.) The reconstruction of the London Bridge in Lake Havasu City had taken a crew of 40 workers three years to finish, without serious injury—in contrast to the original construction in London, which took a crew of 800 seven years to finish, with 40 fatalities. (Courtesy Lake Havasu Museum of History.)

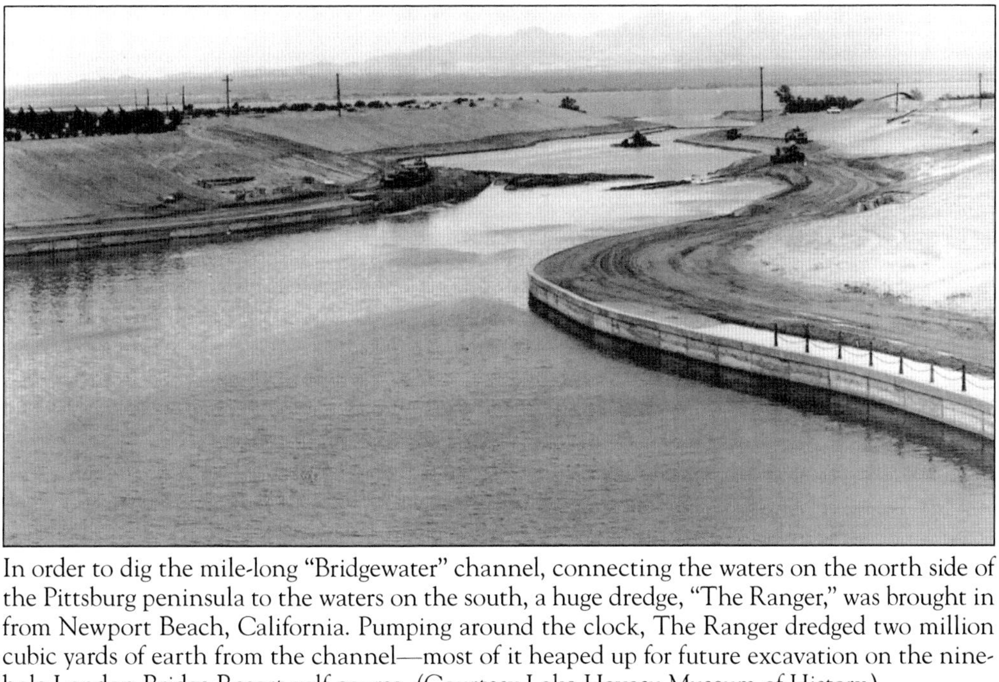

In order to dig the mile-long "Bridgewater" channel, connecting the waters on the north side of the Pittsburg peninsula to the waters on the south, a huge dredge, "The Ranger," was brought in from Newport Beach, California. Pumping around the clock, The Ranger dredged two million cubic yards of earth from the channel—most of it heaped up for future excavation on the nine-hole London Bridge Resort golf course. (Courtesy Lake Havasu Museum of History.)

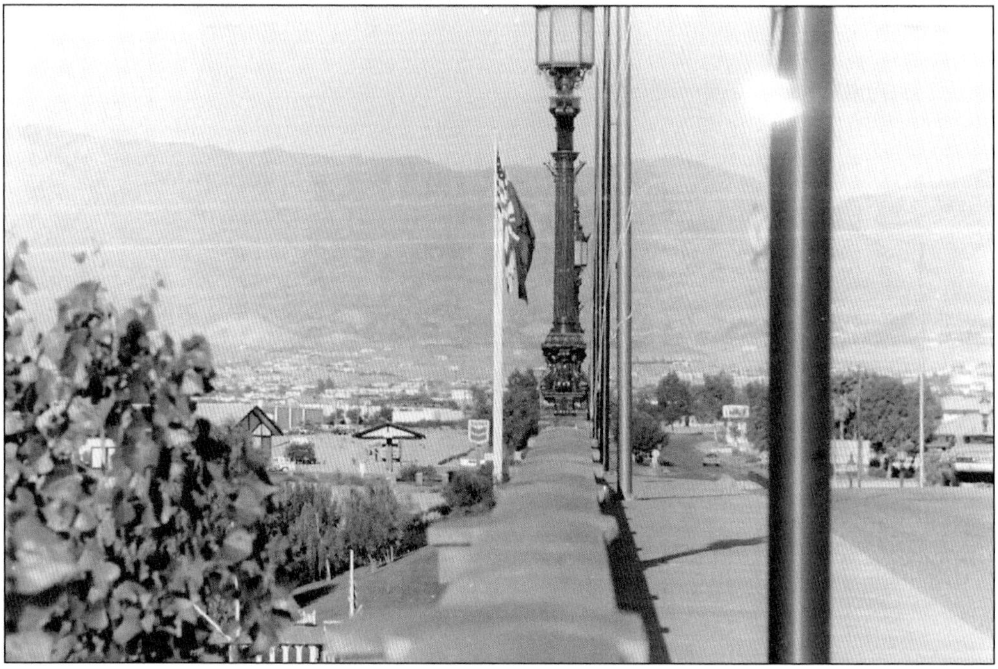

Aside from the unusual circumstances of the bridge's reconstruction and its fascinating history, tourists were also intrigued by such details as the cast-iron lampposts atop the bridge, molded from French cannons captured during the 1815 Battle of Waterloo. The pockmarks in the granite on the sides of the bridge, especially prominent near the "turtlebacks" supporting the piers, caused by exploding German shells during the Battle of Britain in World War II, were another intriguing detail. (Courtesy Lake Havasu Museum of History.)

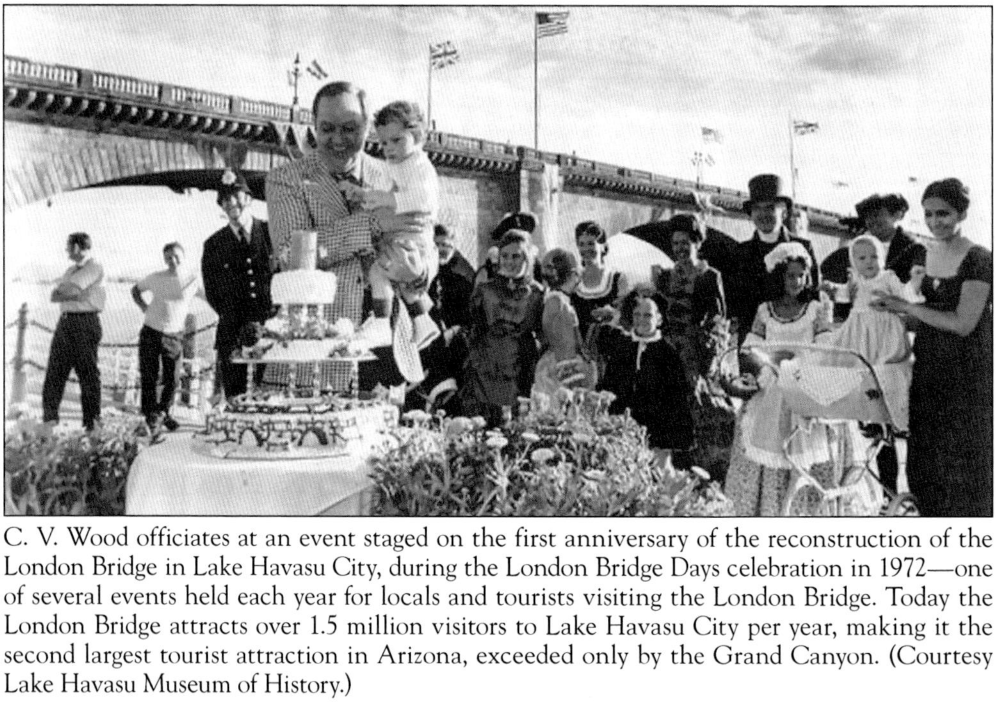

C. V. Wood officiates at an event staged on the first anniversary of the reconstruction of the London Bridge in Lake Havasu City, during the London Bridge Days celebration in 1972—one of several events held each year for locals and tourists visiting the London Bridge. Today the London Bridge attracts over 1.5 million visitors to Lake Havasu City per year, making it the second largest tourist attraction in Arizona, exceeded only by the Grand Canyon. (Courtesy Lake Havasu Museum of History.)

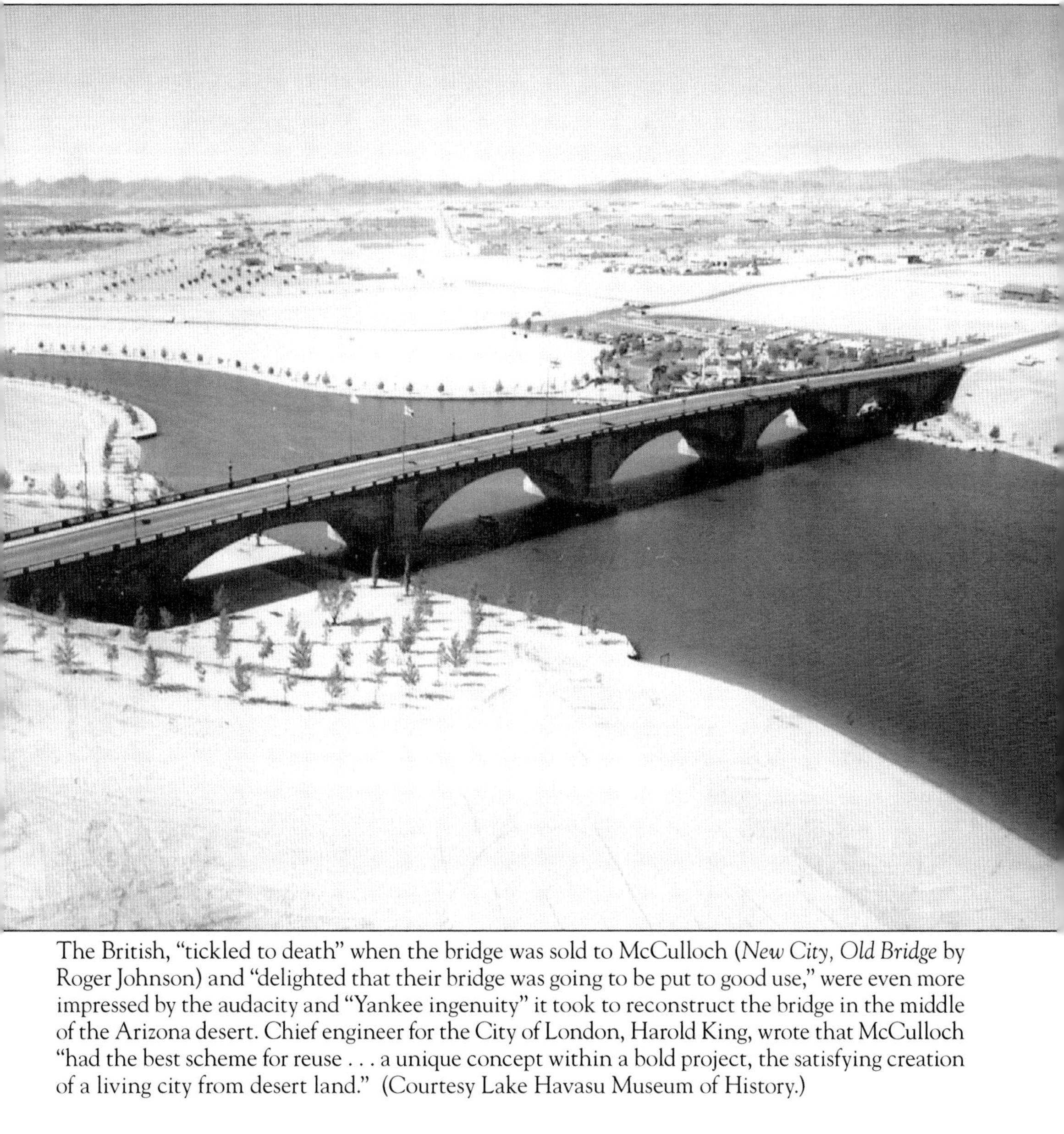

The British, "tickled to death" when the bridge was sold to McCulloch (*New City, Old Bridge* by Roger Johnson) and "delighted that their bridge was going to be put to good use," were even more impressed by the audacity and "Yankee ingenuity" it took to reconstruct the bridge in the middle of the Arizona desert. Chief engineer for the City of London, Harold King, wrote that McCulloch "had the best scheme for reuse . . . a unique concept within a bold project, the satisfying creation of a living city from desert land." (Courtesy Lake Havasu Museum of History.)

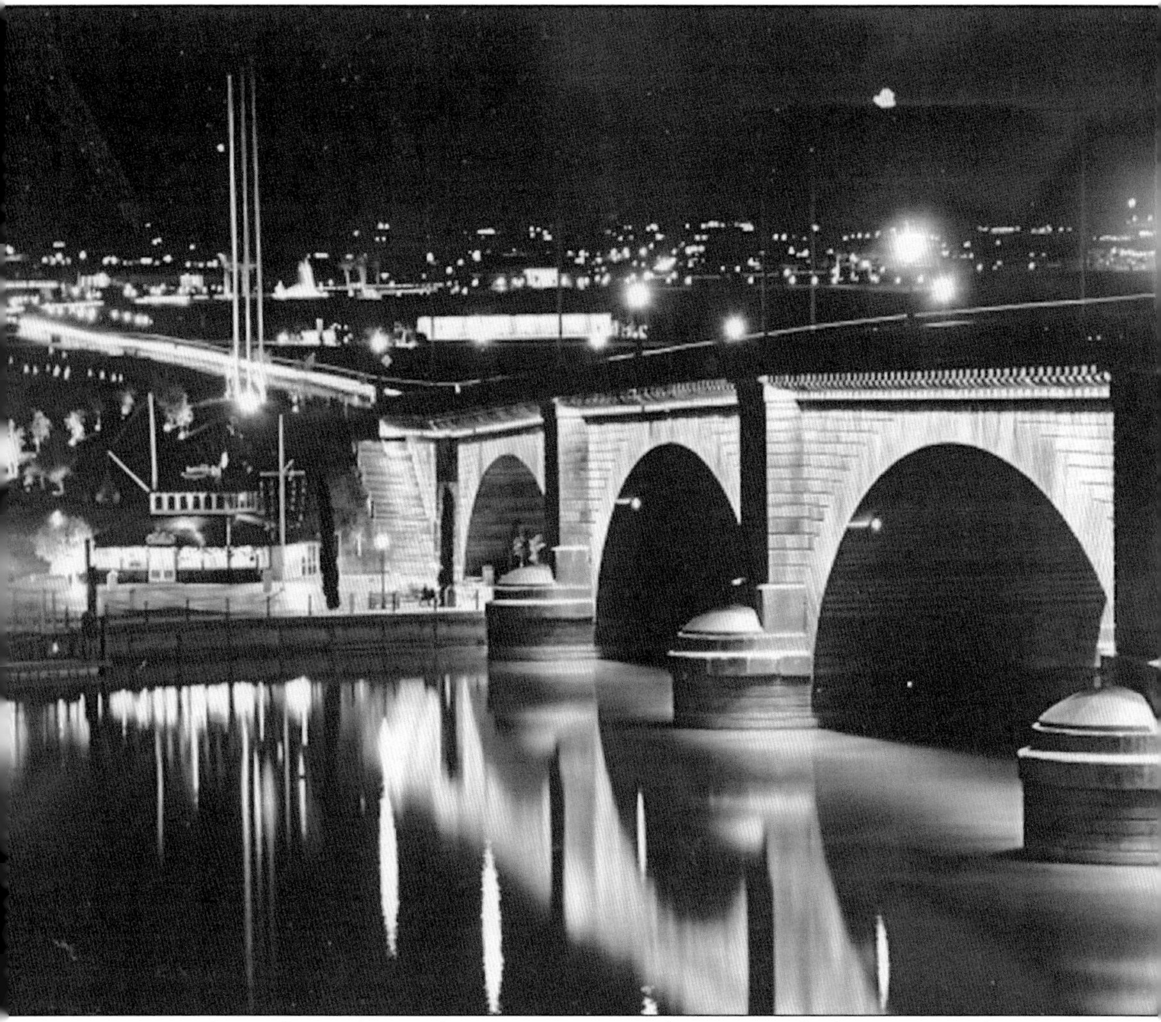

Bringing the London Bridge to Lake Havasu City was Robert P. McCulloch's crowning achievement. The only thing left was for the city to become incorporated, which finally happened in 1978. But McCulloch was not there to enjoy it. Robert P. McCulloch Sr. passed away on February 25, 1977. After his death, his son Robert McCulloch Jr. continued to run McCulloch Properties, Inc. until he died in 1985. C. V. Wood Jr. continued on as chairman of the board and chief executive officer of the McCulloch Oil Corporation, the parent company of McCulloch Properties, until he retired in 1980. C. V. Wood passed away in 1992. (Courtesy Lake Havasu Museum of History.)

Ten

A Gala Celebration

By 1971, the reconstruction of the London Bridge in Lake Havasu City was complete. The gala celebration extended over 10 days and involved some 60,000 participants. It was Lake Havasu City's biggest event ever—an extravaganza to rival the celebration given by King William IV in London, when the bridge was first opened there in 1831. On October 9, 1971, 800 guests attended a cocktail party and banquet held in two giant tents on the island side of the bridge. Crystal chandeliers hung from the ceilings; coats-of-arms, shields, and suits of armor decorated the walls; crystal, china, and silver were set at the tables. It was all great pageantry.

At 6:00 p.m., recordings of Big Ben began to chime. Strolling musicians, madrigal singers, and magicians drifted among the guests as they moved into the cocktail tent. At 7:00 p.m., trumpets sounded and the guests moved out onto the bridge to view a parade of lighted boats cruising up the channel. At 7:45 p.m., trumpets sounded again, accompanied by fireworks. Guests poured into the dinner tent. Actor Lorne Greene introduced the dignitaries, Sir Peter Studd, lord mayor of London, and Jack Williams, governor of Arizona, and dinner began. The menu included lobster, prime rib, cannelloni Florentine, Cornish pasties, glazed baby carrots, and a bevy of fine wines. At midnight, the evening ended with more spectacular fireworks.

On October 10, 50,000 people gathered for the dedication of the bridge. Sir Peter Studd and his retinue came by water from the Nautical Inn on a miniature paddle-wheeler. Then the band struck up and the procession across the bridge began: first, 12 pikemen, each with sword, lance, helmet and breastplate; then, the brigadier in silk robe and crown-cap, carrying his sword of office; the common crier and sergeant-at-arms with his mace; the lord mayor in his gold-lace-trimmed robe and plumed three-cornered hat, the great jeweled chain of office suspended from his neck, the diamond-circled London coat of arms over a fall of lace at his throat; and, last, the high sheriff of London and the chief commoner deputy in scarlet and violet robes.

A 19-gun salute was followed by a trumpet fanfare, and the band launched into "God Save the Queen" and "The Star Spangled Banner."

After short speeches including words from Robert McCulloch, Sir Peter Studd and Governor Williams released a hot-air balloon, along with 30,000 small balloons and 3,000 white doves.

Then came the first annual London Bridge Days parade. American Indians in tribal dress, Londoners in their robes, and locals in historic costumes marched a mile into town. In all, 3,500 participants—150 Boy Scouts, 15 bands, and 10 floats depicting the history of the London Bridge, from the Romans in 43 A.D. to the Vikings in 1014, to the first stone bridge in 1209, to the last stone bridge in 1831, and the reconstruction in Lake Havasu City in 1971—crossed the new London Bridge.

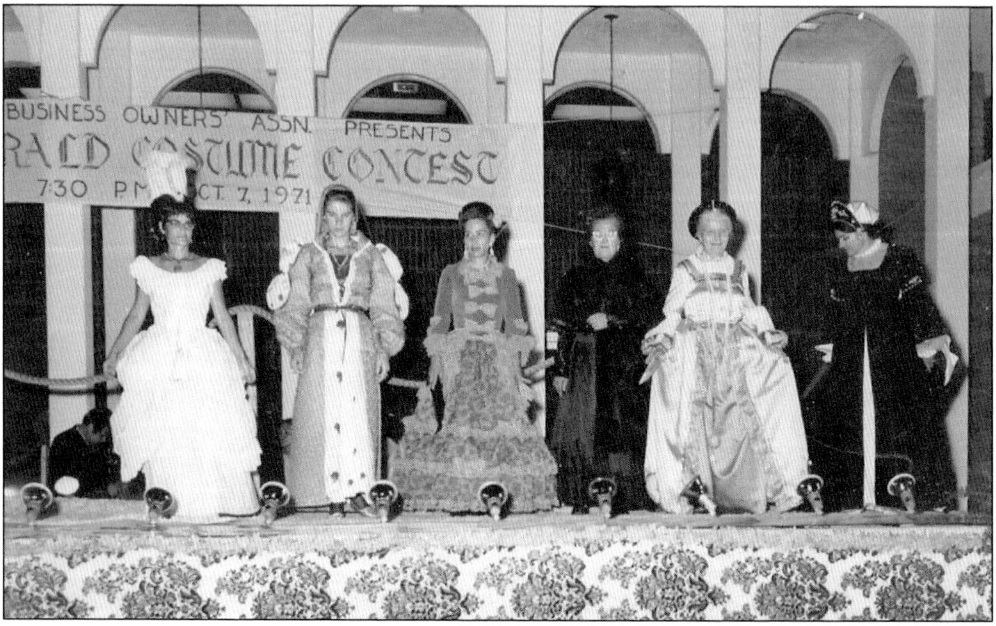

On October 7, 1971, the first event held during the gala celebration week, the costume contest, was staged in front of the First National Bank (now Bank One) on McCulloch Boulevard. Residents dressed for the occasion in British or at least early American costumes. Contestants could be seen in trunk hose, doublets, knee breeches, silk stockings, top hats, frock coats, and gowns in a variety of different historical styles. (Courtesy Lake Havasu Museum of History.)

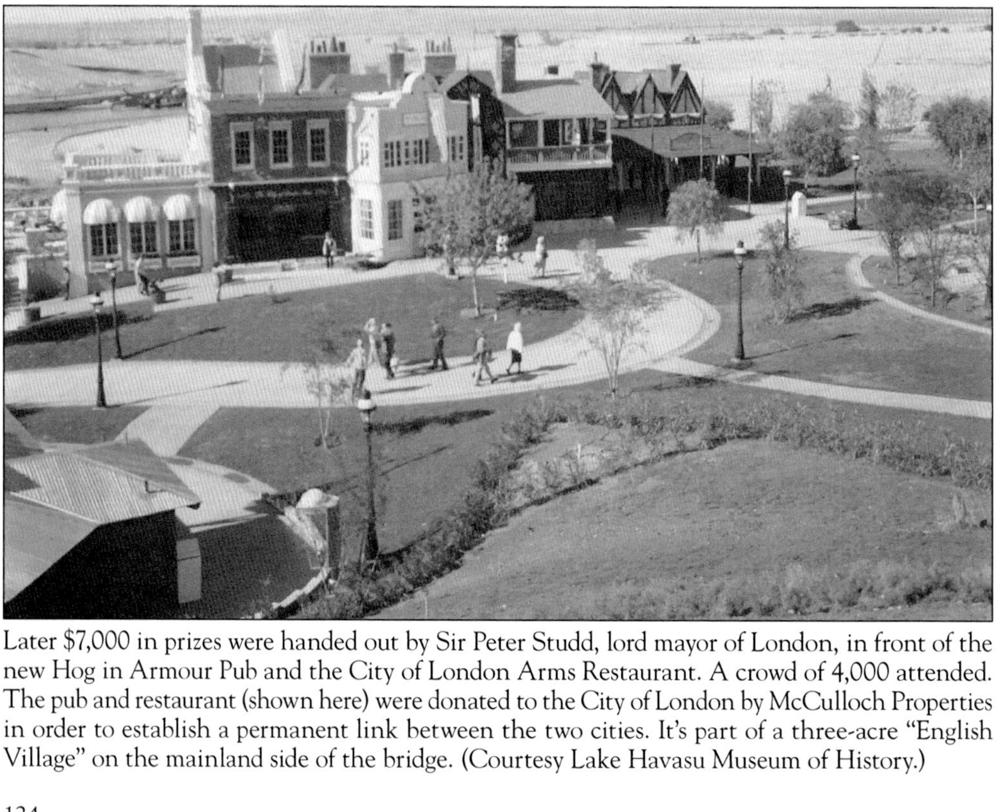

Later $7,000 in prizes were handed out by Sir Peter Studd, lord mayor of London, in front of the new Hog in Armour Pub and the City of London Arms Restaurant. A crowd of 4,000 attended. The pub and restaurant (shown here) were donated to the City of London by McCulloch Properties in order to establish a permanent link between the two cities. It's part of a three-acre "English Village" on the mainland side of the bridge. (Courtesy Lake Havasu Museum of History.)

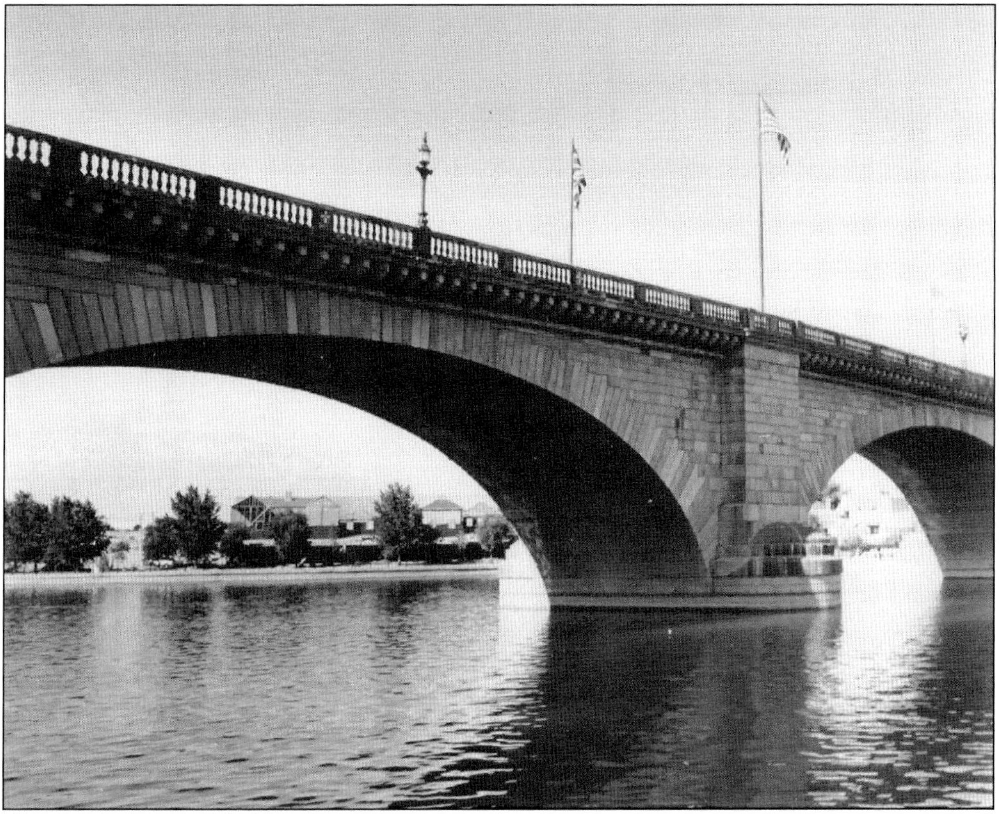

The pub, with a lounge and four dining rooms, was designed by John Rogers, Ltd. of London, a firm founded in 1416 and specializing in traditional English pub reproductions. Extending along a ten-foot wide paved promenade on the waterfront, the village complex featured docks, shops, cafes, and a central park with a fountain and flower gardens throughout. (Courtesy Lake Havasu Museum of History.)

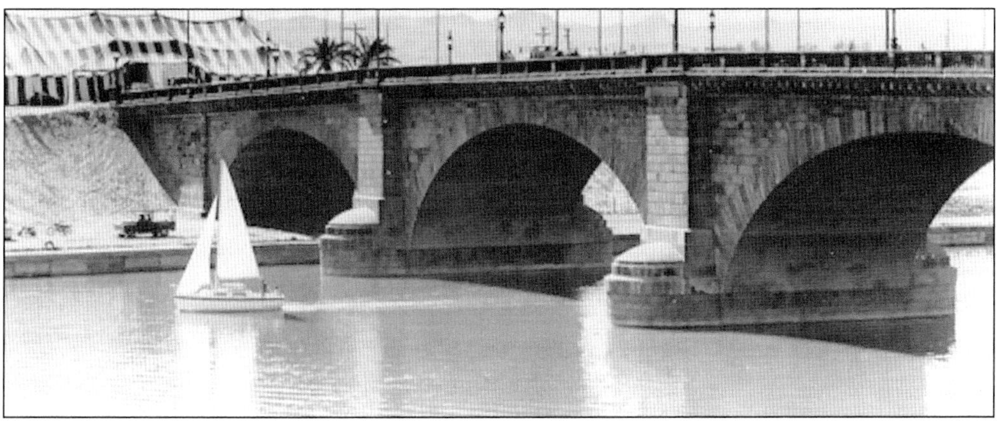

On October 9, the parties—the cocktail party, the banquet, and the ball—were held in two huge, 36-foot high tents erected on the island side of the bridge. The cocktail tent was 40 by 120 feet, and weighed seven tons; the dinner tent was 80 by 160 feet and weighed between 18 and 20 tons. The cocktail tent had to be put up without center poles so that the mile-long grand opening parade could march through it the next morning. (Courtesy Lake Havasu Museum of History.)

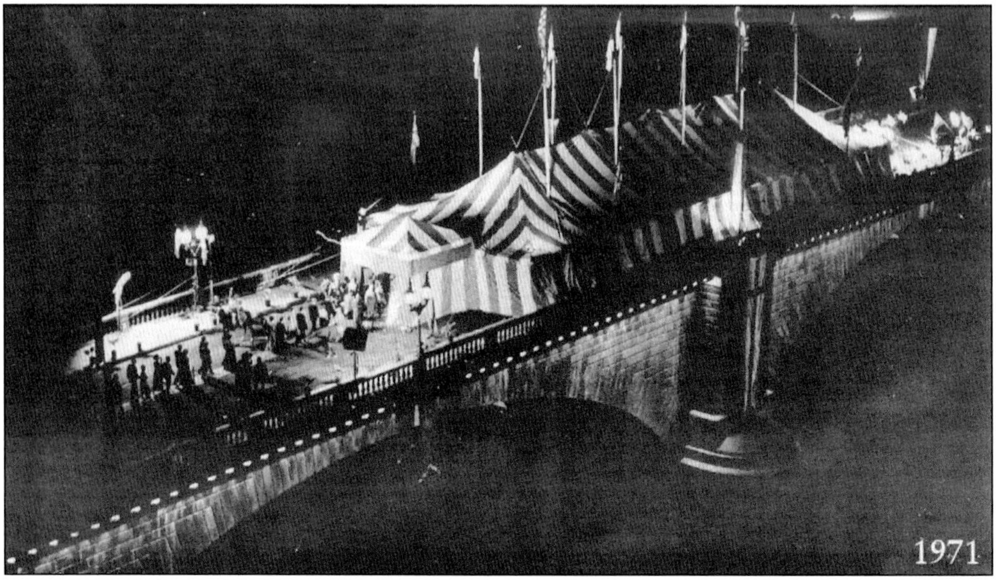

Appetizers at the cocktail party included successive servings of crab Lorenzo, lobster Newburg, cheese straws, miniature Monte Cristo sandwiches, quiche lorraine, rumaki (bacon-wrapped water chestnuts), Chinese eggrolls with apricot sauce, artichoke buttons with crab and avocado, jumbo Guaymas shrimp, Gulf and Spanish shrimp, Alaskan king crab with Louisiana hot sauce, and tidbits of teriyaki steak. (Courtesy Lake Havasu Museum of History.)

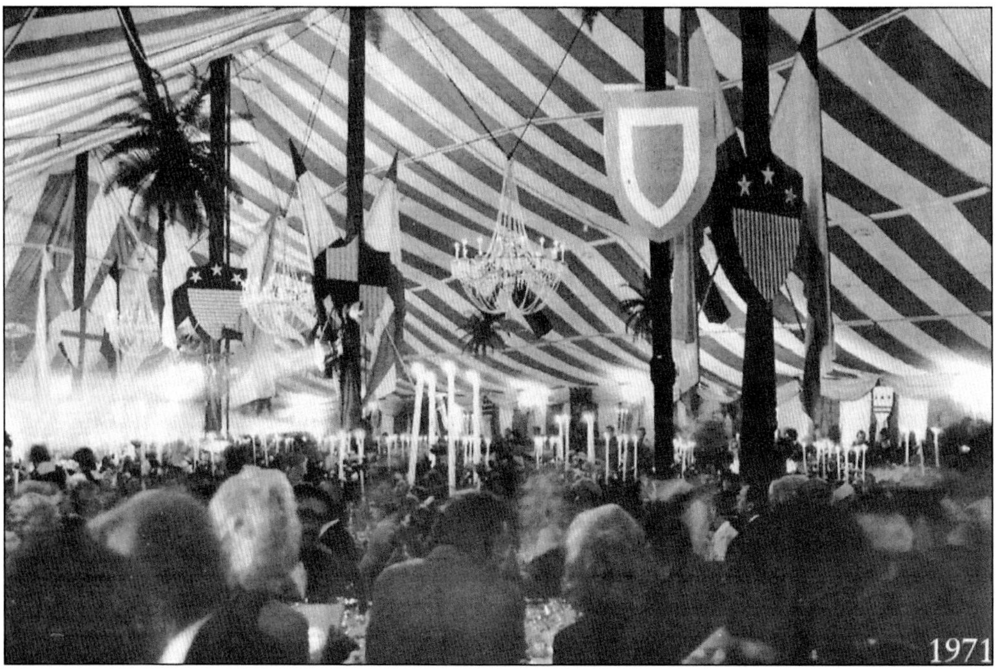

The custom-made dinner tent was filled with 70 tables, 10 chairs each, a 112-foot-long head table, and a 18-by-24-foot stage. Three crystal chandeliers—five feet wide in diameter—hung from the ceiling. Side tables and coffee stations were set up along the end walls. Behind the back wall were the kitchen tents, crew trailers, supply trucks, and a refrigerated van full of foodstuffs catered from Los Angeles. (Courtesy Lake Havasu Museum of History.)

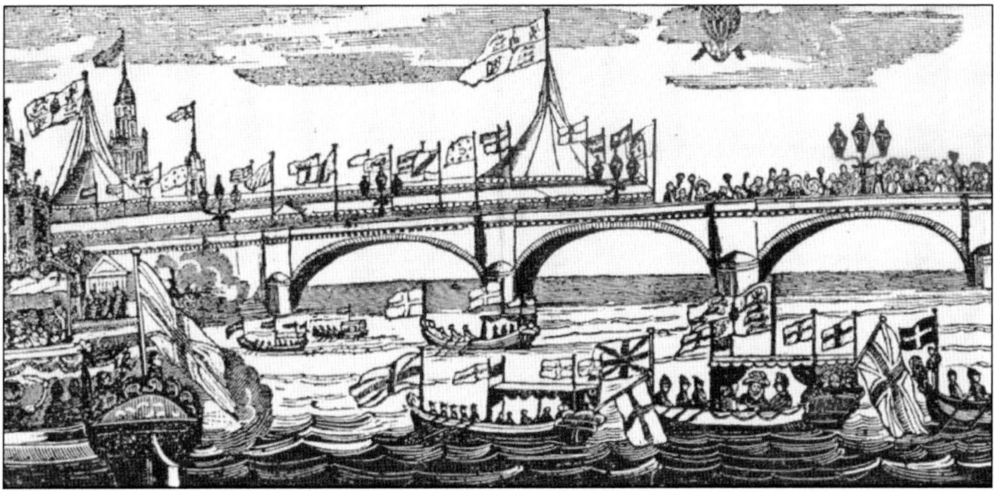

The dedication party given King William IV and Queen Adelaide in London on August 1, 1831, featured in this advertisement, was attended by thousands. After coming by water to the bridge and witnessing the ceremonial ascension of a hot-air balloon, the king and queen proceeded to the royal tent and partook of a rich *dejeune a la fourchette* (breakfast with a fork). (Courtesy Lake Havasu Museum of History.)

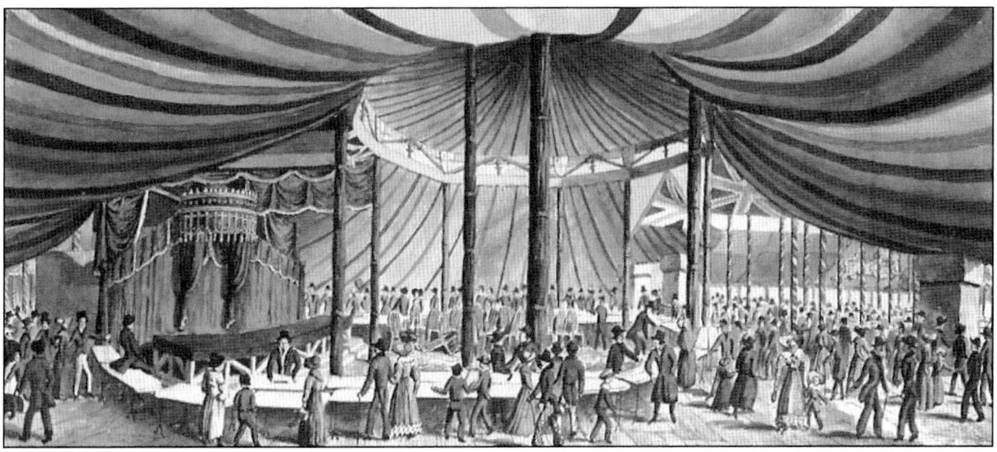

The 1831 menu in London included 370 dishes of chickens, 250 dishes of shellfish, 150 hams and tongues, 75 French pies, 75 pigeon pies, 40 sirloins of beef, 50 quarters of lamb, and 200 dishes of salad. The meal was accompanied by 840 bottles of wine. (Courtesy Lake Havasu Museum of History.)

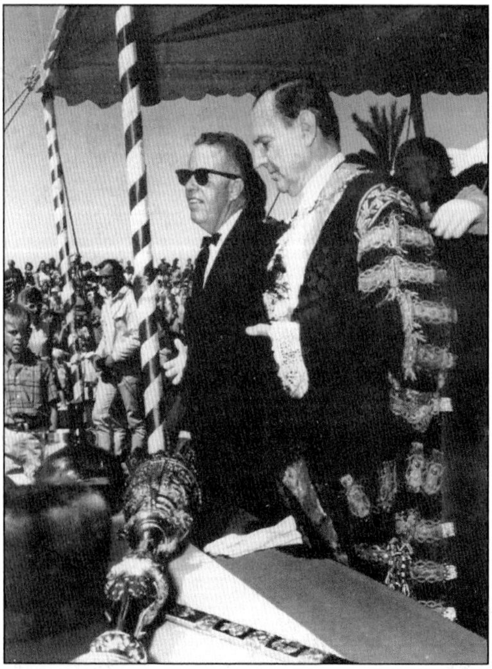

The dedication party given by McCulloch in Lake Havasu City on October 10, 1971, was attended by thousands as well. And the similarities continued. Lord Mayor Studd (right) came by water to the bridge, much the same as King William. Then the lord mayor joined Gov. Jack Williams (left) to witness the ceremonial ascension of a hot-air balloon, much the same as King William and Queen Adelaide. (Courtesy Lake Havasu Museum of History.)

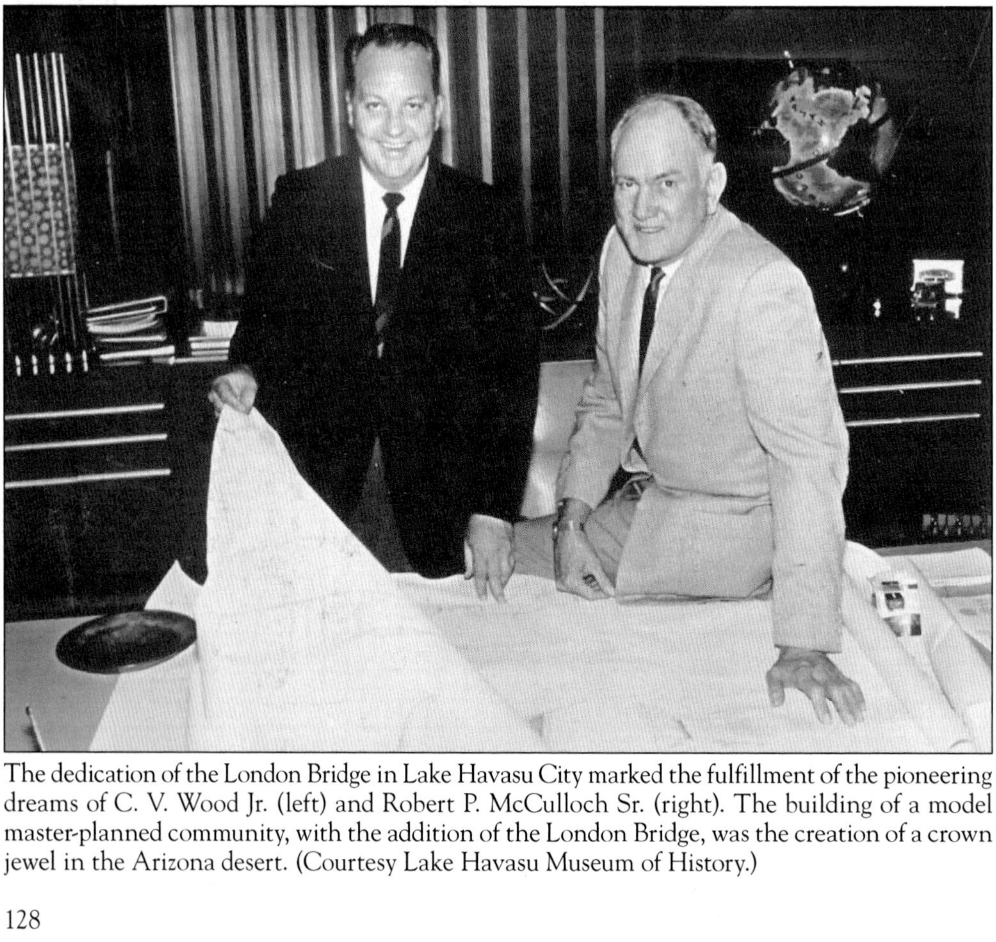

The dedication of the London Bridge in Lake Havasu City marked the fulfillment of the pioneering dreams of C. V. Wood Jr. (left) and Robert P. McCulloch Sr. (right). The building of a model master-planned community, with the addition of the London Bridge, was the creation of a crown jewel in the Arizona desert. (Courtesy Lake Havasu Museum of History.)